The Making of Migration

SOCIETY AND SPACE SERIES

The Society and Space series explores the fascinating relationship between the spatial and the social. Each title draws on a range of modern and historical theories to offer important insights into the key cultural and political topics of our times, including migration, globalisation, race, gender, sexuality and technology. These stimulating and provocative books combine high intellectual standards with contemporary appeal for students of politics, international relations, sociology, philosophy and human geography.

Series Editor: Professor Stuart Elden, University of Warwick

Migration, Ethics & Power: Spaces of Hospitality in International Politics by Dan Bulley

Geographies of Violence by Marcus A. Doel

Surveillance & Space by Francisco R. Klauser

The Data Gaze by David Beer

Circulation and Urbanization by Ross Exo Adams

The Making of Migration

The Biopolitics of Mobility at Europe's Borders

Martina Tazzioli

$SAGE

Los Angeles | London | New Delhi
Singapore | Washington DC | Melbourne

⊛SAGE

Los Angeles | London | New Delhi
Singapore | Washington DC | Melbourne

SAGE Publications Ltd
1 Oliver's Yard
55 City Road
London EC1Y 1SP

SAGE Publications Inc.
2455 Teller Road
Thousand Oaks, California 91320

SAGE Publications India Pvt Ltd
B 1/I 1 Mohan Cooperative Industrial Area
Mathura Road
New Delhi 110 044

SAGE Publications Asia-Pacific Pte Ltd
3 Church Street
#10-04 Samsung Hub
Singapore 049483

© Martina Tazzioli 2020

First published 2020

Apart from any fair dealing for the purposes of research or private study, or criticism or review, as permitted under the Copyright, Designs and Patents Act, 1988, this publication may be reproduced, stored or transmitted in any form, or by any means, only with the prior permission in writing of the publishers, or in the case of reprographic reproduction, in accordance with the terms of licences issued by the Copyright Licensing Agency. Enquiries concerning reproduction outside those terms should be sent to the publishers.

Editor: Robert Rojek
Assistant editor: Eve Williams
Production editor: Katherine Haw
Marketing manager: Susheel Gokarakonda
Cover design: Wendy Scott
Typeset by: C&M Digitals (P) Ltd, Chennai, India
Printed in the UK

Library of Congress Control Number: 2019939508

British Library Cataloguing in Publication data

A catalogue record for this book is available from the British Library

ISBN 978-1-5264-6403-3
ISBN 978-1-5264-6404-0 (pbk)

At SAGE we take sustainability seriously. Most of our products are printed in the UK using responsibly sourced papers and boards. When we print overseas we ensure sustainable papers are used as measured by the PREPS grading system. We undertake an annual audit to monitor our sustainability.

Contents

About the Author vi
Acknowledgements vii

   Introduction 1

1 Migrant Mobs: The (Un)Making of Migrant Multiplicities 15

2 Migrant Singularities: Between Subjectivation
   and Desubjugation 43

3 Digital Multiplicities and Singularities: (In)Visibility and
   Data Circuits 73

4 "Keeping On the Move Without Letting Pass": Dispersal and
   Mobility as Technologies of Government 101

5 Migrant Spatial Disobediences: Collective Subjectivities
   and the Memory of Struggles 130

   Conclusion 152

References 159
Index 173

About the Author

Martina Tazzioli is Lecturer in Politics & Technology at Goldsmiths College, London. She is the author of *Spaces of Governmentality: Autonomous Migration and the Arab Uprisings* (2015), co-author with Glenda Garelli of *Tunisia as a Revolutionised Space of Migration* (2016), and co-editor of *Foucault and the History of Our Present* (2015) and *Foucault and the Making of Subjects* (2016). She is co-founder of the journal *Materialifoucaultiani* and a member of *Radical Philosophy* editorial.

Acknowledgements

Ventimiglia, Calais, Bardonecchia, Lesvos, Lampedusa, Choucha, Rome, Athens, Chios, Berlin, Claviere, Paris, Briancon, Tunis: this book has been written in an attempt to follow the geographies of the so-called 'refugee crisis' and the convoluted geographies of migrations. The idea of this book stems from endless and passionate discussions with Oana Parvan, Claudia Nardini and Simone Vegliò, about the English mob, within and against. Together with them, this book comes out of the constant exchanges with Glenda Garelli, a true comrade, friend and very often co-author in our migration journey, since the time of Lampedusa and the Arab Uprisings.

I would like to especially thank Claudia Aradau, to whom I am particularly indebted, for her unconditional support, and the salient and truly engaging conversations, about biopolitics, the mob and critique. Many sections of this book have been rethought and revised again and again after those discussions. *The Making of Migration* has been very much informed by the debates and questioning with Judith Revel, since the time of Pisa. The focus on collective and individual subjects mainly comes from those endless lessons.

Nicholas De Genova and Sandro Mezzadra have been fundamental philosophical supports and sources of inspiration for orienting this work overall, and for constantly reminding me to keep politics at the core, as *The Making of Migration* tries to do. I would like to thank Barbara Pinelli, for pushing me towards new literatures and authors, and Elena Fontanari, for the discussions on counter-mapping and the beginning of our collective map. Thanks especially to William Walters, who has provided invaluable feedback on most of the content of this book. The collaboration and discussions with Manuela Bojadzijev, Angharad Closs-Stephens, Brenna Bhandar and Jef Huysmans have been crucial for developing and further problematising collective subjects and mobility. Conversations and exchanges with colleagues and friends have nourished and enriched the chapters of *The Making of Migration*: Lauren Martin, Filippo Furri, Gaia Giuliani, Dave Clarke, Amedeo Policante, Emma McCluskey, Maurice Stierl, Lorenzo Pezzani, Stephan Scheel, Leonie Ansems de Vries, Federica Mazzara, Charles Heller, Marcus Doel, Neva Cocchi Aila Spathopoulou, Alessandra Sciurba, Fiorenza Picozza, Paolo Novak, Eduardo Domenech. And Arnold Davidson, a constant source of inspiration over the years and beginning of my Foucaultian journey. The analyses on subjectivity and critique would have not been possible without the invaluable exchange and confrontation over the years with Daniele Lorenzini, Orazio Irrera and Laura Cremonesi. I am also very grateful to Stuart Elden, for supporting this project with no reservations. *The Making of Migration* tries to leave a trace of those who are 'here' and who 'are not going back'.

Introduction

If we confront the geopolitical map of Europe with an imaginative cartography of the actual frontiers for migrants in Europe and the multiplication of punctuated border zones that are also spaces of struggle and refuge for the migrants – such as Calais, Ventimiglia, Eidomeni, the train station in Berlin, the informal encampments in Paris – we would immediately notice a huge discrepancy between the two maps. Indeed, most of these frontiers are not visualised on the geopolitical map, as not all of them correspond to the national borders. Moreover, on the geopolitical map borders are homogeneous; that is, they do not represent the differential and unequal ways in which these impact on and are experienced by subjects. Such an account of the European space contributes to unsettle taken-for-granted state narratives about the existence of a "refugee crisis", as well as analyses that are predicated upon an "emergency politics" (Honig, 2009) of migration. In fact, nowadays the European space is punctuated by mushrooming border zones, spaces of migrant struggles, safe places of temporary refuge and others that have been transformed into hostile environments. Many cities across Europe have become frontier-spaces for the migrants, but at the same time also places where spaces of sanctuary and struggles to stay took place. Notably, many of these border zones – such as Calais – are not exceptional spaces that suddenly popped up, but rather places that have contributed to shape Europe's space. Indeed, a political genealogy and memory of these border zones should be retraced, bringing to the fore Europe's geographies of control and the counter-geographies enacted by migrants.

If we zoom into these border zones, we can observe that they are criss-crossed and shaped by migrant movements, struggles, alliances between locals and refugees, anti-migrant movements, mechanisms of capture and containment as well as operations of data extraction. There, migrants are targeted as part of actual or potential groups – what in this book I call "temporary multiplicities" – and, at once, as individuals – what I refer to here as "singularities". In fact, beyond being hampered in their mobility, migrants are obstructed from building spaces of life and in their freedom to choose where to go and stay. Indeed, racialised bordering mechanisms affect both migrants' mobility and their lives. Hence, a politics of mobility is always mutually intertwined with a specific biopolitics of migration, that is with a series of technologies, knowledges and policies apt at regulating and acting upon life. It is through this entanglement of a politics of mobility and of biopolitical mechanisms that migrants are targeted.

This book investigates how some people are racialised, governed and labelled as "migrants", both individually and as part of multiplicities, exploring what I call *the making of migration*, meaning by that the political, legal and racialising mechanisms through which some people are labelled and governed as "migrants". That is, against the reification of migration into sociological categories, I would point towards the material processes through which in different contexts some subjects are produced as migrants and whose mobility is eventually "illegalised". The *making of migration* retains an ambivalent meaning, since it captures how migrants are both the subjects and objects of such a making. On the one hand migrants are made by laws, policies, discourses. It is indeed through legal, administrative and political mechanisms that the "production of migrant illegality" (De Genova, 2002) is actualised. On the other hand, migrants make and open up spaces (of liveability, of refuge, etc.) and generate unusual collective formations, as a result of their unauthorised movements and presence as well as through their struggles. These collective formations can be seen as "mobile people" (Isin, 2018) that disrupt the constitutive link between people and sedentary ontology (Elden, 2010). Or they can be irreducible to something like "a people", as long as this latter is constitutively predicated upon the reproduction of exclusionary boundaries (Andrijasevic et al., 2012): "those who are either not the people or other than the people", Bruno Bosteel contends, "are relegated more or less violently to the pre-political or nonpolitical realm indicated by the pejorative use of terms such as plebs, populace, mob, or rabble" (Bosteel, 2016: 1). In this sense, the making of migration captures the battlefield and the asymmetries between bordering mechanisms and migrants' subjective drives. In fact, the map of Europe's migrant spaces described above includes both border zones and spaces of control produced through border enforcement, violent evictions and push-back operations, and, at the same time, places of refuge opened up by migrants' struggles and movements and that have contributed to define the European space.

Therefore, the making of migration encapsulates "the making of the subjects" (Cremonesi et al., 2016) – how some individuals are racialised, labelled and governed as migrants and what these individuals produce and open up – while simultaneously gesturing towards the reshaping of Europe's geography as it stems from the multiplication of border zones, border controls and migrants' spaces of movement. The choice of such an expression – "the making of migration" – echoes E. P. Thompson's seminal book *The Making of the English Working Class* (1963), in which "making" refers to the ambivalent production of the working class, as something that "made itself as much as it was made" (Thompson, 1963: 213). "Making", Thompson explains, "is an active process, which owes as much to agency as to conditioning" (1963: 8). Although we cannot speak of migration in terms of class, it is precisely such an ambivalent process of subjectivation and subjection that is taken into account here. The book focuses on the making of migration from the specific angle of migrant singularities and multiplicities, considering how migrants are shaped and targeted individually and as part of temporary collective formations. Which modes of individualisation and totalisation are at play in the making of migration and, thus, how are "*omnes et singulatim*" (Foucault, 1986) articulated to each other? How are migrant multiplicities divided and criminalised as potential or actual collective subjects? Instead of fixing migrants to specific subject-identities, I investigate the process of subjectivation and subjection that migrants are shaped by and in which they engage, not only individually but also as part of temporary collective formations.

In so doing, the book tries to grasp the fields of tensions within which some subjects are racialised and disciplined as migrants, both individually and as part of temporary collective formations. The production of subjectivity is the outcome of a heterogeneity of struggles that stated the irreducibility of singularities and racialised differences to a homogeneous subject. Such an irreducibility is the marker "of the proliferation of figures of subjectivity at the intersection between devices of subjection and practices of subjectivation" (Mezzadra, 2018a: 12). This involves considering the dynamism between subjectivation and subjection as two poles that are constantly both at stake, as the unstable outcome of power relations and of movements of refusal and struggle against subjection. However, as I will explain in Chapter 2, the very meaning of subjection cannot be taken for granted, and a focus on migration entails inquiring heterogenous forms of violence, exploitation and coercion, some of which might be less visible than others. Moreover, an insight into the actual and subtle modes of subjection that migrants are targeted by, leads us to question the analytics of security and humanitarianism as fully adequate to analyse how migrants are interpellated, controlled and treated. Indeed, does the twofold representation of migrants as potential threats and risky subjects on the one hand, and as victims and subjects to protect on the other, allow for capturing the multiple ways in which they are disciplined and depicted?

Through a focus on the twofold level of collective subjects (multiplicities) and of individual subjectivities (singularities), I investigate the processes of subjectivation and objectivation that are at play in the making of migration. By subjectivation I mean here to the material process, that which is legal and the discursive practices through which individuals are known, shaped and governed as subjects. "The question", Foucault argues, "is to determine what the subject should be, at which condition he is subjected, which status he must have […] in order to become a legitimate subject of knowledge" (Foucault, 1984). By objectivation I refer to the modes in which subjects are crafted as possible objects of knowledge, according to which mechanisms of partition, through objectivation, they also become governable. As far as migrants are concerned, multiple modes of objectivation are at stake: objectivation through medicalisation and pathologisation; objectivation of migrants generated by techniques of visibility and detection; objectivation through knowledge production that transforms migrants into statistics, numbers and potential flows. In this regard, it is worth recalling Etienne Balibar's reflections on subjectivation and objectivation: "the questions of the subject and of the object—understood as a double process of subjectivation and objectivation, the subjectivation of the individual by rules and the construction of the 'relation of self to self' according to different practical modalities—are not opposed to one another, but are two sides of the same reality" (Balibar, 2003: 20).

This book takes "migration" as an analytical lens and, at the same time, as an object of study that refers both to collective formations (here called "migrant multiplicities") and to individual subjects. As an analytical lens, migration constitutes a contested terrain through which to rethink some of the central categories of political theory: among these, I take into account collective and individual subjects, and investigate how these articulate with temporality and political visibility. Taking migration as a lens to rethink collective subjects and modes of individualisation also involves problematising the meaning biopolitics: a focus on the racialising mechanisms through which some subjects are labelled and governed as "migrants" pushes us to consider the production of inequalities among lives. Foucault's formulation of biopolitics as a politics of populations needs to be supplemented with an inquiry about inequalities. Concurring with Didier Fassin, biopolitics "does not consist only in the normalisation of people's life but also in deciding the kind of life that they could or could not live" (Fassin, 2014: 28; see also Fassin, 2007). This echoes Veena Das's focus on "disputations over what constitutes life" (Das, 2006: 16).

In so doing, this book is in dialogue with a scholarly debate that assumes migration as a litmus paper for exploring broader transformations at the level of global labour and capitalism (see in particular Mezzadra and Neilson, 2013; but also Boutang, 1998; De Genova, 2013; Mezzadra, 2010; Papastergiadis, 2000). In fact, it mobilises a similar methodological move: it engages with the micropolitical level of governmentality, to rethink collective subjectivities and the production and governing of individuals in light of migration. Bringing specific attention to the dimension of collective subjectivities, it asks: how do emergent migrant collective formations unsettle the logics of numbers and the minority/majority divide (Andrijasevic et al., 2012)? Which modes of subjection are at play that cannot be analysed in terms of making live/letting die ? How are individuals targeted without being interpellated by mechanisms of datafication and data extraction? And how are migrants' lives regulated and disrupted by temporal borders? The heterogeneity of political technologies that migrants are hampered, contained and exhausted by generates a series of grey zones that might be analysed in terms of not making live without letting die. These latter are characterised by the use of mobility as a technology – and not only an object – of government that affect migrants' lives, desires and geographies.

RETHINKING (MIGRANT) MULTIPLICITIES AND SINGULARITIES

In her book *Fare Moltitudine*, Judith Revel has observed that the figure of the citizen is historically the outcome of a fundamental tension between the dimension of the individual and the dimension of collectivity that underpins modern political thought. On the one hand, there is the series of singularities, which includes "the person, the individual, the citizen, that is all those figures of particularism", and on the other, constantly intertwined with the former, the series which "includes the figures of the people, the population, the crowd and the mass" (Revel, 2004: 5). These two series have finally defined the borders and the space of political representation. Instead, the notion of the "multitude" has been historically discredited as non-political and remained under-theorised: it has been conceptualised as "synonymous with the many, that is as an indistinct category" (Revel, 2004: 5). As Etienne Balibar remarks, in the Western modern philosophical tradition only Spinoza put the multitude at the core of his analysis (Balibar, 1997). Similarly, this book focuses on migration to explore singularities and collective subjectivities that are not included in the above series and that are criminalised or disqualified as non-political and as unruly.

In order to account for collective subject formations, throughout the book I use the term "multiplicities" or, better, "temporary migrant multiplicities". Why "multiplicities" instead of using more distinct and well-defined terms such as "groups" or "populations"? "Multiplicity", I suggest, enables tackling collective formations that do not fit into the referent "population", as they are non-homogeneous, highly precarious and temporary. These collective formations do not share an identity but come together in places; in some cases they act collectively towards common political goals and they lay claims, as a result of a shared condition – e.g. being blocked at a border, or not being allowed to stay in a given place. In this sense, they generate unusual forms of political subjectivity that are, however, often discredited as non-political, or criminalised as unruly mobs. The term "population" designates the object and the target of dispositives of security, and it is characterised not only by the reference to the nation-state but also by a certain stability which in turn allows a degree of legibility. Instead, the migrant collective formations that I look at in the book are highly heterogeneous in their composition and temporary in their duration. More precisely, they resemble what Foucault defines as subjects that resist being part of the population (Foucault, 2007).

Second, through the term "multiplicity" I want to keep open the very meaning and category of social composition. Unlike sociological categories such as "group", multiplicity enables de-essentialising migration to shift the attention to the racialised mechanisms through which some subjects are labelled and governed as "migrants".

At the same time, unlike "the multitude", speaking of multiplicity means leaving open questions around the politicalness of these collective formations. In other words, instead of superimposing a conceptual grid for designating collective subjects, establishing in advance what they are, I am more interested in investigating the peculiarities of temporary migrant collective formations.

Third, I analyse migrant collective formations insofar as these latter on some occasions and in some contexts exceed any arithmetic counting. In fact, multiplicity is an ambivalent notion that has a numeric dimension that at the same time cannot be counted (Deleuze and Guattari, 1987). Migrant multiplicities are often discredited as non-political or as unruly subjects, while at the same time they do not fit into sociological categories such as "population" and "the people".

To sum up, the partial undecidability of the notion of multiplicity – at the edges of what is counted and what escapes counting, as well as in terms of its political and social composition – enables interrogating the dimension of collectivity in relation to migration and mobility. In turn, in resonance with the general aim of this work, migration is used as a litmus paper for questioning and rethinking collective subjectivities. The term "multiplicity" is then articulated throughout the book in relation to a series of notions which designate collective subjects, such as "the mobs" and "assemblies". Indeed, the constitutive heterogeneity of migrations and their irreducibility to a distinct and homogeneous "figure" enable us to register both the antagonistic fields in which new collective subjectivities emerge and the inadequacy of the political lexicon usually employed for naming multiplicities.

In particular, what characterises migrant multiplicities, I suggest, is their temporariness, their fleeting dimension and, together with that, their movement. As far as temporariness is concerned, usually migrant collective formations do not last in time for long, as they might be evicted, partitioned and, individually, they might end up with different legal situations (some might be deported, some others might get the refugee status etc.). The unease in conceptualising migrant multiplicities stems also from their movement. Even if they stay put and they struggle in a place or they are blocked there, migrant multiplicities tend to move – not in group or in a coordinated way, but as a result of different individual paths of migration. Therefore, we see that temporariness and movement (being on the move) are tightly connected to each other in shaping migrant multiplicities and our perception of them. In light of that, how shall we account for collective formations that are both temporary and on the move ? For instance, migrants who gather and struggle at different European border-zones? How might a collective political subject emerge not despite being precarious and on the move, but precisely through movement and temporariness?

What does it mean to tackle multiplicity from the point of view of the subjectivation/subjection conceptual diptych? Individual subjects are the outcome of both modes of subjection that shape them (being subject to), and of the process of subjectivation they engage in (being subjects of). I mobilise a similar approach in relation to (migrant) multiplicities exploring how these latter are, on the one hand, produced and divided while, on the other, constitute themselves as collective subjectivities that disrupt or alter power mechanisms. For instance, migrants are managed by being grouped, classified and partitioned – in the refugee camps, at the harbour, in the hotspots and at the border. At the same time, what states have called a "refugee crisis" has been characterised by a series of migrant border crossings and marches that have criss-crossed Europe. Some of these made newspaper headlines, forcing border closures and leading states to let them enter – for example, the migrants walking along the Balkan route in 2015, migrant collective border crossings in Eidomeni, at the Greek–Macedonian border, the migrants' long march from Budapest to Vienna in 2015 that also pushed Germany to temporarily open the borders. Through such an angle on the multiplicities irreducible to homogeneous subjects, this book interrogates the unusual and peculiar temporary collective formations that cannot be described as "a population" nor as "a people".

The other conceptual pole of the book consists of an investigation of the ways in which migrants are targeted individually and, at the same time, how some people are shaped as "migrants". In the book I engage with the issues around the targeting of migrants individually and the making of migration by using the notion of "singularity" as a conceptual catalyst. By foregrounding the term "singularity" instead of "individual" I question the peculiar modes in which migrants are shaped and targeted on an individual basis, without taking for granted the term "individual". In fact, as I will show in Chapter 2, there is a need to rethink processes of individualisation in light of the commodification of migrants, as well as migrants being considered as deceitful subjects incapable of telling the truth (Fanon, 2007).

Such a methodological move allows for not superimposing pre-fabricated conceits of subjectivity and not taking for granted "migrant" as a starting point of the analysis. Indeed, "migrant" is not a sociological category nor an identity; being labelled and governed as a migrant is the outcome of specific laws, racialised policies and administrative measures implemented by the states. I deal with the making of migration at the level of individual subjectivities without considering these as fixed or stable categories, but by looking at how they are shaped and produced as objects of knowledge. The non-fixity of subjectivities depends to a large extent also on migrants' strategies of desubjectivation, struggle and appropriation (Mezzadra, 2016; Scheel, 2013).

By focusing on the making of migration – that is on the political, temporal, legal and economic mechanisms through which some subjects are governed as "migrants" – this book distances itself from analyses that mobilise identity categories – such as the citizen, the refugee, the foreigner – as well as from those that deal with migration as bare life and as subjects stripped of rights. Relatedly, an analytical approach that centres on figures (e.g. the migrant, the citizen, the smuggler) does not help to grasp the peculiar processes of racialisation, exploitation and subjection that shape the individuals, nor the multiple temporary identities that migrants strategically embrace. Hence, the goal is not to find a new paradigmatic figure of migrant subjectivity. Rather, I ask here what are the modes of subjectivation/subjection that shape migrants and that cannot be reduced to the citizen/bare life opposition. Any account of the ways in which migrants are targeted, racialised and disciplined needs to carefully investigate dynamics of power also in their capillary dimension. This involves shifting the attention from any ontologisation of racial processes and subjectivities – which for instance posit the migrants as the racialised subjects or bare lives per excellence – towards an understanding of the how – that is of how in specific contexts some individuals are addressed, racialised and governed as migrants. Ultimately, a focus on *the making of migration,* that is on the processual and conflicting ways through which (some) individuals are enacted as migrants, resounds with approaches to racialisation that conceives race as a technology, apt at constantly producing divisions, hierarchical partitions and exclusions (Atanasoski and Vora, 2019).

GENEALOGIES OF POLITICAL TECHNOLOGIES

The images of overcrowded migrant vessels in the Mediterranean, of amorphous masses of women, children and men landing in Europe, widely circulate on the web, reinforcing the idea of migration as "bare humanity" and as Lisa Malkki (1996: 387) incisively put it, formed by subjects who are deprived of history. More broadly, the media narratives of what states have called a "refugee crisis" have saturated the discursive and the political space, presenting migrants as shipwrecked lives to be rescued or as "swarms" and "unruly mobs" to be chased away. As part of that, migrants are eminently seen as a part of a "problem" to be regulated, contained, or at best, managed. Against this background, I mobilise here a lateral gaze on migration, engaging with a politics of knowledge that delinks migration from the question of "how to govern them?" or "how to govern them better and in a fair way?" Both the security-based approach to migration and the humanitarian one contribute, from different angles, in crafting migration "as a problem" and as an object of government at the same time. In this sense, a critical engagement with the "refugee crisis" narrative consists in rethinking "politics out of security" (Aradau, 2008) and also in producing knowledge out of the security-humanitarian assemblage. In this regard, Angharad Closs-Stephens invites us to reject an approach to knowledge as "a task of counting, ascertaining or measuring that which can already be ascertained", and instead to leave open such a goal, by interrogating how states and nationalisms have been reshaped and how they have resurged in the face of migrants' presence (Closs-Stephens, 2018: 3–4).

In the place of taking for granted the argument according to which there is a "refugee crisis" in Europe, the current politics of migration containment should be analysed according to a historical genealogy of political technologies of governmentality. The partial historical continuity between the colonial context and the current one refers more broadly to the reiteration of a produced distinction between the undisciplined and threatening movements – of the colonised, and of those racialised as migrants today – and the good free mobility of the liberal subject: "the balance presumably achieved within the body of the liberal subject becomes a schism, a contrast, between those who can control their movements, and thus rule, and those whose movement is hindered or excessive, and thus cannot" (Kotef, 2015: 9).

Therefore, in undoing exceptional politics there is a need for historicising techniques of migration control through a postcolonial lens that retraces how similar political technologies have been used for policing colonised populations. Indeed, the colonial experience inhabits and haunts the present, "not only in its most violent forms […] but also through the invisible ones" (Beneduce, 2010: 202); this book retraces a political genealogy of dispersal and concentration, as well as of governing through dividing multiplicities. For instance, tactics of dispersal have been extensively used by the French authorities in colonised Algeria as well as in France in the sixties, as part of urban plans, in order to prevent the consolidation of potential or actual collective subjects. In tracing the genealogies of some political technologies, I build on what Lisa Lowe has called "relations across differences" (Lowe, 2015: 5). Methodologically, this involves "reading across the archives" in a way that "unsettles the discretely bounded objects" (Lowe, 2015: 6), and grasping anomalous details and inconsistencies which can be laboriously spotted in those disparate archives. Despite the different historical and political contexts, it is noticeable how some political technologies for producing subaltern subjects and for governing unauthorised mobility travel across time (Bhandar, 2018). The states' narrative on the "refugee crisis" has contributed to the de-historicisation of the political measures adopted for producing differential hierarchies of mobility. This emerges quite blatantly if we draw attention to how the media depict refugees rescued at sea: they appear as shipwrecked bodies, detached from their own histories, as well as from the political context they come from.

Retracing the genealogies of some notions (such as "the mob") and of political technologies (such as the tactics of dispersal) does not mean disregarding the innovative character of the technologies deployed for containing migration, nor does it entail positing a historical linear continuity. Instead, it is a question of taking stock of the continuities and transformations at the same time as they occurred in the field of migration governmentality and, more broadly, in the governing of unruly populations. To some extent, we can speak of a substantial "nonscalability" (Tsing, 2012) as the methodological starting point to mobilise in migration research: this consists of moving beyond the oppositions between emergency and crisis, on the one hand, and total continuity, on the other, addressing instead the historical contingencies and peculiarities of current power relations. Actually, speaking of transformations is not exhaustive, as long as we do not qualify these further. In fact, do transformations consist of a radical break or a crisis? Or do they instead refer to imperceptible but still relevant restructuring? Some of these transformations have in fact been triggered by specific events, while others consist in re-assemblages of existing power mechanisms, and others in discursive shifts. Situating current migration governmentality within a longer history of population controls and racialised politics of mobility enables us to approach migration from a postcolonial lens (De Genova, 2016).

BIOPOLITICS OF MOBILITY?

In critical migration literature a lot of attention has been paid to bordering mechanisms' politics of control as well as to migrants' resistance and the way in which they exceed security measures (De Genova, 2010; Mezzadra, 2010; Papadopoulos et al., 2008). A growing scholarship has focused on the ways in which migrants' mobility is regulated, selected and contained (Bigo, 2011; Mountz et al., 2013). Overall, these works have focused on the transformations of the border regime (Hess, 2012; Tsianos and Karakayali, 2010). Another relevant migration scholarship has centred on the ways in which migrants' lives and bodies are shaped and targeted as "bare life" (Minca; 2015; Rajaram and Grundy-Warr, 2004) or from the standpoint of the biopolitics of individuals and population (Vaughan-Williams, 2015). However, how are migrants' lives choked, disciplined and displaced in relation to their mobility and to their being on the move? Which political technologies are used to regain control over migrants' mobility and to discipline their lives? What is the relation between biopolitics and mobility?

In the "Security, Territory, Population" course at the Collège de France (1978–1979) Foucault notably conceptualised biopolitics in relation to the governing of circulation. This aspect has remained quite marginal and partially under-theorised both in his work and in contemporary uses of biopolitics, with notable exceptions (Aradau and Blanke, 2010). In particular, while Foucault argues that the main operations of governmentality consist of "making a division between good and bad circulation" (Foucault, 2007: 18), he does not actually analyse how the bad circulation is governed, criminalised and excluded. However, as I will discuss in detail in Chapter 4, if we turn to Foucault's course "The Punitive Society" (1972–1973), we will notice that there he develops an insightful analysis of the criminalisation of popular illegalisms and of acts of vagabondage in the eighteenth century. Therefore, as I explain throughout the book, combining Foucault's analyses on biopolitics from the late seventies with this earlier work might help in our rethinking the biopolitical mechanisms of control which are at play in the present for governing mobility.

A focus on migration today requires interrogating the ways in which biopolitical mechanisms are excised upon and in relation to the governing of mobility. In turn, looking at the intertwining of biopolitical mechanisms and modes of mobility control enables our going beyond the spatial disciplining of migrants, taking into account the effects that borders generate on migrant lives. These cannot be fully grasped in the necropolitical terms of killing or letting die but are, however, associated with heterogeneous modes of violence. In this sense, the use of the term "biopolitics" is not narrowed down to the formula making live/letting die, nor to its sovereign reversal (killing/letting live); rather, it takes into account a spectrum of techniques for regulating life – these also include violent modes, and forms of deprivation and containment which, however, do not necessarily involve making die. Similarly, from such a standpoint, migrants are not tackled in terms of bare life, nor as active-subjects; rather, this book considers how migrants are racialised and the heterogeneous modes of abjection that are generated. Such an analysis of how political technologies shape and impact on migrant lives cannot be done in abstract terms, and necessitates considering the peculiar security-humanitarian technologies that migrants are governed by on a daily basis. In fact, the intertwining of security and humanitarian logics crafts migrants as "risky subjects" and "subjects at risk" at the same time (Aradau, 2004). Therefore, there is not something like a biopolitical technology that applies homogeneously to a definable population. In this sense, we can speak of a series of heterogeneous modes of subjection produced through mechanisms of not making live without, however, letting die. Through such an expression I refer to the proactive operations, enacted by states and non-state actors, for obstructing, choking and disrupting migrants and migrant spaces of life (not making live). Simultaneously, migrants are targeted by humanitarian techniques and interventions that produce migrants as vulnerable subjects and reproduce hierarchies of lives between rescuers and rescued subjects.

How are migrants' lives disciplined by security and humanitarian rationales and interventions, as well by the entanglements of these? According to which political technologies are some subjects racialised and governed as migrants and how do mechanisms of racialisation change over time? Asking these questions means rethinking some of the terms that are widely used in migration literature as well as in political theory to describe modes of subjugation and governing. Notions such as control, protection, identification registration and verbs such as governing need to be deeply revisited in light of the actual (and heterogeneous) practices, knowledges and techniques through which migrants are managed. Migrants are often subjected to modes of governing through partial non-registration and control is overall enacted in an uneven way. On many occasions state authorities are not interested in registering migrants' passages, as for instance is the case at some internal frontiers, nor in identifying migrants individually. Such an enquiry relies on an analytical approach that retraces the continuity of certain concepts, more than of theories, as such a continuity "attests the permanence of the same problem" (Macherey, 2009: 54). The opening and framing of a problem is what theoretically matters for orienting the direction of the analysis. Here, it is the very nexus between migration and governmentality, that is the taken-for-granted idea that migration should be governed, which is posited as a problem, as something to critically undo.

This enquiry into migrant multiplicities and singularities responds to a politically informed investigation that aims at unsettling and stretching the borders of the political. Such a methodological gesture could consist of asking questions such as "what is a struggle?", "what is a political act?", "who is a political subject?". Here, however, I mobilise a slightly different approach, shifting away from a normative-based approach towards an analysis that rethinks the politicalness of mobility, as well as of certain struggles and practices of movement, by paying attention to the current migration battlefield, without superimposing on them pre-established political and epistemic boundaries. Given the irreducible heterogeneity of migration and the difficulty of producing a stable theory out of it, the fact of assuming migration as a lens involves moving from the "what" to the "how" of politics: How do some unruly and unauthorised mobilities disrupt the codes of the political? How are some struggles discredited as non-political? How can we reinvent the political lexicon in light of, and treasuring, migrants' presence and claims? Instead, projecting on the migrants the image of active citizens – and asking if and to what extent migrants do have agency or do resist – I question how migrants' struggles and claims, as well as migrant collective formations, lead us to rethink political spaces and subjectivities. As I will show, both the paradigm of the bare life and the image of the autonomous subject that acts according to free will are inadequate for understanding the modes of subjection and constriction exercised upon migrants. Conversely, this involves paying attention to mechanisms of subjection and constriction that migrants are targeted by, and which often are not exercised through direct physical coercion, nor through a thanatopolitical logic. That is, migration is taken here as a terrain to rethink categories such as "struggle", "agency" and "resistance" and, simultaneously, to come to grips with modes of power and violence that are not highly visible nor overwhelming. Feminist and postcolonial scholarship is used for rethinking jointly practices of subversion from within cramped spaces and modes of subjection through debilitation, obstruction and containment (Hartman, 1997; Mahmood, 2011; Puar, 2017).

While the twofold rationale of incorporation-integration asks "how to bring and codify migrants' claims into the space of citizenship?", it is worth interrogating "how, building on migrants' claims and presence, do we produce and transform political spaces?". It is also in such a way that, as I mentioned above, *the making of migration* acquires an ambivalent meaning: on the one hand, it addresses the political, material and legal processes through which some subjects are shaped, racialised and governed as migrants; on the other, it hints at what migrants generate or contribute to transform, in terms of spaces and languages. The making of migration entails a collective dimension, and it is never a solitary and individualist endeavour: indeed, people who are labelled and governed as migrants are usually subjected to exclusionary partitions and classifications that generate fictitious populations and groups. At the same time, migrants open spaces and enact political subjectivities as long as they turn out to be actual collective formations – migrant groups laying political claims and struggling together – or they appear as virtual multiplicities – irrespective of individual practices of mobility, that is as collective movements, that are depicted by migration agencies and states as "flows".

Methodologically I take spatial chokepoints, partial interruptions and frictions as the starting point of the analysis and not as the by-products of smooth circulations. In fact, in order to rethink biopolitical mechanisms of control we need to bring attention to the moment of partial dis-connectivity, fractions and protracted interruptions that characterise both digital and physical movements. The chokepoint highlights both a spatial bottleneck – which might involve selective processes – and a temporally protracted interruption – which consists for instance of protracted migrant strandedness at certain frontiers. Rethinking the governing of mobility from the standpoint of chokepoints and protracted temporary disruptions means challenging analyses that re-propose the model of the so-called "Fortress Europe" and posit migrants as bare lives; at the same time, this enables questioning works that on the contrary stress the smooth circulation of data and people. Hence, the book engages in conceptualising the operations of power starting from and building on these interruptions, repeated frictions and chokepoints that are not, however, full blockages. Ultimately, as Anna Tsing has famously contended, in order to think and see global connections, we need to start from the multiple frictions that underpin them (Tsing, 2005).

Chapter 1 deals with what I call throughout the book "temporary migrant multiplicities"; that is, migrant collective formations that emerge when migrants become organised to struggle, as well as collectives that are produced by state and non-state actors to discipline migration. Through a genealogical approach, I briefly retrace the history of "the mob", in order to explore the partial continuity among diverse collective subjects that have been discredited as unruly, non-political and dangerous. Following the same methodological approach, Chapter 2 investigates the political technologies that target migrants on an individual basis, and shows that biometric identifications and controls are combined with modes of governing through opacity and non-registration. It brings attention to the peculiar ways in which migrants are governed individually, and building on Fanon's works it points to the depiction of the migrant as a deceitful subject, as a subject incapable and unwilling to tell the truth. Chapter 3 draws attention to virtual multiplicities that stem from the circulation of migrant data. The chapter addresses modes of objectifying migration; that is, producing migrants as objects of knowledge, focusing both on techniques of detecting and governing migration at a distance (e.g. through the use of radars and satellites) and on techniques of data extraction that depend on the mediation of digital technologies (e.g. debit cards for asylum seekers in Greece).

Chapter 4 revolves around mobility as a technology used for governing unruly migration: migrants, the chapter shows, are disciplined and obstructed not only through temporary blockages and forced strandedness but also by being kept on the move, and forced to undertake convoluted geographies across Europe. The chapter retraces the genealogy of dispersal as a technique used for managing colonial populations in the past and that today holds centre stage as part of the policing of migration. It takes into account what I call "the traps of humanitarianism", meaning the active role played by humanitarian measures and actors in restricting migrants' geographies and in producing migrants' vulnerability. Chapter 5 develops the analysis about migrant multiplicities, engaging with recent debates in political theory about collective political subjects, and it foregrounds the idea of migrants' spatial disobediences as collective and individual refusals in front of the spatial restrictions imposed by the Dublin Regulation and by the asylum regime. As this chapter points out, there is a need to enquire about the difficulties of keeping in our memory the multiplicity of migrant struggles that have shaped the European space, as well as border violence. In fact, the spaces of control and the spaces of mobility that are the outcome of border conflicts are highly ephemeral and temporary, and hardly become part of official Europe's history.

A critical approach to "refugee crisis" states' narrative cannot be limited to a deconstructive move which debunks and unveils the political as well as epistemic assumptions this latter relies upon. Unpacking, challenging and undoing are verbs that designate what a critical attitude should gesture towards, with respect to discourses that take for granted and as a starting point the existence of something like a "refugee crisis". Nevertheless, my contention is that the theoretical and political task cannot stop there. The twofold analytical angle of migrant multiplicities and singularities foregrounds the importance of rethinking (the making of) migrant subjectivities, as well as building a political memory of such a hidden and apparently ephemeral but constitutive presence.

1

Migrant Mobs

The (Un)Making of Migrant Multiplicities

INTRODUCTION

Ventimiglia, French–Italian border, 4 August 2016: around 140 migrants, mostly from Sudan, manage to enter France, and yet, after few hundred metres they are caught by the French police and pushed back into Italy. Italian authorities decide to divide the group of migrants, transferring them ten by ten to different reception centres in Southern Italy and Sardinia: "in order to solve the problem, and to prevent Ventimiglia becoming a new Calais on Italian territory, we need to decompress the frontier, which means migrants need to be taken away from there"[1]. These words from the Head of the Italian Police, Franco Gabrielli, in response to the ongoing presence of migrants stranded at the Italian–French border, encapsulate well the tactic of dividing and scattering that characterizes the management of migrant groups in critical border zones. As long as migrants who assemble at a certain frontier or in an urban area organise themselves and appear as emergent collective subjects, they become the target of divisive measures and dispersal strategies. What are the peculiarities of these emergent collective subjects, insofar as their migrant composition is very heterogeneous and that they are often the outcome of temporary alliances? How can we mobilise migration as an analytical lens for coming to grips with collective formations that cannot be described as populations and groups, nor be conceptualised as "the people"? And, how can we think about the politicalness of collective subjects that are temporary and on the move – not as groups who move together, but as result of different individual paths?

This chapter focuses on the production and government of migrant multiplicities, taking these latter not as a pre-existing and fixed category but, on the contrary, as what should be critically tackled in their making. Thus, instead of starting from pre-given collective entities and groups and engaging in a sociological analysis, it explores the ambivalent character of multiplicities. In fact, it looks, on the one hand, at how multiplicities are produced as a result of governmental strategies and at the sorting mechanisms they are subjected to. On the other, it considers how migrant multiplicities do also give rise to unusual forms of collective political subjectivities that are not a population, as long as they do not share an identity or organisation but come together in places. The chapter starts by exploring the peculiarities of migrant multiplicities and of their temporary character, bringing attention to the political technologies through which they are assembled and divided. Then, it retraces a political genealogy of "the mob", highlighting partial continuities between migrant multiplicities and the criminalisation of other forms of unusual collective formations. The chapter moves on by analysing in detail how migrants are governed by being assembled into temporary multiplicities at the harbour, soon after landing, and at the border – in places like Calais and Ventimiglia. In the final section, it takes into account migrant multiplicities as collective subjects, drawing attention to how they are divided, criminalised and discredited as non-political by state-authorities.

Migrant multiplicities in border zones are distinct from other kinds of collective formations since they are governed *through* and *for* the sorting and scattering of the migrants, channelling them, producing differentiations and then individualising the "hold" on their lives in order to hamper the formation of collective political subjects. The difficulty that many migrant groups encounter in finding a common political and legal solution for everybody reflects the way in which migration policies and administrative procedures made on a case-by-case basis contribute to undermine the very possibility of a collective subject emerging. "Mob" and "crowd" are the disqualifying terms through which heterogeneous migrant multiplicities are designated, denying in this way from the very beginning the "politicality of migration movements" (Mezzadra, 2016; see also Stierl, 2018). I suggest that the "fear" of the migrant mob reflects the impasse in fitting migrants' conduct into categories and the irreducibility of migrant subjectivities to a clearly shaped profile and, thus, to a single reason for migrating. Migrant groups are presented as unruly mobs in order to downplay the political dimension of their struggles for movement and to thwart the possibility of a multiplicity becoming a collective political subject. I dwell here on the ambivalent character of the mob, as a multiplicity that is disqualified as amorphous and non-political and that, at the same time, is feared for its troubling potentialities. Nevertheless, there is something specific to migrant collective formations, which mainly depends on their temporariness and precarious character, together with movement (being on the move).

Thinking about migration historically enables our dodging the traps of presentism which are at play in the narratives about the "refugee crisis" and "predisposes us to an analysis that allows that mobility just not happen within ordered social and political structures, but rather it undermines, reshapes and reinforces power relations and institutions. This brings centre stage questions such as: "when is mobility imagined as a problem?" (Anderson, 2013: 12). The Hobbesian model of the collective subject nowadays still looms over philosophical and political conceits of collectivities through a peculiar articulation of the multitude/sovereignty divide, numbers and representation. First, there is no political unity without the translation and reduction of the multitude into one person, "when they are by one man, or one person, represented" (Hobbes, 2008: 109), partially hampering a rethinking of collective formations that cannot be reduced to such a unity without, however, being amorphous multiplicities. In terms of political representation, this involves, as Sandro Mezzadra aptly explained, a "profound separation between the sovereign representation of the political unity of the people and the inarticulate multiplicity of the individuals forming the 'multitude' (2018a: 49).

Migrant multiplicities redefine the edges of non-representability: without being fully excluded, as long as they are interpellate (as potentially threatening subjects), migrant multiplicities unsettle the political operations of representation. They constantly do not fit within the order of political representation, but at the same time are partially incorporated by being interpellated and criminalised. Second, as far as numbers are concerned, it is worth noticing that according to the Hobbesian model the preservation of the multitude is connected to a calculation about adequate numbers. Such a numeric dimension is neither the disordered "many" of the multitude and nor it is considered in absolute terms, rather it is set in comparison to the actual or potential enemy's size. The migrant multiplicities taken into account here are, as I will show later, scanty in numbers, while at the same they are presented in the media as the source of crisis and emergencies. It is precisely by focusing on such a numeric migration paradox – being few, being too scanty in numbers for becoming a hegemonic political subject, but the same time provoking the fear of threatening numbers – that we can engage in rethinking collective subjectivities. Rutvica Andrijasevic and colleagues have compellingly pointed to the emergence of collective subjects that disrupt the binary opposition between minority/majority by strategically appropriating the very "numerical abstraction" used by the state to objectify them (e.g. by speaking of flows and migrant mobs): it is precisely by claiming to be big in numbers that, they argue, emergent collective subjects escape the trap of particularism and minoritization and can lay universal claims (Andrijasevic et al., 2012).

In this regard, the analytical grid on subjectivation and subjection as two mutually interrelated process in the making of individuals needs to be supplemented with a reflection on the making of collective subjects that, as I mentioned in the Introduction, remains by far marginalised in Foucault's work. Or better, in analysing disciplinary mechanisms of power in the mid-seventies, Foucault has actually linked the mechanisms of division and serialisation with the aggregation of these singularities into groups, populations, for controlling them better and making them more productive. In fact, Foucault stresses how disciplinary institutions have worked by producing "identifiable singularities" while at the same time "constituting fields of possible comparison" among them, and generating "phenomenona of groups and populations" (Foucault, 1974). In particular, disciplinary powers act by preventing the consolidation of collective subjects, as Foucault explains in *Discipline and Punish*: "Each individual has his own place; and each place its individual. Avoid distributions in groups; break up collective dispositions; analyse confused, massive or transient pluralities" (Foucault, 1977: 143).

I tentatively use the expression "migrant multiplicities" to designate migrants who temporarily assemble together in a certain space, often building tactical alliances, and whose collective dimension can be captured neither through the notion of population nor in terms of (consolidated and homogeneous) groups. This enables keeping open and interrogating the specificity and the actual composition of migrant *incipient collective subjects* and of their politicalness instead of assuming a pre-established collective subject – like the multitude, the people or the population. In the history of political thought the very notion of "the people" is associated with the territory, and, therefore, "mobile people find it impossible to constitute themselves as political subjects precisely because they cannot be coextensive with a territory, as they remain peoples without geography" (Isin, 2018: 120; see also Elden, 2010). In so doing, it becomes possible to disjoin the collective dimension from numbers, to the extent that a (migrant) multiplicity can also be scant or quite irrelevant in a number sense while being politically significant. Ultimately, the term "migration" works as a sort of abstract placeholder for a plurality of individuals, as well as for heterogeneous groups and migrant multiplicities, that in this way become part of the indistinct and atemporal "migration" figure. As Nicholas De Genova has poignantly pointed out, "migration scholarship (however critical) is implicated in a continuous (re-) reification of 'migrants' as a distinct category of human mobility" (2013: 253). Thus, "migration" is the name of an operation of abstraction and translation of *migrations* (as plural, as multiplicities, as migrant groups) and *migrants* (not as sociological categories but as people who are racialised and governed as migrants) into an abstract over-catching referent that visually corresponds to the image of the (migration) "flow". In fact, the figurative referent of "the flow" operates by subsuming migrant singularities and the concrete reality of migrant multiplicities, in their heterogeneity. Speaking of "flows" means suspending the (heterogeneous) temporality of migration: the image of the migration flow is not the result of a snapshot taken in a certain place at a given time, but of a more complex elaboration of data and information collected over time and then translated and abstracted into an atemporal figure. Nevertheless, in light of migrant multiplicities being characterised by being temporary and on the move, we could think about a way to appropriate, twist and reverse the very image of the flow. The limits of theorising migrant multiplicities through sociological categories (such as group and population) rely precisely on the fact that very often these multiplicities do not last in time, not only because they might be evicted but also because they do also move. For the citizens of towns like Ventimiglia or Calais, the presence of migrant multiplicities also when these have engaged in collective struggles is indeed perceived as a passage, that might last a few days or weeks. Therefore, the movement of "migration movements" is what needs to be conceptualised further, as it is crucial for grasping the specificities of migrant multiplicities, too. In this regard, it is worth noticing that in the literature on collective subjects, the dimension of movement remains under-theorised: echoing Foucault's consideration that in speaking of "class struggles" Marxism never actually dwelled upon the notion of "struggle" and its dynamism, similarly we can argue that theories of "social movements" downplayed "movement" as such (Foucault, 2000a).[2]

The production and government of migrant multiplicities has been relatively marginalised in migration scholarship, although with notable exceptions (Agier, 2011). To be more precise, such a topic has been addressed in migration literature from diverse perspectives, although often while taking for granted the collective units in which migrants are included. Moreover, reflections on the production and government of collectivities can also be extended beyond scholarship on border controls to critical analyses about race and racism (Gilroy, 2013; Keith, 1993), showing the racialized and constructive character of migrant group membership (Sharma, 2013). Here I scrutinize the effective modalities and techniques through which migrants are targeted, classified and partitioned as part of multiplicities in order to be governed, showing that what distinguishes migrant multiplicities in border zones is their *temporary and divisible character*. That is to say, migrants in border zones are grouped in order to be managed and controlled, and at the same time they are grouped to be divided. Then, I investigate the ambivalent character of migrant multiplicities, showing that, although multiplicities are the outcome of techniques of identification and government, potentially they can also form *incipient collective subjects*. The "migrant mob" is in fact what is feared by states and migration agencies that constantly try to divide and scatter the migrants.

As I will illustrate further, migrant multiplicities can be the result of a *spatial proximity* – migrants who arrive at the same border; they can be a *virtual multiplicity* formed through the assemblage of migration data giving rise to generalizable singularities and profiles; or, finally, they can be a *narrated and visualised multiplicity*.

GENEALOGIES OF "THE MOB"

"Democratic theories have always feared the mob", Judith Butler argues, "even as they affirm the importance of expressions of popular will, even in their unruly forms" (Butler, 2015: 1). The mob is not only feared but also criminalised and disqualified as an amorphous collective subject, whose actions are not deemed to be political. The fear of the mob as well as of migrant multiplicities should be situated in a longer political genealogy about the criminalisation of colonised subjects. Such a continuum of criminalisation does actually involve a series of racialised subjectivities: "every act, as long as it is made by a slave, an indigenous person, a colonised subject, or a Black person... become a criminal act" (Dorlin, 2017: 28). If, on the one hand, migrants arriving in groups become objects of government – insofar as they are managed as temporary divisible multiplicities – on the other, the level of the multiplicity corresponds to what cannot be fully captured by the selective and exclusionary criteria of migration management. As an important stream of literature has explained, the mob as a dangerous unruly multiplicity has a long history: the term "the mob" has its etymological root in the Latin expression *mobile vulgus*, designating the "unstable common people" (Hayes, 1992: 6; see also Shoemaker, 2007; Thompson, 1963), and has been used in the English vocabulary since the seventeenth century to name tumultuous popular multiplicities. Dimitris Papadopoulos and colleagues have rightly observed that "it is no coincidence that the word mobility not only refers to movement but also to the common people, the working classes, the mob" (2008: 56). The mobility and instability of the mob is of particular relevance, I suggest, for dealing with migrant multiplicities, whose main characteristic is precisely their being fleeting and on the move – yet, not as a group of people which move together but as a collective formation whose individuals might follow different pathways and be subjected to different restrictions.

Notably, Karl Marx and Friedrich Engels used the term *Lumpenproletariat* to designate, through a negative connotation, all those heterogeneous people who were not part of the proletariat, and who were not part of the productive process. However, Nicholas Thoburn has remarked, Marx and Engels actually have not defined Lumpenproletariat in a precise way, and indeed this latter appears as a "nebulous non-class" which "takes multiple guises" (Thobourn, 2002: 438).[3] The mob, Engels contends in *The Peasant War in Germany*, fails to be consolidated into a party, and it is the tumultuous "scum of the decaying elements of all classes" (Engels, 2015: 8).

As Peter Linebaugh (1975) has shown, in eighteenth-century England, the "scum of the people" as poorly disordered individuals, and the tumultuous working class, get blurred in the use of the term "the mob". More precisely, the mob revealed that the very "separation between the criminal and the working class" was hardly tenable (Linebaugh, 1975: 82), due to the increasing criminalisation of infra-legal activities). Subsequently, since the end of the eighteenth century, "the mob" came to designate an unruly minority formed by vagabonds, beggars, lazy people and criminals that were not part of the working class or of the people – therefore, it encapsulated all those subjects who, as described by Michel Foucault, were considered guilty of "debauchery", of refusing to be "fixed to a productive apparatus" (2015a: 207) and the "geographic pinning" (p. 43) associated with that. In this regard, Foucault's lectures at Collège de France in 1973, "The Punitive Society", can be seen as a pioneering text of an important critical literature that traces a genealogy of the ways in which unruly conduct consisting of acts of vagabondage and vagrancy had been regulated and disciplined over time (Anderson, 2013; Boutang, 1998; Papadopoulos et al., 2008). In the lecture series "Penal Theories and Institutions" (1972) Foucault focuses on popular seditions in the seventeenth century, employing the term "seditious plebs". However, an important change takes place between the two lecture series. While in "Penal Theories and Institutions" Foucault mobilises the expressions "*seditions populaires*",[4] one year later in "The Punitive Society" he uses a different vocabulary, speaking of "popular illegalisms", and such a change in the terminology reveals a critique of Marxist analyses of the role of popular seditions and of the mobs. In particular, Foucault's criticism is directed towards the Marxian historian E. P. Thompson, who referred to the actions of the mob to explain the increase of repressive measures against popular classes. If in the course of 1972 Foucault in part supported such a hypothesis, in "The Punitive Society" he situates the analysis in a more complex economy of power: "popular illegalisms" appeared to him as a more operational and effective notion because it captures the productive role that the "illegal" conducts of the popular classes had for the rise of early capitalism and of the bourgeoisie. The moralisation and criminalisation of popular illegalisms started only when these latter became counterproductive for the bourgeoisie:

> Now I am not sure I am right in using the term "seditious mobs [*plèbe séditieuse*]." Actually, it seems to me that the mechanism that brought about the formation of this punitive system is, in a sense, deeper and broader than that of the simple control of the seditious mobs. What had to be controlled [...] is a deeper and more constant phenomenon of which sedition is only a particular case: lower-class or popular illegalisms. (Foucault, 2015a: 140)

Therefore, Foucault distances himself from analyses that use the term "mobs", not because he refuses to consider popular riots, but because such a terminology has been adopted for giving a specific historical explanation about the emergence of apparatuses of control. Here I am interested in interrogating how to repoliticise "the mob" in light of the current migrant collective formations and the ways in which these are constantly divided, governed and neutralised by state authorities. I do not consider the term "the mob" in relation to our present as a lens to analyse the enforcement of border politics and repressive measures, but instead as a way to investigate the emergence of temporary (migrant) collective subjects and how the ways in which these were disqualified were non-political. What is important to retain from Foucault's courses at the Collège de France from the early seventies (1971–1972 and 1972–1973) is the attention paid to what can be called the irreducibility of multiplicities to the population. In fact, while five years later, in "Security, Territory, Population" (1978–1979), he focuses on the historical emergence of the population as an object of government, those two earlier lecture series shed light on movements and collective formations that are criminalised as unruly subjectivities, and at the same time break any potential unity of the population. Actually, in the lecture of 18 January of "Security, Territory, Population", Foucault opposes the people to the population, showing that historically the people have constituted what has resisted their incorporation into the population as an object of government:

> The people comprise those who conduct themselves in relation to the management of the population, at the level of the population, as if they were not part of the population as a collective subject-object, as if they put themselves outside of it, and consequently the people are those who, refusing to be the population, disrupt the system. (Foucault, 2007: 43–44)

Yet, the incommensurability between the people and the population is the outcome of individual and collective refusals and of resistances: in the eighteenth century the people, Foucault explains, are those who do not act as members of the population, that is those who do not behave according to the economic rationale and who end up provoking riots. In *Pouvoirs et Strategies* (1977) Foucault describes such an irreducibility of some multiplicities to the population by using the term "the plebs": indeed, "the plebs" is not a sociological entity, according to Foucault, but rather it exists in groups, classes and in the civil society as something that tries to disengage from power relations, not by being outside them but working as "their limits", as a sort of "centrifugal movement" (Foucault, 2000b: 421).

Thus, the unruly multiplicities that Foucault takes into account in 1972 and 1973 recall to some extent the irreducibility of "the people" to the population, although with some important differences. Indeed, "the people" that Foucault talks about in "Security, Territory, Population" is in a relation of internal exclusion with respect to "the population", as long as "the people" is ultimately formed by individuals that do not behave as they were expected to – and, as a consequence of their refusals and misconducts, are marginalised and exclude themselves from it. Instead, "The Punitive Society" and "Penal Theories and Institutions" point more to conducts and movements that deliberately act against the constituted order (the seditious revolts of the Nu-Pieds) or that act by constantly subtracting from disciplinary obligations (the vagabonds). In particular, as far as the seditious revolts are concerned, it is relevant that they are characterised by the constant blurring between political struggles and ordinary crimes. In fact, in this way these revolts highlight how practices of refusal turn out to be discredited as non-political and, at the same time, as ordinary crimes (Foucault, 2015b). Despite the recurrent use of the term in the English literature, "the mob" remains a fundamentally under-theorised notion and a term that tends to be dismissed more than reactivated in the present to grasp collective formations that are not reducible to the population.

If the mob is not reactivated for thinking about marginalised political subjectivities in the present, it is, I suggest, also because of the negative connotations that it has assumed throughout the centuries. In fact, the mob is nowadays associated in the media with groups rioting, subjects that clash with the police, and it is usually inflected by racialising features – e.g. "black people". Thus, the mob is used for disqualifying collective subjects, being very often associated with mechanisms of criminalisation. Relatedly, in political theory the term has been dismissed and depicted as amorphous masses or groups that act violently (Schlesinger, 1955). However, it is by starting from such a negative connotation that, I suggest, the notion of the mob can be revitalised, retracing its genealogy, precisely to point to the misrecognition and to the criminalisation of emergent migrant collective formations. In other words, we can ask "is that another way to mobilise that term, even forcing a certain break with its legacy?" (Butler, 2015: 147).

The use of the term "the mob" can be made through a sort of strategic appropriation which enables drawing attention to the modes in which collective subjects are divided, targeted and disqualified by state authorities. To be clear, my goal is not to restore "the mob" – in this case "migrant mobs" – as a positive political notion; rather, such a notion becomes a sort of analytical lens for grasping the emergence and governing of migrant collective formations. In turn, through such a move I question the way in which collective political subjectivities are object of hierarchisation – and, thus, some collective subjects are considered more political than others, or are disqualified as not at all political. Ultimately, a focus on the *(un)making of migrant mobs* enables us to grasp in a transversal way the *making of the people* and the exclusionary criteria upon which this latter is produced and renewed. Through such an analytical lens it becomes possible to question the exclusionary thresholds of the political, and to come to grips with temporary collective formations that in many cases, even if they do not lay claim or demand, simply struggle to stay or move (Rancière, 1999).

In the *Outlaws of the Atlantic*, the historian Marcus Rediker retraces the formation and the struggles of what he calls the transatlantic motley crew in the years 1760–1780. Far from representing a unitary collective subject, this latter was formed by "multiracial mobs" (Rediker, 2014: 138) of sailors, slaves and workers that struggled against a series of law reforms in the British colonies in North America. What is remarkable, in Rediker's account, is the heterogeneous composition of those motley crews, both in terms of social and economic positions and in terms of origins. Through his analysis of the motley crews, he provides a sort of counter-history of British colonialism, putting at the core what remains rather concealed in official historical narratives: the struggles of the multiracial hydra mobs – that is, people who were part, as sailors or as slaves, of the transatlantic trade. Importantly, Rediker retraces a counter-punctual genealogy of the mobs at sea – as plural, to avoid any homogenising account of that – by highlighting the radical political claims that the motley crews laid about freedom. It is precisely through the struggles of the mobs that the English principle of liberty became resignified in a radical sense, pushing forward the battle for freedom together with the abolitionist campaign. Yet, even if the motley crews have their origin in the Atlantic Ocean, Rediker's work sheds light on the reverberations that they triggered on the mainland: sailors, workers in the ship sector and slaves became organised in many towns along the East Coast of the United States, going on collective strikes, or hampering the departure of merchant vessels, or rioting against the local powers. Moreover, we could find important similarities between the motley crews and others: "The second meaning describes a social-political formation of the eighteenth-century port city [...] Motley crew in this sense was closely related to the urban mob and the revolutionary crowd" (Rediker, 2014: 119).

Despite emergent organisational forms, the multiracial mobs have never become a homogeneous collective subject; on the contrary, their political strength relied precisely in their heterogeneous composition that had, however, been put to work for building transversal alliances which criss-crossed different classes and racialised conditions. Therefore, Rediker's analysis of the motley crew allows the restoration of an image of the mob that undoes depoliticising narratives of it, showing the revolutionary drive that it actually constituted for a decade. The *Many-Headed Hydra* by Peter Linebaugh and Marcus Rediker, which also focuses on the motley crew, equips us, I suggest, with an important methodological tool for tackling multiplicities beyond the singularity of specific episodes. Indeed, they retrace the emergence of the motley crew by taking into account "acts of resistance" not in an isolated way, but rather by "situating them in relation to each other" (Linebaugh and Rediker, 2013: 193). In fact, they suggest that only by reconstructing the historical continuity and the mutual relationship among different episodes is it possible to keep a memory of these collective subjects that is not narrated by the official historical narratives and is missing from the archives.

To sum up, "the mob" refers at the same time to the people who form it – being an unruly and marginalised minority or the common people – and to the troubling activities in which they engage, in particular as undisciplined mobile workers (Shoemaker, 2007). In this sense, a genealogy of the mob intersects from the very beginning a series of anti-vagrancy laws, and the techniques and legislation for disciplining the poor and social disorder (Anderson, 2013). This point is also related to the choice of using the term "the mob" instead of "the crowd" for designating migrant multiplicities – both as they are produced and governed by states, and as multiplicities of migrants that are feared insofar as they trouble the exclusionary order of citizenship (Nail, 2015). As Peter Hayes underlines, the "the crowd" has been historically associated with a majority subject (the mass) that, moreover, is characterised by an external drive that leads it and influences the behaviour of the people who are part of the crowd, not as individuals but as a mass (Hayes, 1992). Here I use the term "the mob" in a very specific way, one that does not fully overlap with "deviant" conducts that refuse any territorial bondage – like vagabonds – and that designate migrant multiplicities in border zones – and, how they are governed as multiplicities.

Claudia Aradau and Jef Huysmans advocate "for recovering the 'mob' as a category of democracy rather than as its outside", hinging on the extra-legal character of the mob, on its irreducibility to the demos (2009: 601): "While the people as the demos was perceived as the orderly force that democracies needed to foster and to sustain, the mob was the antinomy of the demos, the excess and unrest that could only be perceived as threatening for democratic forces" (Aradau and Huysmans, 2009: 602). It is precisely this opposition between the people and the mob, they contend, that needs to be challenged, looking at the mob as the constitutive internal excess of the people. It is along these lines, I suggest, that the migrant mob should be addressed as part of a critical project that aims to grasp what unsettles and cannot be contained into the partitioning criteria of migration politics. Yet, the migrant mob is not simply the unruly minority, it is formed by the temporary co-existence of subjects who are outside of the space of citizenship. Also, by speaking about "migrant mobs" we should be careful not to overstate what can be called *the political size of numbers* – that is the fact that a given number of migrants is perceived and presented as massive in its impact on the society. For this reason it is important to keep the meaning of a minority that troubles the established order of citizenship, irrespective of numbers. Indeed, in the field of migration it is not only a question of contested "big" numbers but also of the production of remnants – that is, of a "few" people that after any sorting or classifying operation remain outside of categories, as uncountable bodies in excess. The term "migrant mob" can be mobilised also to refer to a mob that is numerically in default – a *dearth mob*.

ASSEMBLING, GROUPING AND DIVIDING IN THE BORDER ZONES

How are migrants managed and partitioned as part of multiplicities in border zones? The sorting processes of categorisation, partition and channelling are particularly visible and work more incessantly than in other spaces, and consequently border zones are privileged ethnographic sites for grasping the formation and the government of multiplicities. What distinguishes multiplicities in border zones from other kinds of migrant collective formations that emerge in other contexts and during different experiences of migration is their temporary divisible character. This is very different, for instance, from subjects who are governed as part of migrant communities in the cities, both for their persistence in time and for the relative homogeneity in terms of migrant composition. The migrant multiplicities I address here should not be confused with ethnic communities or with stable groups with collective identities.

The volatile character of migrant groups in border zones makes difficult the emergence of collective identities that are instead at play in many migrant communities. In border zones migrant multiplicities are produced on a temporary basis and not with the goal to govern migrants as part of stable collective units but, rather, to divide them and to disperse and scatter migrants across space, in part invisibilising their presence. Importantly, by using the term "multiplicity" I do not refer to big numbers. On the contrary, by disjoining multiplicity and big numbers, we can see a resonance between multiplicity and Deleuze and Guattari's account of minorities, according to whom the difference between majority and minority is not given by numbers; minorities can in fact also outnumber the majority, but they remain non-numerable (Deleuze and Guttari, 1987). However, it is not only these multiplicities that constantly mismatch the arithmetic counting (what is counted) that Jacques Rancière notably talks about in *The Disagreement* (Rancière, 1999): migrant multiplicities as potential or actual collective political subjectivities do not always even ask to be part of the geometric counting, that is to claim their right to count, since they are often irreducible to traditional forms of political representation.

What does happen to migrants when, after being rescued at sea by the Navy, they are disembarked at the harbour in Italy? How are they divided and how are they treated as migrant groups in transit points, refugee camps and border-crossing points? The temporary dimension of migrant multiplicities while people are in a refugee camp or when they are blocked at the border crossing point makes it difficult to understand on which basis people are grouped and partitioned, and the kind of multiplicity that is produced and targeted. The term "population" is often used to describe the simultaneous presence of many migrants in a certain place – a space of detention or a refugee camp. However, I suggest that the referent "population" appears inadequate to account for the heterogeneity and the temporary dimension of migrant multiplicities that are formed when migrants are facing national authorities or humanitarian actors in charge of governing and partitioning them. Indeed, if we go back to Foucault's definition of "population", we see that a certain degree of homogeneity – a commonality of naturalised features – among the subjects who form it is required together with a stability of that collective dimension: a population designates "a multiplicity of individuals who fundamentally and essentially only exist biologically bound to the materiality within which they live" (Foucault, 2007: 37).

Yet, it could be objected that populations are not only groups characterised by the same nationality: since the nineteenth century the production of populations has also been done by starting from statistics about specific phenomena – like pathologies and deviances – that concerned sub-groups of the national population and that had been mapped and calculated in order to govern them and produce degrees of normality and abnormality (Brighenti, 2014; Hacking, 1982; Hannah, 2000; Legg, 2005). However, what is relevant for understanding the transformation in the government of individuals and multiplicities is less about these two levels taken in themselves than their mutual relationship (Foucault, 2007). Thus, the theoretical challenge consists precisely of undoing the unquestioned nexus between populations and states that has been historically crystallised with the emergence of the modern system of nation states. In this regard, he has highlighted that "our analysis of the government of the state should itself be located in a more general examination of the government of populations" (Hindess, 2000: 119), and conversely that "the state is not the only agency involved in the government of its population (2000: 132).

Migrants who arrive in border zones are managed as individuals who are part of a multiplicity. This essentially involves two things. Firstly, the way in which migrants are governed and labelled[5] depends to a large extent on a question of percentages and numbers – for instance, given a certain group of migrants who have arrived in a refugee camp, some of these will be denied international protection, as the asylum system is based precisely on the partition between refugees and people who are rejected. The political context has a great influence on the approach of the police and humanitarian actors, as well as the choice of targeting specific individuals among the migrant mass. A blatant example is given by arrivals of migrants rescued in the Mediterranean within the framework of the Triton operation and who were disembarked at Italian harbours:[6] at any time, among the migrants rescued, Frontex officers would single out one or more presumed smugglers who will be treated differently from all the other people in the group and put in the line for detention and deportation. In addition, temporary multiplicities are actually produced in order to partition the migrants, dividing between asylum seekers and "fake" refugees, allocating some to special hosting centres and activating for others fast deportation procedures.

I use here the expression "temporary divisible multiplicities" to refer to the ways in which migrants are addressed and treated as part of various groups by national authorities, border guards or humanitarian actors when they arrive in crucial border zones. Temporary divisible multiplicities are characterised by their volatile and temporary dimension, as well as by the goal of selecting, channelling and partitioning the migrants. As mentioned above, such a temporary divisible character cannot be generalised to any space, and in fact there are contexts, beyond the border zones, in which migrant multiplicities correspond to more or less stable and homogeneous groups. The migrants who are part of a certain temporary governable multiplicity will then form new temporary groups and multiplicities. In his book *Ambiguous Multiplicities* Andrea Brighenti (2014: 14). contends that the government of multiplicities also entails strategies and "forms of spatial containment" that, building on civic engineering, shape the effective and material manageability of collective formations, preventing the eruption of unruly multitudes. The logic of containment and mechanisms of capture that often actualise in forms of preventative detention are at stake also in the government of migrant multiplicities: the potential impact of migrants arriving in groups is managed through measures of temporary spatial segregation that make the heterogeneous migrant composition a governable multiplicity of bodies to identify. Nevertheless, the spatial containment of migrant multiplicities in the border zones is not aimed exclusively at controlling individuals. Rather, actions of spatial bordering pave the way for classifying and dividing migrants, and, further, it is not only a question of sorting out migrants: partitioning mechanisms serve and contribute to produce asymmetrical differentiations and exclusionary boundaries among them.

AT THE HARBOUR

The heterogeneous migrant composition and the "turbulence of migration" (Papastiergiadis, 2000) is what policy makers, states and migration agencies try to govern by constantly crafting new taxonomies to capture and discipline practices of migration that do not fit within existing migration profiles. After being rescued at sea, migrants are firstly identified and fingerprinted at the harbour upon disembarkation. The first identification procedure aims to establish their biometric *traceability*, verifying if someone already has a criminal record as an irregular migrant in Europe, and marking all their entrances by storing the data in national and European databases, such as the European Asylum Dactyloscopy Database (EURODAC).[7] At the harbour, migrants are also interrogated by Frontex officers who ask them questions about their journey. However, it is not at this stage that the *biographical records* of migrants are used for assessing individual cases and deciding on their asylum claim: the data collected are anonymised and then used to generate migration profiles that are independent from individual stories, and produce maps about migrants' routes and migrants' modus operandi.[8] Therefore, the "hold" on migrants at this stage is intended less for governing them individually than for archiving migrant stories and geographies in order to produce risk analysis. This does not (only) mean that individualising processes come later with respect to the management of multiplicities; rather, mechanisms of individualisation take place in the frame of partitions and exclusions that address the migrants as part of a multiplicity.

Migrants in the places of first arrival are subjected to sorting processes with the twofold aim of tracing exclusionary partitions (dividing potential asylum seekers from those who are quickly returned to their countries of origin) and, simultaneously, of preventing collective subjects from emerging around a common claim. This tactic of quickly dividing migrant multiplicities has been especially visible on the island of Lampedusa: indeed, many times the Italian authorities divided groups of migrants who were collectively refusing to be fingerprinted – when the migrants made collective protests, they were transferred to the mainland in small groups and forced to give their fingerprints with the use of violence. In that way, the police's goal was both to identify any single migrants and to neutralise migrants' collective formations.

The government of a migrant multiplicity entails a technique and a politics of counting in order to assess its governability and to trace exclusionary boundaries.

The practice of counting works on a twofold temporal dimension: counting is functional to the immediate management of the migrant multiplicity but also to statistical purposes; the data collected are stored and assembled, detaching them from the contingency of that specific migrant multiplicity. Therefore, it not only serves the goal of numbering subjects but also of sorting them. Taxonomy and classification, on the one hand, and quantification, on the other, are, in fact, as Alain Desrosieres illustrates in his historical account of the "politics of great numbers", the two main functions of counting (Desrosieres, 1993). In order to challenge the image of migration management as an exhaustive practice of control, it is important to confront the proliferation of statistics on migrant arrivals and the daily counting of migrants in border zones with the *production of uncounted remnants*.[9] These uncounted remnants correspond to the "few" migrants that remain unclassified or not of concern for humanitarian actors and migration agencies. The uncounted could also refer to unmapped presences and movements of migrants. Therefore, the "uncounted" encapsulate a series of subjects and phenomena that remain under the pertinence and the interest of the governmental counting.

A case that is particularly timely today with the increasing number of asylum applications in Europe is provided by the rejected refugee population in the European space; that is, asylum seekers who have been denied international protection. What happens after asylum seekers are produced by the criteria of asylum as irregular migrants on the European territory? In this regard, Nicholas De Genova has aptly remarked that "in systematic and predictable ways, asylum regimes disproportionately disqualify asylum seekers, and convert them into 'illegal' and deportable 'migrants'" (2013: 1081). Over the last two years the asylum system has worked as one of the main mechanisms of illegalisation of migrants. Indeed, about 220,000 asylum seekers have been illegalised between 2013 and 2015 as they have been denied international protection.[10] However, this number says very little about the actual presence in Europe of those people, as well as of their internal displacements within the European space or eventual returns. This means drawing attention to the production of a multiplicity of rejected refugees who become not of concern for governmental agencies: asylum seekers "disappear" from the United Nations High Commissioner for Refugees (UNHCR) official statistics and reports as soon as their legal status changes with the rejection of their asylum claims. Or better, while the number of rejections is quantified, their movements and their effective condition after illegalisation remain fundamentally unmapped. Yet, not being counted should not be confused with not being governed: the life of those who remain out of any count is not less governed and affected by migration policies than the life of those who fit into specific migratory profiles and are finally counted. Rather, there are always subjects who are (governed as being) not of concern. To put it differently, in order to make migrant multiplicities governable, there are some who remain unclassified or uncounted.

THE PRODUCTION OF GENERALISABLE SINGULARITIES

The government of migrant multiplicities is not based only on the direct action upon many migrants who gather in a border zone and who are thus managed as a group, as a multiplicity. The production of a governable multiplicity consist also in databases of migrant profiles generated through the assemblage of data. Actually, the production of what I call generalisable singularities, starting from the collection of personal data, is not peculiar to migration governmentality only. Rather, data extraction and assemblage activities in the field of migration should be situated in a much broader context of data double production that concerns all subjects. Starting from a given composite population, different sub-groups – among which are also migrants – are singled out through mechanisms of data extraction and generating profiles of risk (Adey et al., 2012). Yet, the practices of data extraction that I address and that are devised for targeting migrants work in a slightly different manner: what is produced are less distinct categories of risk profiles and sub-groups than a narrated map of migrants' modus operandi that is combined with statistics about the nationality and the status (e.g. asylum seekers, "irregular" migrant, refugee) of the migrants.

This activity of data-extraction is usually conducted by Frontex or by the national police at border crossing points, or when migrants are apprehended for control inside the European space. Then, the information gathered becomes the material for the production of Frontex risk analyses and is also stored in the Europol database. The data collection conducted across Europe in October 2014 under the Mos Maiorum operation clearly shows the modalities and the implications of the knowledge extraction on migration. For 15 days the national police of European Union states were in charge of stopping migrants in cities and in crucial sites like rail stations. On that occasion, migrants were asked to provide details both about their nationality and actual status and about their journeys and modus operandi (costs, use of smuggling networks, routes) and their final destination. All the data collected were then anonymised, and thus the information concerning migrants' identity – such as age and nationality – was not connected to any single person but detached from the individuals and reassembled in order to trace a picture of the composition and modus operandi of the migrants.

The result of this "biographical interrogatory" for the migrants has been an EU report combining information on *who* the migrants are who cross irregularly the external and internal borders of Europe with details about *how* and *where* they crossed.[11] It follows that what is at stake in the production of a virtual migration population is a peculiar relationship between the level of singular identities and conducts – from which data have been extracted – and the level of multiplicities and big numbers. The production of *generalisable singularities* is the outcome of the combination of anonymised data concerning the "who" of the migrants and data about their *conduct of migration*, that is the activities and strategies in which these migrants engage. At a closer glance, it appears that a threefold process is at stake: *extraction* – of data from individual migrants; *abstraction* – from the materiality of migrant biographies and data; and *assemblage* – of different data to craft profiles that actually correspond to generalisable singularities, namely migrant profiles that then are used for labelling and categorising heterogeneous practices of migration and individual trajectories. Hence, the production of generalisable singularities translates the materiality of individual stories and identities into a virtual population that has not only a descriptive function but also an anticipatory one that works as a blueprint for partitioning migrants.

The question of the production of virtual populations as a reality that does not result from statistics but from pre-emptive knowledge is an issue that cannot be addressed only through Foucault's analysis of the emergence and government of population. In *Security, Territory, Population* governmentality and dispositives of security are tackled in relation to actual multiplicities of subjects that become effective "populations". Indeed, the reality of the population is defined by Foucault through its "penetrable naturalness" (2007: 72), and it is the outcome of political economy and statistics. Moreover, as Foucault clearly explains, the issue of population in modern governmentality is inherently connected to the problem of the interventions needed for its regulation. Instead, the virtual populations that stem from the data extraction and data elaboration activities are not actionable realities, nor do they represent a collective subject. Virtual populations constitute the projection of potential future multiplicities formed by a series of profiles and trends that have been shaped on the basis of the information and data collected from singular bodies.

WHICH MULTIPLICITY? THE MIGRANT MOB BETWEEN ROUTES AND CROWDS

Up to now, this chapter has addressed the political and administrative techniques through which multiplicities are produced and migrants are governed as part of them. However, the level of representation is also part of the range of techniques mobilised for making up a migrant multiplicity from the point of view of its visual capture and of the public perception of it. As Ian Hacking has demonstrated, subjects are not merely made up in a passive way; on the contrary, tactics of strategic appropriation are a constitutive part of processes of subjectivation (Hacking, 2002). The struggles over the asylum illustrate well how migrants sometimes strategically overturn the function of categories. If we consider asylum-seekers who have been denied international protection, it is noticeable that in many European migrant transit points – such as in Milan and Marseille, and in Ventimiglia, at the French–Italian border – these rejected refugees claimed to be the real subjects of humanitarianism, as people fleeing wars and living in a state of insecurity. They unsettled in this way the exclusionary criteria of the asylum, defining themselves as refugees and considering the international protection as what should be granted on the basis of the war and insecurity they experienced, not necessarily in the countries of origin but also in the countries where they were living.[12] Thus, up against UNHCR that labels as "people not of concern" all asylum-seekers who do not meet the criteria and become rejected refugees, these migrants engaged in a sort of "politics of the governed" (Chatterjee, 2004), demanding to be protected as war escapees and recrafting the very category of the asylum.

If we consider the images through which unauthorised migrants enter the European space, it is noticeable that migrant multiplicities are presented through the visual operators of migration governmentality. The news and pictures of thousands of migrants blocked in summer 2015 at the external borders of Europe have circulated widely on the web, presenting those people seeking asylum as unruly crowds, formed by women, children and men, clashing with the police. The lengthened presence at the borders of many of the migrants, temporarily stranded in the attempt to cross the borders of Europe, has in fact contributed to depict and narrate them as "crowds", "masses" and "mobs". The captions under the images finalise the illustration of bodily presences as unruly multiplicities, as if a sort of coordinated attack by transnational populations on the European frontiers was under way. The resurgence of the terms "crowd" and "mob" used for naming the massive numbers of people fleeing wars in the attempt to reach Europe to seek asylum reveals a partial shift away from the image of the flow that has largely characterised the narrative of migration management. Indeed, in front of the images of migrants stranded at the borders or waiting in many European rail stations, the fluid and abstract visual descriptor of the "flow" appears as inadequate. In addition to this, the stubbornness of the migrants in reaching Europe, and the "incorrigibility" (De Genova, 2010) of their practices of movement, contributed the depiction of those people as "migrant crowds": the resolution of women, men and children in crossing borders and moving on could hardly have been encapsulated in the elusive and moving image of the flow. The study of migration flows performed by migration agencies such as Frontex actually entails a refocusing from border lines to migrant itineraries for crafting new migrant routes – "the ways in which migration management seeks to channel movements into migration routes" (Casas-Cortes et al., 2015: 900). In other words, the presence of mass migrations in route requires that these are scrutinised in their spatial strategies of mobility. Nevertheless, this spatialisation of migration movements that migration agencies undertake in order to contain and channel mobility as a phenomenon of great numbers and multiplicities does resolve the issue of qualifying the composition of these migrant multiplicities.

If we consider the political economy of visibility at stake in the media representation of migration, the migrant vessel plays a paramount role and has become "a visual trope that migrates across information and media platforms" (Walters, 2015: 475). Indeed, the migrant ship is part of a complex *scene of rescue*: disembarkation has become the dominant image and moment with which migrants rescued at sea are associated in the media. Moreover, it is important to highlight the kind of visibility that is at stake when migrants are detected on a vessel. At that stage, the migrant multiplicity is captured by media as an indistinct group of people, and what matters is neither the exact number of migrants on board nor to identify who they are. Instead, what is relevant is to assess the governability of that multiplicity – how to intercept and rescue the migrants – whose physical borders are given in that moment by the migrant vessel itself. This makes the visibility of the migrant group matter on the level of the approximate number of people on board: "when we detect and approach a migrant vessel to rescue" the Coastguard says "what is important to us is to grasp the size of the group of migrants, that is their indicative number".[13]

A critical engagement with the indistinct and abstract migrant multiplicities produced by state maps and migration agencies should be attentive in not reproducing the image of the "flow", getting rid of the heterogeneity of migrants' subjective drives and desires that cannot be reduced to nor contained within overarching explanations about why migrants move and what they want. The widespread depiction of migrants as abstract collectivities (flows), as indistinct unruly multiplicities (mobs) or through the use of animal terminology (swarms) shows the importance of paying attention to the irreducibility of subjectivities and to the experiences of emergent collective subjects in their singularity. "Migrants in Calais are like cockroaches": Katie Hopkins' shocking and violent public speech actually captures well, together with the declaration by the ex-British Prime Minister David Cameron who defined migrants coming from Calais as a "swarm", the animal vocabulary through which migrants are discredited and demonised. However, the bug lexicon used by racist politicians and those in the media for naming migrant multiplicities in this case pertains less to the register of criminalisation than to one of infestation: migrants are portrayed less as threats – they are bugs to be chased away. Thus, the migrant-hunt that takes place on a daily basis in border zones like Calais and Ventimiglia does not frame migrants as enemies but, rather, as burdening presences or swarms of undesired bodies.

THE MOTLEY MIGRANT MOB[14]

The practice of dividing the migrants and of keeping the multiplicity only on a temporary basis does not depend only on the exclusionary goal of migration and asylum policies – which differentiate between migrants deserving of protection, "irregular" migrants, etc. – nor on the governability of a multiplicity of migrants. For state authorities and migration agencies the temporary and divisible character of migrant multiplicities is also a way of preventing the formation of a collective political subject. Actually, the "fear of the mob" and the governmental techniques for ruling and dividing mobile flows and temporary collective formations go well beyond the government of migrant multiplicities. Scholars have analysed the dynamics and the techniques that sustain the government of unruly collective formations, such as crowds, especially when these are related to riot events and social protests (Della Porta and Reiter, 1998; Parvan, 2017). Tactics for crowd control, from repression and tolerated transgression during public demonstrations to preventive strategies to hamper the formation of collective subjects in the streets, are mobilised to manage and disperse mobile flows (De Biasi, 1998). It goes beyond the scope of this work to compare the governing of migrant multiplicities and the policing of crowds at large. Yet, it is important not to conflate the object of this analysis (migrant multiplicities as potential mobs) with crowds and riots. The "turmoil" generated by migrant multiplicities is not of the same order as that produced by crowds and riots: migrant mobs are not "minority groups" who are part of the space of citizenship and who, from within such a space, lay political claims. Rather, by focusing on migrant mobs in border zones I bring attention to subjects who are not there for protesting: their presence in a mass is in itself considered a source of trouble and becomes an object of control. Migrant multiplicities as potential mobs are taken here by highlighting how they are divided and scattered, more than how they are policed as a group. A focus on migrant transit points across Europe allows us to grasp the tactic that national authorities usually put in place for managing migrant multiplicities: migrants are grouped in border zones and governed as a spatially located "X" – for instance, the migrants stranded in Calais – and then they are partitioned or scattered as soon as they appear to have a collective strategy or to be building a common political identity that emerges from the very fact of sharing space and the same condition of "illegality".

Paris, July 2015, Lycée Jean-Quarré, XIX arrondissement: after being evicted from La Chapelle square, the heterogeneous group of migrants who were part of the movement "La Chapelle en lutte" occupied a disused college in Paris to which about 700 migrants moved. In the first stage migrants were allowed to stay in a big group – and governed as the "squat at Lycée Jean-Quarré" – since this facilitated the governability of a considerable number of individuals. Yet, when the migrant multiplicity started to appear as a more coherent collective formation, laying common political claims,[15] the goal of the municipality was to divide them. When the squat was evicted in October 2015, the strategy of the municipality consisted of thwarting the migrants' ability to find another common space, and distributing them instead to small centres in the French countryside in order to avoid any possible collective formation or stable group. The exclusionary channels of the asylum are spatially materialised through the scattering of migrants across places. A similar tactic of *grouping and scattering* migrants is also periodically used by French authorities in Calais. The informal migrant transit camp in Calais is in fact indirectly managed by the French police through a twofold mechanism of spatial *stranding and draining*: migrants are constantly blocked and violently hampered from crossing the Channel, and many of them never succeed in reaching the UK. Nevertheless, any time that the number of people at the camp becomes huge and can be a source of disorder, the police on the sly let a few of the stranded people go; sometimes, alternatively, migrants are transferred by force to detention centres in France.

The difficulty that many migrant groups encounter in finding a common political and legal solution for everybody reflects the way in which migration policies and administrative procedures made on a case-by-case basis contribute to undermine the very possibility for a collective subject to emerge. "Mob" and "crowd" are the disqualifying terms through which heterogeneous migrant multiplicities are designated, denying in this way from the very beginning the politicalness of migration movements. I suggest that the "fear" of the migrant mob reflects the impasse in fitting migrant conducts into categories and the irreducibility of migrant subjectivities to a clearly shaped profile and, thus, to a single reason for migrating. Migrant groups are presented as unruly mobs in order to downplay the political dimension of their struggles for movement and to thwart the possibility of a multiplicity becoming a collective political subject.

In this section I draw attention to two forms of migrant mobs that, from the point of view of numbers, appear at opposite extremes – a multiplicity of "few" people and a migrant mob huge in number. These two examples taken together illustrate the co-existence of migrant mobs that become visible because of their numeric "size", and of multiplicities formed of "few" people that are the outcome of the exclusionary procedures of asylum and of migration laws. The first concerns war escapees from the Libyan conflict who went to Tunisia in 2011 and who were migrant workers in Libya. Some of those who had been denied international protection by UNHCR Tunisia decided to remain at Choucha refugee camp, and continued to do so after the official closure of the camp in June 2013. They continued to stay there because they didn't have another space to stay in, but the existence of "Choucha beyond the camp" (Garelli and Tazzioli, 2017) was also a sort of struggle carried on by the rejected refugees who demanded to be resettled in Europe as the escapees of the Libyan war. Beyond their discursive political claim, in which they stressed that they were refugees – despite not being so according to the UNHCR – by staying there they effectively opposed their own "disappearance". Those who were still at the camp, according to the UNHCR, were by now only "a few nomads living in the desert"[16] and have been erased from official statistics about refugees and migrants in Tunisia. The political relevance of the "irrelevant few people" relies on the political and statistical invisibility of those migrants produced by migration agencies: instead of governing the migrant multiplicities, in that context the very dimension of the group was considered not-existent by state and non-state actors. The multiplicity of a few rejected refugees at Choucha camp appeared to humanitarian actors and to Tunisian authorities as a troubling dearth mob, despite the scarcity in number, due to the common claims they made beyond any dividing and individualising criteria.

In some way they built on their very exclusion from the asylum, reversing it as a common ground of struggle, based on the shared condition of being "rejected". Through their spatial persistence at Choucha camp they stressed the lack of a space to stay and the unsafe place in which they were living: in this way, the group of rejected refugees presented themselves as the subjects who have been affected by the politics of asylum despite being rejected by it.

The second snapshot focuses on a migrant mob which is huge in number and is feared because it appears as an ungovernable motley multiplicity. This is the march to Europe made by thousands of refugees from the city of Budapest to the Austrian border in September 2015. Thousands of people coming from different countries arrived simultaneously in the span of a few weeks in Hungary in order to seek asylum in Europe. Due to the family contacts that most of them had in countries like Germany and Sweden, and given the low rate of successful asylum claims in Hungary, once in Budapest their common goal was to reach Austria, in order to then move to other European countries. Hungarian authorities blocked the trains to Vienna with the aim of hampering the refugees from crossing the Austrian border. Thus, after days of waiting, on 4 September, all the refugees decided to move together on foot, marching on the main motorway heading to Austria. The mass of people stranded at the train station in Budapest suddenly became a motley migrant mob that neither Hungarian nor Austrian authorities could stop at that point. Faced with the sabotaging of their movements due to the national authorities blocking the trains, the refugees enacted a self-resettlement strategy, moving on their own to the Austrian border. Instead of laying claims they opened up a *route to refuge* by marching to the places in which they wanted to settle.

The reference to the Vienna–Budapest refugee march sheds light on the ambivalent dimension of multiplicity as part of migration governmentality as an antagonistic field: migrant multiplicities are governed, divided and produced by states and non-state actors for regaining control over unruly mobilities. At the same time, migrant multiplicities also designate collective movements and practices of border crossing that have multiplied over the last few years due to the increase in border enforcement. In some cases, these temporary collective movements took the form of exodus, as was the case of migrants walking along the so-called Balkan route and actually opening such a *migration path*. What states call a "refugee crisis" has been constituted also by the materiality of collective struggles and movements, made of people from different nationalities who temporarily marched together and forced border controls. This happened between 2015 and 2016, at the Greek–Macedonian border, in Eidomeni, that for thousands of migrants had represented the Greek outpost towards the Balkan route. Nevertheless, it was not a matter of an interrupted flow, nor did migrants always pass through it collectively. Rather, as is the case of many frontiers, since border enforcements have been subjected to an irregular, desultory temporality, even migrant collective crossings and marches are highly irregular. Similarly, with

France's suspension of Schengen in May 2015, the French–Italian border has become a site of repeated collective migrant (attempts at) crossing. If, on the one hand, it is important to highlight the sheer temporariness and the heterogeneous composition of migrant multiplicities, on the other it is likewise worth noticing that they constituted an active force in opening borders and in this way reshaped the European space. Therefore, rethinking multiplicity through the lens of migration means considering it as a constitutively ambivalent notion that refers to governmental techniques for partitioning and dividing migrants, as well as to the artificial populations created for disciplining them, and at the same time, to the reality of temporary collective subjects.

"SOME WILL PASS MORE QUICKLY AND SMOOTHLY THAN OTHERS"

The year 2015 was characterised by a succession of (partial and selective) openings and (differential) closings of border crossing points along the Balkan route. In summer 2015, Germany's decision to temporarily allow migrants to enter and stay in the country made the Balkan route appear as a refugee corridor to Europe, partially replacing the Libyan corridor which is the central Mediterranean route. In this regard it is important to remark that "hydraulic" terms such as "channels" and "corridors" have gained centre stage in the political debate on migration and the lexicon of refugee agencies, and are usually inflected in a humanitarian sense (Kasparek, 2016): "humanitarian corridors", "safe channels" and "humanitarian channels" are largely employed by international organisations such as the UNHCR and by non-governmental organisations (NGOs) for naming legal safe routes for migrants to enter European countries. Yet, the ubiquitous use of "channel" conceals its constitutive dual character: the channel is in fact what hauls and protects mobility, making it possible, while at the same time it is by nature an exclusionary and selective infrastructure that keeps out unauthorised movements. The way in which I refer to "channel" here is in a quite material way, as illustrated by critical migration scholarship that has recently pointed to the "migration infrastructure" (Xiang and Linquist, 2014), the "logistic of crossing" (Alternied et al., 2018; Garelli and Tazzioli, 2018) and the centrality of means of transport – as noted by William Walters, who has coined the notion of "viapolitics" (Walters, 2015).

The spatial trope of the channel refers to the material corridors migrants pass through, facilitated by refugee support groups, smuggling economies, or temporarily and partly crafted by state policies. A disparate range of selective restrictions and differential access criteria had been implemented along the Balkan corridor: the mechanism of differential and exclusionary "sluice gates" put in place in November 2015 worked according to a sort of north–south trickle-down movement that generated the largest blocked-space frontier in Eidomeni, at the Greek–Macedonian border. Indeed, Slovenia's decision to restrict access from Croatia[17] and finally to close the border had immediate repercussions along the whole Balkan route: the other states of the region suddenly enforced border controls and limited migrants' entry. In this scenario, the progressive closure of the Balkan corridor took place according to highly selective measures: indeed, far from decelerating and stopping migrants in a homogeneous manner, border-enforcement measures were enacted through exclusionary partitions mainly based on nationality. Thus, what in the European political debate was presented as a "migration flow" to be decelerated and stopped turned out to be a sort of thick mass to sift through. Yet, the selective filtering mechanism was not only a way to reduce the total number of those who could enter Europe. Indeed, beyond that, the sudden transformation of some areas from spaces of transit into crowded clogs and border zones was also functional to produce further divisions among migrants – through selective access – and to prevent the formation of collective subjects. More precisely, what I want to suggest is that border zones along the Balkan route have functioned as pre-emptive frontiers of the European asylum system, crafting new exclusionary racialised divisions. What do these partitioning criteria consist of? And how have they been effectively enacted by national police and European agencies?

Nationality has been used as the main selective criteria for deciding on migrants' "right" to enter Europe and claim asylum. In particular, Syrians have represented the *yardstick of humanitarianism* of the refugee crisis and at the same time the only truly humanitarian subjects. Indeed, they have been the sole migrants' nationality that used to be labelled "refugee" on the spot – although after the signature of the EU–Turkey agreement Syrians also started to be rejected as asylum applicants in the hotspots in Greece. At the same time, Syrian nationals have become a sort of humanitarian yardstick for all other people seeking asylum: that is, a series of degrees of vulnerability was established putting Syrians at the top, with all other nationalities being in need of demonstrating that they were deserving protection. Syrians and (albeit with less guarantees than them and in a more conditional way) Afghans and Iraqis have been presented and treated by member states and European agencies as the *good and deserving exception*, within a general frame where asylum seekers are to some extent considered to be *guilty until not proved otherwise*. Ultimately, as Elsa Dorlin points out, the western juridico-political tradition has been characterised by the "production of non-defendable subjects, as they are deemed to be dangerous [...] and always at fault" (Dorlin, 2017: 29).

Instead, people coming from "North Africa" have been preventively denied the right to claim asylum and blocked or returned straight away. A blatant actualisation of this nationality-based treatment has been in place at the Greek–Macedonian border since November 2015 when the Macedonian authorities started to deny migrants entry, except to Syrian, Iraqi and Afghan nationals. As soon as the racialised measure was implemented, the police detected an increased number of "fake Syrians", that is of people from other nationalities who declared to be Syrians, sometimes holding a fake Syrian passport. However, ultimately the hunt for the fake Syrians was less important, from the point of view of partitioning criteria, than the racialised biopolitical management of migrant populations that during the ongoing refugee crisis in the Mediterranean region has been reshaped along new dividing lines.

Yet, by focusing in an exclusive way on the dividing and partitioning effects of migration policies, we run the risk of overlooking the productive dimension of those mechanisms of government and of the racialising components that, far from being side effects, are constitutive of the biopolitics of migration. By "productive dimension" I refer to the exclusionary and classifying procedures by which subjects are not only labelled and divided but are also racialised and subjectivised into specific profiles. In his book *Habeas Viscus*, Alexander G. Weheliye points out that racialised categories, such as Muslims, do not only put into place "the conditions of possibility for violent exclusions but also [serves] as the foundation for policing borders between bare life, life and death" (2014: 65). Weheliye pushes forward this argument grounding on a twofold critique of Giorgio Agamben's notion of "bare life" and analyses of biopolitics. According to Weheliye, racism has historically worked not only by producing divisions within populations or between different populations but, more radically, by instantiating new normative orders and differentiated politics of/over life. Such an analysis helps in not reducing the production and government of migrant multiplicities to the partitioning mechanisms – for instance of the asylum system – that exclude certain subjects and illegalise others. At the same time, it enables studying racialisation in its making; that is, by shifting the attention from the racialised migrant body and subject towards the constantly changing racialising partitions and differences among migrants.

The nationality-based criteria that were at play at many European border zones in 2015 and 2016 had been enacted for enforcing exclusionary criteria that instantiate degrees of protection and non-protection. Furthermore, the exclusionary classifying procedures of the asylum regime do not only produce divisions between deserving refugees and "bogus" refugees; they also contribute to reshape the biopolitics of mobility, by strengthening new hierarchies among the refugees themselves. It could be argued that the "crisis" as an epistemic frame through which events and phenomena are read and conceptualised and measures of intervention are decided is also characterised when it is related to migration by a multiplication of categories and denominations for labelling and classifying migrants and refugees. Ultimately, in the face of transformations in practices movements, the labelling activity in the field of migration governmentality becomes particularly incessant and categories get multiplied (Zetter, 2007). In fact, this is in part the result of an "epistemic crisis" that occurs any time that migrant practices of movement exceed and trouble the existing governmental labelling frame. The restructuring of what I call the *epistemology of the asylum*, meaning by that the set of exclusionary categories that designate different degrees of protection and non-protection, is usually formed by a combination of legal and extra-legal categories. The designation of "people in clear need of international protection", for instance, has been put at the core of the EU Relocation and Resettlement Scheme,[18] although such a denomination has no juridical basis and works rather as a sort of preventative watershed of illegalisation, that posits from the beginning that a huge part of the people claiming asylum will be rejected as not being in "clear need". Moreover, Roger Zetter illustrates in detail that the result of such a multiplication of categories is a substantial decrease in the numbers of people who are granted international protection.

CONCLUSION

The increasing number of migrant arrivals in Europe characterised by people in groups escaping wars to seek asylum highlights multiplicity as a crucial dimension at stake in the government of migration. Far from being an object of government that is already there, migrant multiplicities are the outcome of processes of grouping and partition enacted by migration agencies and states to make migrants manageable, and also by scattering migrants across space. These produced multiplicities are not stable collectivities; on the contrary, they are formed in order to then divide and select the migrants through an individualising power. More precisely, as I have highlighted, their fleeting and precarious nature depends on the conditions of temporariness and movement (being on the move) they are subjected to. The production of *temporary divisible migrant multiplicities* is a better way of governing migrants and, simultaneously, a tactic for hampering the emergence and consolidation of collective political subjects. That is to say, the governmental dividing of migrants cannot be detached from the *mob-question*: migrants are divided not only in order to classify and partition them in a smoother way but also for neutralising incipient collective formations.

Retracing the ambivalences of the term "the mob", I have shown that migrant multiplicities appear as an object of government and, at the same time, as a potentially troubling collective subject. "The mob" encapsulates this ambivalent and fleeting subject that is the product of governmental techniques, and that at the same time corresponds to a troubling multiplicity that exceeds and undermines the partitioning power of classification and mechanisms of dividing through individualisation. Keeping the heterogeneity of migrant mobs and highlighting the political dimension of migrant struggles for movement, it is possible to grasp multiplicity as the outcome of governmental practices and, at the same time, as an incipient subject often in excess to mechanisms of control. As Oana Parvan shows in relation to the Tunisian uprisings in 2011, there is in fact a strong connection between unruly mobility, the transformation of labour conditions and the emergence of criminalised collective formations (Parvan, 2017). Relatedly, an insight into migrant multiplicities enables the questioning of binary oppositions couplets that sustain Western political thought – e.g. between individual and collective – and to rethink the nexus between minorities and majorities beyond the dimension of numbers (Sibertin-Blanc, 2009, 2013). In the next chapter I undertake a critical investigation of the modes of individualisation that are at stake in governing migration, engaging in the same methodological move that has sustained this analysis on migrant multiplicities. That is, by refusing to adopt taken-for-granted sociological categories, I explore the effective mechanisms through which some subjects are produced, labelled and governed singularly as migrants, and the biopolitical "hold" that is exercised upon them as individuals.

NOTES

1. https://voce.com.ve/2016/08/08/185873/ventimiglia-gabrielli-i-migranti-vanno-portati-altrove/
2. Indeed, Foucault argues: "Marx has in fact contended that class struggle is the drive of history [...] nobody has expanded on the question about what a struggle is. What is a struggle when we say class struggles? Indeed we say struggle, but it is a question of conflict and war" (Foucault, 2000b: 606).
3. More than an under-class, the Lumpenproletariat is the non-class and, as Thobourn stresses, the term Lumpeproletariat does not come from "Lumpen" but from "Lump" which refers to the "knave" people.
4. The term "mob" does not exist in French but by referring to popular seditions he de facto addresses those multiplicities that are not reducible to the population.
5. For instance, considered as economic migrants or as asylum seekers, as well as the chance of "success" of their asylum claim.
6. http://europa.eu/rapid/press-release_MEMO-14-566_en.htm.
7. The EURODAC database was created in 2003 to fight against so-called "asylum shopping" – meaning when a person demands asylum in different European countries. In fact, EURODAC is used to determine which Member State is to be responsible pursuant to the Dublin Convention for examining an application for asylum lodged in a Member State.
8. This information is the result of the interview I conducted with Frontex officers at Frontex's headquarters in Catania (Italy), December 2015.
9. By bringing attention to the uncounted remnants I refer here to the fact that some migrants who are part of a multiplicity are not always classified and counted by the states and international organisations. For instance, the UNHCR stops to count asylum seekers whose claims have been rejected, as they are no longer of "concern", even if they are still living in a refugee camp.
10. http://ec.europa.eu/eurostat/statistics-explained/index.php/Asylum_statistics
11. Final report on Joint Operation "MOS MAIORUM"/ 5474/15 LIMITE FRONT 22 (22 January 2015).

12 Article 51 of the Geneva Convention establishes that it is in relation to the country of origin, and not to the country of residence, that the asylum seeker's claim should be assessed.
13 Interview with coastguard officers at the Coastguard headquarters in Rome, June 2015.
14 The expression "motley migrant mob" is a way to rephrase Peter Leinebaugh and Markus Rediker's expression "motley crowd" (Linebaugh and Rediker, 2013) that designates the heterogeneous composition of piracy in the seventeenth and eighteenth centuries.
15 They asked for a place to stay and they claimed their right to protection.
16 Interview with UNHCR officer, Tunis, August 2014.
17 Slovenia closed its border with Croatia erecting razor wire a few days after the terrorist attacks in Paris (13 November 2015). A much more massive border closure strategy in the Balkans took place in March 2016, when many states decided to hamper migrants' access. Yet, already in October 2015 Hungary had closed its border with Croatia.
18 http://europa.eu/rapid/press-release_IP-16-829_en.htm

2

Migrant Singularities

Between Subjectivation and Desubjugation

INTRODUCTION

With the strengthening of border controls at the French–Italian border along the coast, many migrants who want to go to France have had to reroute towards the Alps. The small cities of Oulx, Bardonecchia and Claviere in the Susa Valley constitute the Italian outposts and at the same time the starting points for the migrants who, coming by train from Turin, head towards Briancon, an Alpine French city located about 20 kilometres beyond the border. Since October 2018, a local NGO has been running an informal shelter of transit next to the rail station of Oulx where migrants can stay overnight before trying to cross to France. The Alpine passage has remained relatively invisible in comparison to other routes and, despite the muscular border enforcement on the French side, migrant identification is fundamentally opaque. "We do not know if the French police fingerprints all migrants who are pushed back", the mayor of the city of Oulx declared to me, adding that

> what we do, as a networks of municipalities and local NGOs, is to count all migrants who arrive at the rail stations in the Susa Valley, as well as those who are returned by the French. For instance, we know that approximately 2500 migrants passed through Oulx between August and November 2018.

However, we are speaking about "passages and not people", as he clarified, since the same migrants could eventually be counted twice, or more, if they are also pushed back, while others could be absent from the statistics, if they had not been detected at the rail station.

This snapshot of the politics of counting along the Alpine migration route foregrounds some of the key themes of this chapter. What does "migration control" mean, and how it is connected – or not connected – to processes of individualisation? What is of relevance for states and non-state actors about individual migrants? To what extent are migrants requested to speak and to what extent are they rather objectified into data to be shared? And which temporalities of control affect migrants' lives? This chapter focuses on migrant singularities, investigating the modes of individualisation, subjectivation and objectivisation migrants are shaped by and resist. The theme of (migrant) singularities is tackled here from the standpoint of the intertwining of modes of objectivation and subjectivation, following the main conceptual thread of this book.

The chapter reverts around three main axes to critically explore the making and the governing of migrant singularities: subjectivity, control/government and discourses of truth. These conceptual focuses constitute mutually intertwined analytical angles for investigating migrant singularities. Engaging with these analytics enables our understanding of the actual battlefield through which some subjects are produced and racialised as migrants, as well as the struggles and resistances that migrants engage in. Relatedly, it allows us to highlight how spatial confinement and temporal borders do shape and impact on migrant lives. The chapter starts with some preliminary considerations about singularity, pointing to the need for historicising subjectivities as well as the production of some subjects as "refugees" or "migrants". It moves on with the section "Subjectivity", questioning analyses that are centred on the citizen as the yardstick of politics and that tackle migration through the binary opposition between victimhood and agents. As part of that section, the chapter also considers the modes of objectivation that migrants are framed by. The section entitled "Rethinking Control: Disjointed Knowledge, Fragmented Visibility" interrogates modes of governing that work not through constant monitoring and surveillance but through partial non-registration, non-control and opacity. It also enquires into temporal borders and the modes of knowledge that underpin these modes of control.

The final section entitled "Untruthful Subjects" gets to grips with the relationship between subjects and discourses of truth in the field of migration: building on Frantz Fanon's reflections on the discursivity requested from the colonised subject, it shows that migrants are not only seen as essentially liars but also as subjects incapable of telling the truth. It concludes by arguing that migrants are in fact subjected to mechanisms of knowledge extraction more than the injunction to tell the truth.

The term "singularity" draws attention to the effects of power on subjects – how these are regulated and objectivised. In *Discipline and Punish* Foucault refers to singularities to speak about the disciplinary disposition of the bodies in space – for instance, in relation to the medical space he argues that this latter "tended to individualize bodies, diseases, symptoms, lives and deaths; it constituted a real table of juxtaposed and carefully distinct singularities" (Foucault, 1977: 144). Therefore, "singularity" captures the work of political technologies on the bodies. The second reason for using such a term is because it is employed not only for addressing individual subjects but also for engaging with the relationships between these latter and the disciplining of multiplicities. Interrogating migration from the analytical angle of singularity involves questioning the methodological individualism that underpins political theory literature as well as migration scholarship. Ethnographic and sociological works on migration focus on either migrant groups and communities or on individual migrants.

A way of challenging methodological individualism consists of gesturing towards the peculiar mechanisms of individualisation through which subjects are shaped and governed. By speaking of modes of individualisation I refer to a methodological approach that would explore the material and discursive ways in which some subjects are governed as migrants, as well as the forms of interpellation through which the subject is called and addressed (DuBois, 1903; Macherey, 2014). This chapter focuses on the ways in which migrants are individually targeted by techno-political measures apt at extracting data and, at the same time, by the injunction to speak (coerced discursivity), while they are considered, however, incapable of telling the truth. Therefore, a focus on migrant singularities involves studying how some subjects are discursively and materially produced as migrants, while at the same time investigating how individuals are digitally scattered across multiple databases. It follows that singularity is not the opposite pole of multiplicities; rather, as long as none of them designates a stable or fixed dimension, focusing on *the making of migration* means looking at the mutual interaction between the two. For instance, processes of datafication make individuals more traceable and, at the same time, the individual as a homogeneous subjectivity fades away. Yet, migrant singularities should not be taken as ahistorical or neutral subjects, replicating the "dehistoricizing universalism" (Malkki, 1996: 378) which is at play in the humanitarian rationale. Ultimately, as Roberto Beneduce has stressed, "humanitarianism needs a simple theory of suffering" (Beneduce, 2010: 37) which contributes to flatten all experiences of migration and violence into objectifying and dehistoricising categories. For this reason, a critical account of border violence requires us to recognise the effects of subjugation and, as Saidiya Hartman suggests, of pain, in their historicity (Hartman, 1997).

Hence, the term "singularity" should be inflected in light of the norms through which subjects are shaped and divided, as well as the racialised and gendered mechanisms of governing. In this regard, Rey Chow has expanded on the need for inflecting the analyses on subjectivities with an enquiry about the racialised and gendered conditions through which subjects are admitted into a community and are recognised into the public space – what she defines as "the politics of admittance" (Chow, 2010: 56).[1] Along similar lines, I discuss how migrants' singularities are targeted not only by techniques of identification but are also subjected to the injunction to speak about themselves, interrogating the peculiar relationship between subjectivity and production of truth.

A genealogical account that retraces differences and partial continuities with colonial modes of governmentality allows an undoing of the persistent and silent "presentism" of migration analyses, which consists of flattening individuals and phenomena on an ahistorical surface – depriving them of any historical "thickness" and of the "temporal depth in which the subject is constituted" (Das, 2006: 66). This is strictly connected to caution in the face of perspectives that replicate a fundamental presentism; that is, works that consider the present migration context as an unprecedented context due to the refugee crisis that, according to these analyses, would affect Europe. In light of that, Barbara Pinelli has stressed the importance of "keeping a historical trace of migration, in order to understand how institutions function at the horizon in which they take place" (2017: 7; see also Biehl et al., 2007). Lisa Malkki has cautioned against the "dehistoricing constitution of the refugee as a singular category of humanity" since this makes "refugees stop being specific persons and become pure victims in general" (1996: 378). Mobilising the analytical diptych of subjectivation and subjection allows the shaping and governing of migrant singularities to be situated in a field of tension, and no consideration of biometric techniques and border controls as fully determining migrants' subjectivities. Indeed, we cannot narrow our analysis of migration to the techniques of control that shape and target migrants' bodies and movements.

SUBJECTIVITY: UNDOING THE MIGRANT ACTIVIST/VICTIMHOOD DIVIDE

Grappling with migrant singularities involves looking not only at how migrants are targeted and shaped by political technologies for controlling, exploiting and disciplining them, but also at how migrants themselves deal with such a condition, how their lives are affected and which tactics of appropriation and subjectivation they engage in. A focus on the political technologies through which migrants' mobility and presence are obstructed beyond the production of "border spectacle" (De Genova, 2013) enables a close examination of the modes of migrants' subjection and subjectivation. Both in political theory and in migration scholarship, the theme of migrants' subjectivities is mainly tackled through the binary opposition between migrants as subjects of agency and resistance, on the one hand, and migrants as subjects of victimhood, on the other (see Squire, 2017 for a similar questioning). Neither the "making live/letting die" biopolitical formula, nor the oppositional representations of migrants as bare lives on the one hand and agentive subjects on the other, are adequate for taking into account the whole array of effects of subjection, confinement, feelings, desires and modes of destitution. In fact studying this means undoing binary oppositions as well as an exclusive focus on life and death as such. For instance, migrants who are constantly chased away from Calais as well as from other border zones across Europe and not allowed to settle are neither targeted by a direct thanatopolitics nor are they just reduced to bare lives. Rather, they are constantly deprived of a space to stay and repeatedly harassed in front of any attempt to build spaces of life. Similarly, migrants who have been stranded on the Greek islands for one year or more are subjected to a sort of lifetime sequestration – what Shahram Khosravi defined as "stolen time" (Khosravi, 2018) – and at the same time they are forced to act according to specific timeline and temporal borders. As far as the other pole of the binary opposition is concerned – agency – in critical scholarship migrants are often depicted as active and resistant subjects. As part of such a conceptual framework, migrants are presented as subjects who revitalise citizenship and political agency. In this way, the analytical attention is narrowed to modes of struggle that respond to and corroborate the image of the migrant as an active citizen – e.g. public protests in which migrants deliberately lay political claims. But is agency always seen as desirable, independently of the subject who acts? Actually, we should consider that when migrants act, their actions, struggles and refusals are often criminalised or seen as potentially suspicious and threatening. Indeed, while "agency" usually has a positive connotation in political theory, it is important to consider how the same ability to act might be associated with dangerousness, vulnerability and suspiciousness.

Relatedly, an exclusive focus on the moments of active resistance overshadows situations of "obstructed agency" (Ngai, 2005: 2) as well as contexts in which migrants simply do not resist. Sianne Ngai refers to "ugly feelings" explaining that these "ramify beyond the domain of the aesthetic proper" (2005: 2). Through a similar move, when it comes to migration governmentality we have to investigate all their nuances, modes of subjection and confinement that work by depriving lives without killing them, by wearing out and exhausting migrants, by hampering the building up of spaces of life and by stealing migrants' time. Methodologically this entails refusing "the drive for resolution" (Lisle, 2016: 425) about finding and conceptualising migrant agential subjectivities.

How to register modes of governing that choke and constrain migrants without, however, necessarily killing them? And how to account for border struggles that do not necessarily entail resisting or clashing with power but, rather, consist of tacit negotiations or invisible flights? The binary opposition between victimhood and agency does not allow for retaining the variety both of modes of subjection and of subjectivation that shape migrants' lives. Indeed, migrants are often portrayed as subjects who cannot but act and whose politicalness is determined by their being active subjects. In this regard, it is worth asking why we are so interested in finding in migrants their capacity to resist. In order to undo the biopolitical binary opposition between migrants as bare lives and migrants as activists or active subjects we need first of all to start with an enquiry into the wide array of political technologies and tactics of appropriation that remain fundamentally opaque if approached in terms of making live/letting die. From such a perspective, a critical account of the making of migration, and in particular of how migrant subjectivities are shaped and targeted, entails paying attention to modes of governmentality that *work by obstructing,* namely that hamper migrants not only in their mobility but also by choking and cramping their "spaces of livability" (Aradau, 2017a: 7).

Jasbir Puar's theorisation of debilitation as a technology for governing populations equips us with helpful analytical tools to come to grips with the nuances of biopolitics in contexts that are characterised by structural violence, such as Palestine: "alongside the 'right to kill' I noted a complementary logics […] that of creating injuries and maintaining Palestinian populations as perpetually debilitated, and yet alive, in order to control them" (Puar, 2017: x). In so doing, the biopolitical stake does not mainly consist in "the right to life, or even letting live", but in "the logic of 'will not let die'. Both are part of the deliberate debilitation of a population […] and are key elements in the racializing biopolitical logic of security" (Puar, 2015: x). Although Puar's analysis is about the Palestinian political context and Israeli domination, I contend that her critical rethinking of biopolitics beyond the binary opposition of making live/letting die enables our interrogating the specific power's hold over migrant lives as something that works by obstructing and working them without (necessarily) letting them die. It is in fact important to reflect on the heterogenous mechanisms of violence which are exercised on migrants and that are not narrowed to the most blatant, spectacular and horrific modes of domination. In this respect, Saidiya Hartman's argument that violence does not always lie "in these exhibitions of extreme suffering or in what we see but in what we do not see" (Hartman, 1997: 25) is particularly instructive for further problematising how violence might be exercised beyond the most horrific and deadly sovereign operations.

Cramping, choking, hindering, chasing away, constricting, confining, dismantling: these verbs capture the ways in which migrants' mobility and presence are fundamentally disrupted without being erased. Considering this means mobilising an analytical sensibility which gestures towards non-spectacular forms of violence that are, however, not less constrictive nor less harmful for the migrants with respect to the other most blatant and visible modes of border violence. As long as we challenge the migrant activist/victimhood divide we also question, more broadly, a series of binary oppositions that sustain theoretical analyses about migration as well as debates on political theory – such as, between inclusion and exclusion, between positive and negative biopolitics, between integration and marginalisation, between citizenship and legal destitution. Taking subjectivation and subjection as the two main analytical angles also means considering that borders do not only impact on subjects, shaping and transforming them; jointly, it is important to grasp what of the subject is made visible and knowable. In other words, it is a question of drawing attention to *how* subjects are affected by borders and, simultaneously, to *what* of the subject is filtered, looked at and made the object of concern. Such an operation enables undoing the image of the subject as a fully graspable entity, or as something that is targeted and visibilised in its totality. For instance, migrants at times can be targeted and made visible to power mechanisms as gendered subjects, they can be radicalised on the basis of their nationality, or they might be controlled and monitored as bodies in motion. Borders do not only select what of the subject is of interest and what should be known; they also contribute to rub out the history of subjects (Ticktin, 2008). In fact, biopolitical techniques exercised on migrants in part produce subjects without and out of history. The stripping out of the subject's history is not only the result of the state and humanitarian narratives about refugees; rather, it is also the outcome of material and non-discursive techniques through which migrant bodies are targeted, securitised and controlled.

A case in point is constituted by the securitising and partitioning procedures that take place when migrants are disembarked at the port. The shipwrecked refugee fished out from the water is at the same time detached from and stripped of his own story: it appears as a racialised body to be scanned and identified, and, in a second stage, as an individual to be eventually interrogated. Hence, an account of biopolitical mechanisms that shape singularities involves bringing to the fore and challenging the processes of dehistoricisation that migrant bodies are subjected to: in order to investigate what of the subject is made knowable, visible and to be controlled, we cannot stick to a spatial analysis of border functioning; nor by speaking of "subjects" can we take for granted what of the subject is actually shaped, governed and considered of concern. Frantz Fanon equips us with analytical tools for repoliticising the migrant's body as a surface for power's hold and moulding both discursively and on a more directly material level. In particular, Fanon's analyses of the effects of colonisation on the individual help in addressing the mutual entanglements between discursive practices, bodily mechanisms of subjection and spatial domination pointing to the necessity of historicisation of the body itself:

> French colonialism has settled itself in the very centre of the Algerian individual and has undertaken a sustained work of cleanup, of expulsion of self, of rationally pursued mutilation. There is not occupation of territory, on the one hand, and independence of persons on the other. It is the country as a whole, its history, its daily pulsation that are contested [...] Under these conditions, the individual's breathing is an observed, an occupied breathing. It is a combat breathing. (Fanon, 1965: 65).

Thus, Fanon recalls the historical articulation between spatial dispossession and violent bordering mechanisms, on the one hand, and the shaping of the colonised subjectivities, on the other. Hence, what emerges from such an insight is the inadequacy of analyses that centre exclusively on borders and border controls. In other words, an "open the border" politics and claims for free mobility cannot be disjoined from an in-depth investigation of the forms of exploitation and racialised partitions that are not visible through a border-centered perspective. Relatedly, a transformative politics would fight not only the spatial containment of migrant mobility but also engage with the inequalities of lives that are produced and reinforced by the border regime.

Fanon's reflections on the colonised subject and the mechanisms of subjection at play in the colonies equip us with a useful analytical angle to address this. In *Black Skin, White Mask*, where Fanon focuses on the pathologies that the Algerian colonised suffered from as a result of the French domination, the verb "to breathe" – or better "not to breathe" – appears in many occurrences, to describe the condition of the colonised subject in Algeria: a fundamental difficulty and irregularity of breathing characterises the daily life of the colonised: "she is short of breath", "the call of Europe like a breath of fresh air", "breathing that accelerates or slows" (Fanon, 1965). In particular, in the conclusion of the book, Fanon connects the difficulty of breathing to the subject's decision to revolt: "It is not because the Indo-Chinese has discovered a culture of his own that he is in revolt. It is because quite simply .. it was, in more than one way, becoming impossible for him to breathe" (Fanon, 1965: 226). The impossibility of breathing and the perception of the intolerable go together. Such a lack of or difficulty in breathing is in fact very telling, I argue, of the conditions of many irregularised migrants, as long as it is taken both as physical breathing, and in an economic-political sense writ large. Materially and physically speaking, migrants do often move and find themselves in cramped spaces, and it is not uncommon to hear about migrants who have been at risk of suffocating or who in fact did, inside cargos, trucks or vessels.

The difficulty of breathing encapsulates a series of conditions – being cramped, being choked even without being totally immobilised or blocked, and being obstructed or losing material and legal ground – that characterise migrants' experience. Fanon's final words– "the real leap consists in introducing invention into existence" – points precisely to the need to get out of the condition of being choked, of being suffocated through spatial fixation on the one hand and the effects of displacement on the other. His words in *The Wretched of the Earth* about the disciplinary fixation imposed upon the colonised subject succinctly speak about the choked presence and mobility in space: "the first thing the colonial learns is to remain in his place and not overstep its limits. Hence the dreams of the colonial subject are muscular dreams, dreams of action, dreams of aggressive vitality. I dream I am jumping, swimming, running, and climbing" (Fanon, 2007: 15). The politics of containment, implemented both inside Europe and at its external frontiers through cooperation with third countries, takes material and legal ground away from the migrants and, at the same time, chokes them: confined and cramped spaces, clandestine means of transportation, legal obstacles and induced psychological diseases are some of the many ways in which the difficulty of breathing characterises migrant lives. The lack of breath which could appear as a minimal biopolitical issue actually speaks about a political technology of producing and governing vulnerable lives, even beyond migrants per se: "governance seems no longer interested in only the physical punishing of bodies.

It now wants to control, monitor and, when necessary, cut off the supply of the medium that forms the elementary condition of life itself" (Nieuwenhuis, 2015).

THE MULTIPLE FORMS OF OBJECTIVATION

The modes of objectivation I am referring to are constitutive of and inherently entangled with the making up of people (Davidson, 2004): modes of subjectivation cannot be detached from the processes by which individuals are objectivised. Bringing attention to processes of subjectivation entails, simultaneously, "determining under what conditions something can become an object for a possible knowledge ["*connaissance*"], how it may have been problematized as an object to be known, to what selective procedure ["*procedure de decoupage*"] it may have been subjected […]. So it is a matter of determining its mode of objectivation […] This objectivation and this subjectivation are not independent of each other" (Foucault, 1984). In *The Subject and Power* Foucault distinguishes between different forms of objectivation: the subject which becomes the object of scientific knowledge; dividing practices through which "the subject is either divided inside himself or divided from others"; and finally those procedures through which "the human being turns itself into a subject" (Foucault, 1982: 778), which consist of the subject engaging in transformative practices. These practices of resistance and refusal do not only concern the possibility of subjecting oneself differently and subtracting oneself from modes of domination and exploitation. They also involve practices of de-subjection ("*desassujetissement*") through which the individuals reject, resist and dodge their own multiple objectivations (de-objectivation) (Lorenzini and Tazzioli, 2018).

What are the specific modes of objectivation through which some individuals are produced as "migrants"? How is objectivation actualised through mechanisms of registration, identification and techniques of datafication of bodies and mobility? In fact, objectivation can be the outcome of racialising labelling mechanisms and forms of interpellation. It can also be produced by mechanisms of data extraction that do not involve modes of interpellation: these include, for instance, the datafication of the body through biometric techniques; the digital images of the radars that detect migrant crossings; migrants' personal data collected at the border by national authorities and circulated into databases. Therefore, the modes of objectivation through which some individuals are labelled, shaped and governed as "migrants" are heterogenous and cannot be subsumed into a master signifier. An insight into modes of objectivation makes it possible to grasp the political technologies of migration governmentality in the material effects that they engender on migrant lives.

As Bridget Anderson has put it, "'migration' signifies problematic mobility […] Not all mobility is subject to scrutiny, but 'migration' already signals the need for control and in public discourse is often raced and classed" (Anderson,

2017: 1532). Thus, a focus on the techniques of objectivation allows us to reconstruct how through laws, policies and administrative measures some individuals are racialised as migrants. Indeed, if "juridical power inevitably produces what it merely claims to represent" (Butler, 2002: 5), understanding the legal and political operations that sustain the *making of migration* enables the undoing of the supposed ontological stability of "the migrant" as an epistemological category. Processes of objectivation play a crucial role in the racialisation and disciplining of some people as "migrants". Data-extraction activities as well as techniques of visibility and surveillance do materially contribute to the objectivation of migrants. Modes of objectivation refer to the multiple nexus between knowledge production, exclusionary criteria and power relations. However, if we consider the work of authors like Achille Mbembe we see a different inflection of the term "objectivation" which concern the processes of commodification of the human body – the production of "human-commodities" (Mbembe, 2017: 2) and "disposable people" (Ogilvie, 2012). In fact, by focusing on the making of migration and on the racialising processes connected to that, it is fundamental to pay attention to the ambivalent meaning of objectivation, at the crossroad between an epistemic dimension – turning subjects into objects of knowledge – and the commodification of the body. Indeed, the ongoing shifting "between subjecthood and objecthood" (Mbembe, 2003: 26) is at the core of the racialised production and government of migrants' bodies.

INVISIBLE VIOLENCES AND GOVERNING THROUGH VULNERABILITY

An approach to migration that is exclusively geographical and spatial is not sufficiently adequate to assess the impact that laws, measures of containment and restrictive policies have on migrant lives: migrants are not only spatially restrained and obstructed in their possibility to freely move or stay in a given place. Rather, the spatial disciplining of migration is in fact combined with a specific biopolitical hold on migrant lives. I refer in particular to the pathologisation of migration, which includes the use of vulnerability as a blurred category for selecting migrants, and to the mental health diseases that are triggered by protracted detention and indefinite waiting. The two phenomena are intertwined with each other. The use of vulnerability as a governmental tool for tracing exclusionary partitions among migrants is by now a consolidated measure that relies also on EU texts. Therefore, we cannot speak of exceptional measures in order to describe the governmental uses of vulnerability in the field of migration. On the contrary, the playing out of vulnerability as an ambiguous and constitutively blurred category has become more and more normalised at the level of daily practices of refugee governmentality. In some contexts that governing through vulnerability has been functioning not only for dividing migrants and producing hierarchies among them, it has also worked towards restricting the access to mobility. This is the case for Greece since the signature of the EU–Turkey deal in

March 2016, where the entire refugee system on the islands now pivots around the nexus between (recognised) vulnerability and (access to) mobility. Under the EU–Turkey deal, Greece has imposed geographical restrictions upon migrants who land on the Greek islands, which means that they cannot move to the mainland until their asylum claim is processed – and only if it gets a positive answer – with an exception being made for vulnerable cases (Kofman, 2018). Vulnerability becomes the only way for migrants to be released from the geographical restrictions and to move to the mainland: thus, proving to be vulnerable appears as the condition for getting access to rights and mobility. Or better, vulnerability per se is not enough: indeed, migrants need to convince the doctors from the Ministry of Health inside the hotspot that they are highly vulnerable. In fact, until 2018 only those migrants who were deemed to have a "severe vulnerability" were released from the geographical restrictions, while those with recognised "moderate vulnerabilities" had to remain on the islands for the duration of the asylum process.

In August 2018, under pressure from the European Commission that criticised the rate of vulnerability recognition as being too high, Greece implemented new criteria – "non-vulnerable", "non-vulnerable with special reception needs" and "vulnerable" – in order to reduce the number of people who are deemed to be affected by some vulnerabilities. Therefore, the recognition and misrecognition of vulnerability has become a battlefield with multiple lines of tension: between migrants and the Greek authorities in charge of assessing vulnerability, as well as between the European Commission and Greece. The current under-recognition of vulnerabilities that many NGOs have denounced in Greece concerns particular kinds of violence that are invisible at a first medical screening, but at the same time are also the result of a more or less tacit struggle between migrants' will to move away from the islands and Greek authorities facing pressure from the EU about keeping them there. Who is in charge of doing the vulnerability assessment in Greece? On the Greek islands, the doctors of the Greek Registration and Identification Service are in charge of conducting the medical screening – and yet, the vulnerability assessment is de facto collapsed into the medical screening, which means that vulnerabilities generated by mental health issues or kinds of invisible violences are less likely to be recognised. Plus, on the basis of the EU mandate, the European Asylum Support Office (EASO) has deployed "vulnerability experts" who are in charge of supporting the Greek authorities when a vulnerability arises. The figure of the "vulnerability expert" is actually a quite indistinct one: on what expertise is it based? And which vulnerabilities are scrutinised and how? As an EASO officer declared to me at the EASO Headquarters in Athens, "vulnerability experts" are not necessarily doctors nor psychologists; "on the basis of the EU's criteria, we check if we spot any marker of vulnerability".[2]

In fact, the vulnerability assessment procedure does not simply assess vulnerable cases, but also contributes to shape degrees of vulnerability. Importantly, even in EU law there is no clear definition of "vulnerable persons" as the 2013

European Directive on Asylum refers to disparate categories that should be granted "special reception needs".[3] In so doing, vulnerability as a governmental tool for restricting and regulating (access to) mobility and asylum appears to be a necessary condition that migrants need to prove and, at the same time, something that is constantly non-recognised. Therefore, the nexus between vulnerability and (access to) mobility actually hinges on the hierachisation of vulnerabilities, on the one hand, and on the misrecognition of less-visible vulnerabilities, on the other. In particular, the gendered dimension of violence is precisely what is underplayed, either being conflated into the blurred catchword of vulnerability or remaining fully non-recognised.

At the same time, the discourse on vulnerability in the field of refugee humanitarianism is situated in a twofold process of the pathologisation and medicalisation of migration. The conditions of sheer unliveability in the hotspots and the indefinite wait in Greece generate serious mental health illnesses: this is the result of the constant exposure to violence and uncertainties that migrants face, as well as to the "stolen time" (Khosravi, 2018). Hence, the produced mental illness and increased vulnerability concern not only the *here and now* but also involve a future-oriented temporality: migration policies do not only hamper free movement, they also make the future hard to be imagined and dreamed, and even more than uncertain. "Staying here, we are becoming all mad. They [the authorities] want to govern us by driving us crazy, it is impossible to get out of here without being insane": an Iraqi man who had been in Lesvos for one year succinctly describes the effects that migration and asylum policies produce on migrant lives, well beyond mobility restrictions. Thus, as Doctors without Borders have poignantly remarked, the hotspot of Lesvos "is a European camp that is traumatising people".[4]

The production and assessment of vulnerability are often used by states as political technologies to regulate migrants' presence, mobility and access to rights. If, on the one hand, the category of vulnerability is used for producing hierarchies of mobility and protection, as well as to restrict the access to rights, on the other it corresponds to a condition that is at the same time produced and misrecognised by the multiplicity of actors involved in governing migration. As I noted above, an attentive analysis of the effects of the border regime should move beyond a spatial approach, which looks at the mobility restrictions that migrants encounter, and consider also how migrant lives are affected – at the level of social relations, the possibility of imagining one's own future and psychological conditions. Heterogeneous modes and conditions of *being exposed to* (violence, blackmail, mental illnesses, a lack of social support, etc.) are de facto subsumed and homogenised under the category of vulnerability. What I am interested in here is to highlight that the exposure to violence, as well as the psychological and physical vulnerabilisation generated by migration policies, directly shape migrant singularities. How could we designate the operations of violent destitution that migrants are subjected to? In fact, the effects of destitution and protracted vulnerability are not narrowed down to punctual sites and moments, but are the outcome of the multiple legal, economic and social restrictions imposed by migration policies and bordering mechanisms. Hence, an enquiry into migrant singularities from the standpoint of the biopolitical mechanisms that shape subjectivities – what throughout the book I call *the making of migration* – requires interrogating the temporality of violence beyond delimited time-spaces and beyond the staging of the border spectacle.

Robert Castel's work on social insecurity helps in better defining the effects of economic destitution and social disaggregation generated by multiple processes of precarisation. Although Castel does not refer to migrants and speaks instead of social and economic policies that target a much broader population, his reflections around the question "what does it mean to be protected?" (Castel, 2003) enable foregrounding the *undoing and unmaking of subjectivities* that migrants are affected by, beyond mobility restrictions and visible violence. He speaks about the "desocialisation of the individuals" as a characteristic of our present (Castel, 2003: 47; see also Castel, 2000). Such an expression also evokes, I suggest, the breaking up of any legal, social, and economic terrain that is triggered by different bordering mechanisms on migrants. However, the vocabulary of economic destitution, social "disaffiliation" and "disposability" is not adequate enough, I suggest, to render the undoing and unmaking of subjectivity that migrants are subjected to. In most of the cases, "illegalised" migrants who enter Europe are not just stripped of their rights, nor they are destitute; they are put in the condition of not being able to envisage future plans and are obstructed in the possibility of building solid or longstanding networks.

Relatedly, far from being a mere negative gesture – making lives disposable – the bordering mechanisms that produce and strengthen migrants' protracted exposure to violence and vulnerability hamper, erode and undermine spaces of life.

RETHINKING CONTROL: DISJOINTED KNOWLEDGES, FRAGMENTED VISIBILITY

THE ALPINE MIGRATION ROUTE

As I have illustrated in the opening vignette, due to the increase in violent border controls along the coastal crossing point (Ventimiglia), since 2017 migrants have been forced to reroute to the Alps in order to try to cross from Italy to France. Although a few migrants had already crossed there in 2016, in 2017 the relative increase in numbers and the media spotlight transformed the Alpine passage into a migration route. Nevertheless, overall, the Alpine migration route has remained relatively invisible in comparison to other border zones. Is this because of the relatively "scanty" number of migrants who try to cross, since it is a question of a few dozen per day? Actually, if we ground on a politics of counting, there is a risk of reproducing the "migration crisis" narrative, as long as it means implicitly assuming that elsewhere, for instance in Ventimiglia, migrants are "a lot" or that they constitute a problem because of their relevant number. It is instead worth noticing that at the Alpine frontier migrants arrive piecemeal; they try to cross without assembling, moving as far as possible and on the sly, taking a brief rest of a few hours only before trying to cross. "Migrants there do not want to be spotted, they do not want to be seen as a problem, they seem to tell us 'don't look at us, we are here but not to stay'. Even if their presence is visible as we are not used to see black people around here":[5] one of the locals who mobilised in support of the migrants in transit summarised in this way the migrants' tactics and attitude centred on not being under the spotlight.

The Alpine migration route is a site where *modes of governing through partial non-registering* and through asymmetrical identification are quite frequent. How are push-back operations at the border registered by the authorities? The French police return migrants to Italy by force every day, on the top of Colle d'Echelle – which can be reached by hiking from the city of Bardonecchia or at the French border in Montgenevre, which is located two kilometres away from the Italian village of Claviere. Local authorities and citizens who monitor the push-back operations speak of about 20 to 30 migrants who are usually returned by force every single day. When the French police spot and block the migrants along the route, they usually fingerprint and identify them before pushing them back. However, firstly this is not always the case: for instance, there are also push-backs that are enacted without identifying the migrants, with these latter being just dropped on the Italian side of the border. And secondly, the French police randomly give expulsion decrees to the migrants: sometimes they do, sometimes they do not. It follows then that not only the border is asymmetrically controlled – as the Italian do not stop the migrants, while the French do; more than that, there is also a discrepancy in terms of who has the traces of the push-back: if a migrant is fingerprinted in France but does not receive any expulsion paper, neither the migrant nor the Italian authorities have any proof of the push-back operations.

How are migrants' passages counted? On the Italian side, the police cooperate with the municipality of Oulx and Bardonecchia, with the priest, with two local NGOs and with the Red Cross, using a common WhatsApp, where they communicate to each other in real time how many migrants have been detected at the rail stations of Oulx and Bardonecchia and how many return after being pushed back. But this count concerns the passages, not the actual presences, as some migrants are counted twice or more – as the same person can arrive in the city of Oulx, then go to the border and being pushed back come to Oulx again. Migrants are often pushed back and go back by themselves to Turin without stopping in Oulx and Bardonecchia, in which case their passage is not registered. Therefore, what is going on along the Alpine migrant passage is a mode of governing through asymmetrical identification and partial non-registering. These forms of governing through partial non-control generate a substantial opacity for the way in which the border works. Such an opacity concerns not only external observers but also some of the actors involved in managing and hampering migrants' crossing at the frontier. Indeed, as I mentioned above, there is an asymmetrical knowledge about who is detected and returned from the border. Even more than speaking of opacity, which hints at a reality which is obfuscated and partially veiled, we can rather refer to a sort of disjointed knowledge and opaque visibility. Indeed, both the visibility and the knowledge of the functioning of border control are spatially fragmented and asymmetrical, while at the same time also scrappy, incomplete.

The Alpine frontier shows that what is often going on at the border zones is a fundamental fragmentation and unevenness in the techniques of control as well as in the "regime of visibility" at play there – that is, what is made visible and what is left or made partially invisible. Therefore, none of the actors involved has a clear and overwhelming picture of what is going on at the border. However, this should not lead us to conclude that migrants are not obstructed in their movements; rather, the violent policing and the tactics of physical obstruction are coupled with modes of governing through partial non-registering. The Alpine passage is far from being an easy crossing point. The extreme weather conditions and the French police's migrant-hunt across the mountains have transformed the Alps into a deadly frontier for migrants. However, as some activists who occupied a church to host migrants in the Italian village of Claviere argued, "the problem [is] not the mountains, the problem is not the snow, the problem is the border".[6] In other words, the Alps have become a deadly frontier for the migrants because they had been forced to cross the mountains, due to the hardening of controls along the coasts. Border zones, as Tugba Basaran has remarked, are peculiar legal spaces, characterised by "an extension of border policing and/or the contraction of borders of rights" (Basaran, 2010: 47). The configuration of different legal borders, she argues, should not be confused with exceptional and outside-of-the-law places: on the contrary, the legal making of border zones and "spaces of legal exclusion [is] created by means of ordinary law" (Basaran, 2008: 340). In other words, if we can speak of border zones, this is not in the sense of spaces excluded from the law but, rather, as places that are produced through the specifics in intertwining bordering mechanisms. Even migrants who have a temporary permit to stay in Italy are pushed back by the French police at the border due to France's suspension of Schengen in May 2015.

On the Italian side of the border, Italian police and even local humanitarian actors sometimes approach the migrants before they try to cross: "You should not dare crossing now. Crossing the Alps it is too dangerous now, with the snow. And also if you manage, the French will take you back here, in Italy. Go back to Turin and try in one month, when there will be no snow." The words uttered by an Italian policeman in front of four migrants who arrived in Bardonecchia by regional train from Turin illustrate quite well the mix between tactics of deterrence and partial non-control. An insight into modes of governing through partial and uneven non-governing and non-registration counter-balances analyses which centre exclusively on how migrants are tracked and identified, and which highlight states' "legibility" (Scott, 1998) as well as the will and the effectiveness of controlling migration. The partially missing records of migrants' passages at some border zones, as well as other forms of non-control, should not be seen only as technical failures or as states' inability to identify migrants but also as a way of coping with migrants' presence in the territory.

In this regard, focusing on Greece, Katerina Rozakou uses the expression of "practices of incomplete recording" defining "irregular bureaucracies" as "nonrecording practices and modes of dealing with irregular migration in improvised ways" (Rozakou, 2017: 37). According to Rozakou, these non-recording practices are constitutive of statecraft processes, and should not be read as states' lack or failure. Rather, Italy and Greece have been trying to dodge the spatial impositions imposed by the Dublin Regulation on people seeking asylum, thus avoiding being responsible for their asylum claims. States' tactics of *not holding responsible* through non-recording have been rife, not only in relation to the asylum process but, more broadly, concerning migrants' presence in the territory. In this sense, non-recording entails a state's apparent withdrawal, although, I suggest, a different analysis is required in this respect. To put it better, on the one hand the effective partial withdrawal by states is a way of getting rid of institutional responsibilities towards migrants as subject to rights, while on the other it is precisely through partial non-control that states manage to get hold of migrants, not through direct surveillance but on the contrary by generating the effect of exhaustion, making the state unaccountable for push-backs and irregular practices. The preventive exclusion of migrants from the asylum through irregularities is a consolidated operation at the French–Italian border: the French police tend not to register the passage of many migrants who are then pushed back to Italy in order not to be accountable for the violation of international law; most of the migrants who manage to cross are in fact denied the very possibility of claiming asylum. Zachary White has introduced the neologism of "myopticon" to designate the regimes of visibility that migrants are targeted by in reception centres. Unlike the panopticon, the myopticon "relies more on uncertainty than on accurately knowing or disciplining its subjects" and is characterised by discontinuous surveillance (Whyte, 2011: 18). Along these lines, Barbara Pinelli has drawn attention to the opacity and confusion that underpin the hosting and governing of asylum seekers in Italy. The fuzziness of the asylum regime should not be approached, she argues, in terms of lack or failure; on the contrary, opacity and legal blurriness are precisely what allow states to govern migrants' lives through uncertainty: the effectiveness of disciplinary controls is enforced through "blurriness, which creates confusion, uncertainty and distress in the asylum seekers", and it is "guaranteed by the confusion and opacity generated by this system of surveillance/care" (Pinelli, 2015: 11–13). In so doing, White and Pinelli show that a specific epistemic regime, grounded on uncertainty, and a peculiar economy of visibility, characterised by discontinuous surveillance and opacity of control, are mutually intertwined in migration governmentality. This book echoes these analytical perspectives but instead of focusing on enclosed spaces – such as detention centres and hotspots – it turns attention to mobile borders and people on the move. That is, it interrogates the modes of knowledge and the regimes of visibility that are at stake in governing migrants on the move – at the border and while they move.

I introduce the expression of "disjointed knowledges" to account for the fragmentariness of knowledge and partial lack of data and information sharing at the border. Indeed, far from being a fully legible and controlled space, that frontier is criss-crossed by modes of partial non-registration and by an opaque visibility. Despite monitoring operations taking place on a daily basis with migrants being chased by the police across the mountains, control cannot be exhaustively described in those terms: the fragmented and asymmetric knowledges about migrant crossing on the two sides of the French–Italian border show that the different actors at play there try rather to roughly take stock of the phenomenon, in order to keep it governable. Control at Europe's border zones is more about disrupting, deterring migrants' passages, and at the same time containing the political visibility of migrants' presence. Fragmentariness and blurriness are neither fully the effect of failures nor the outcome of a deliberate state strategy: they stem in part from political controversies and in part from a non-interest and unwillingness in knowing too much and making the frontier too legible.

TEMPORAL BORDERS, DISORIENTING EPISTEMIC CONFUSION

The irregularities performed by the French authorities at the border concern not only the non-registration of asylum claims but also the counterfeiting of migrants' ages. Oxfam denounced the illegal push-back of many under-aged migrants who received the decree of expulsion (*Refus d'entree*) soon after being apprehended on the train to France: on the decree of expulsion their date of birth is very often falsified by the French police. Once they are sent back to Italy, even the Italian authorities engage in what can be called a *politics of disregard*: the same unrecognised minors are not accounted for, not protected and not looked at. They are just dropped after the border by the police and they wait to find a way to try crossing the border again. In fact, proving evidence of the state's non-compliance with the law turned out to be one of the few legal weapons that NGOs and lawyers have for twisting European and national policies to the advantage of the migrants. For instance, the spatial restrictions imposed by the Dublin Regulation can be partially dodged as long as the migrant demonstrates that the first EU country where she/he had been transferred back is refusing to process his/her asylum claim. The legal side is only the most recordable aspect of such a politics of disregard, which consists of a much broader range of state interventions through withdrawal. By interventions through withdrawal I refer to the ways in which state authorities, often in collaboration with non-state actors and humanitarian organisations, hamper migrants from staying in a place or make their permanence quite difficult, being deprived of material, legal and social support. Hence, state authorities and non-state actors take terrain away from the migrants (Tazzioli, 2017). State withdrawal should not be read as a mere passive inaction, nor as a way of stripping migrants out of their rights; rather, it is an active subtraction (interventions through withdrawal) that in many cases entails the deployment of huge costs and numbers of personnel, as in the case of the police actions for dismantling migrants' informal camps in Calais. Susan Bibler Coutin has pointed to "spatial practices" that states enact in order to "prevent irregular migrants from accessing the legal rights conferred by territorial presence", in such a way that migrants ultimately appear to be "ambiguously as outside of national territory even when, physically, they are within" (2010: 200–201).

To define the ambiguous (il)legal presence of migrants excluded by being inside, she speaks of "national territories as zones of confinement" (Coutin, 2010: 205). Such an analysis nicely captures the condition of spatial entrapment and legal destitution at the same time, where migrants find themselves. Like Coutin, I bring attention to the discrepancies between actual spatial presence and the spaces of the law that in border zones appear even more blatantly, where migrants are subjected to their preventive exclusion from the channels for asylum. Yet, I also suggest using rather the notion of "containment" to refer to the disruption of migrant stay and autonomous movement, as well as to their obstructed access to protection. As I will illustrate in detail in the next chapter, legal destitution coupled with the hampering of movement and of their protracted presence in a given space, does often result in a convoluted and uneven hyper-mobility, more than in a detention-like condition. In this regard, William Walters' critical reflections on disciplinary mechanisms help in problematising what we mean by governing and control. According to Walters, neoliberal economic policy is characterised by "a microphysics of police": "These little techniques are not for the most part motivated to train, domesticate or enhance the productive capacities of the migrant bodies that are their target. Instead, they aim mostly to pacify, neutralize, order, contain and remove" (Walters, 2016: 71).

The second aspect of non-recording consists of governing through confusion and chaos. This should not be taken as an exceptional aspect of governmentality but, rather, as a usual practice enacted in crowded spaces, such as detention centres or landing places for dividing, managing and selecting migrants. Confusion can concern documents and papers delivered to the migrants – what can be named *bureaucratic confusion* – and the actual physical management of migrants, as part of temporary multiplicities, in space – *spatial confusion*. Yet, together with this spatial and bureaucratic mess, modes of governing through confusion are at stake also at the level of the epistemologies of migration, that is in the economy of knowledge production about migration. "Non-knowledge", Claudia Aradau argues, "is enacted as uncertainty, ignorance, secrecy, ambiguity, and error, assembled and reassembled to reconfigure attributions and subjects of knowledge and non-knowledge" (2017b: 328). In the migration context, this clearly emerges insofar as we can look to the multiplication of decrees, policies and bilateral agreements implemented for regaining control over migration. Taking stock of the ways in which migration policies work on the ground is a strenuous endeavour not only for researchers but also for officers and personnel from NGOs, migration agencies and state authorities. This is in part due to the constant frantic changes that occur in the field of migration law and policies, and in part due to the fragmentation of policy responsibilities associated with a proliferation of actors. That said, the opacity of administrative procedures and policies functioning in the field of migration should not be seen only as a technical limit caused by the too wide range of measures adopted but also, more importantly, as a political technology of government as such. Indeed, migrants are subject to the *confusion of the law*, which makes it hard for them to unravel it and get an understanding of how to proceed in order not to make any fatal mistake.

For the NGOs deployed on the ground this involves a sort of telescopic visibility, meaning by that a quite restricted range of knowledge about the wide and constantly changing assemblage of laws and administrative measures. In the end, there are no actors that have an overwhelming gaze over the effective functioning of the border regime. Broad EU programmes very often clash with the reality of petty bureaucracy – which, however, has a tangible impact on migrant lives – and with political frictions between the national and international authorities involved. For the migrants, the chaotic illegibility of how migration and asylum policies concretely work, means not knowing what (not) to do. Importantly, such a constitutive opacity is often further enforced by not informing the migrants of what they are entitled to.

Identification and registration procedures might also turn out to be an unintended informal laissez-passer for the migrants. This takes place also in those border zones depicted as highly monitored by European actors where the spatial and legal leeway for migrants appear to be minimal, as is the case for Lampedusa and Lesvos. Nevertheless, writing about the alterations of the actual meaning and use of certain documents involves a methodological and political caution: the tactics of appropriation that migrants engage in should not be reported in detail, as this would mean contributing to analyses that point to the 'failures' of the European border regime, and produce a narrative that could undermine migrants' leeway in terms of movement. I limit the analysis here to two cases that have also been reported in the local and national media and that do not unveil any strategic secrecy. The first one refers to the management of the 'chaotic' migrants' presence on the island of Lesvos in 2015. The opening of the Moria hotspot did not signify total mobility restrictions for the migrants: on the contrary, for a few months migrants had to register inside the hotspot as a condition for then taking a ferry ticket and moving to the mainland and continuing their journey.

Moreover, registration did not necessarily involve the migrant becoming a digital trace in the European databases, since initially only some fingerprints were sent to EURODAC. The registration procedure represented for the migrants the condition for moving on, and therefore it also represented an unofficial travel document. Similarly, in Lampedusa and at a time when the hotspot had already been in place for over two years, migrants who were disembarked on the island, after being fingerprinted and denied the possibility to claim asylum, often received a seven-day decree of expulsion (Sciurba, 2016). Through such a decree, in principle migrants must leave the country by their own means in seven days; de facto, the paper had a twofold state-effect preventively denying – access to the channels for asylum, and consequently producing a sort of illegalised migrant population whose presence on the territory was juridically and politically made invisible. Yet, for the migrants the decree of expulsion was a double- edged sword: it meant being officially expelled from the country, irrespective of their actual presence, as well as from the channels of asylum, but at the same time it constituted the material inscription of a strategic invisibilisation that, de facto, enabled them to move on or to stay without being deported. In fact, the struggle of thousands of Tunisian migrants who arrived in Lampedusa in the span of a few months in 2017 played out around their being or not being deported, with the latter meaning receiving the decree of expulsion which was the only unofficial way for Tunisian migrants to remain in the territory – due to the repatriation agreement between Italy and Tunisia.

The disorienting confusion that migrants experience is also the result of temporal borders, meaning by that the multiple and heterogenous deadlines that migrants have to comply with, and that have been enforced by states and non-state actors to regulate and restrict access to the asylum procedure. Far from being fixed and stable, temporal borders do frantically change over time; plus, they are characterised by a deep heterogeneity: there is not something like a linear temporality of control or a homogeneous temporal border. It is precisely their unevenness and constant change which generate confusion and disorientation on the migrants. They are intertwined with mechanisms of spatial confinement and, even more easily than these latter, can be quickly re-organised and altered according to different logics of control. The Greek context represents a case in point for investigating how different and constantly changing temporal borders have been enacted to regain control over migration and how these impact on migrants' lives. In particular, since 2015 temporal borders have multiplied to impose restrictions on the migrants, in terms of access to the asylum procedure and the modes of support they can get. For instance, compulsory temporal deadlines and lapses of time have been implemented by the International Organisation for Migrations (IOM) as a condition for migrants to apply for "voluntary returns" to their country of origin from the Greek islands. Indeed, migrants are allowed to apply only if they do so within five days after they receive the denial of the refugee status and if they renounce appealing against the negative decision.

Thus, temporal borders have in this case a deterrent function – discouraging migrants from appealing – and a pro-active one – forcing them to act and claim for a "voluntary return" within five days. They do not only impose restrictions; they also generate confusion and disorientation on the migrants, as long as they are often enacted tacitly and in a less visible way from spatial frontiers. The frantic rhythm and alteration of the multiple temporal borders make it hard for migrants to keep them up to date with the changes and act accordingly. "Nobody told me", a Pakistani migrant revealed to me in the premises of the hotspot of Lesvos, "that in order to be eligible for the 'voluntary returns' Programme I should not appeal against the rejection of my asylum claim, and so I am now excluded from that, I cannot longer get access to the Programme and the same happened to four friends of mine." Temporal borders and the multiple temporalities of control are strictly bound up with the production of obfuscated knowledge and with disorienting effects. Hence, the nexus between temporality, knowledge production and subjectivity constitutes an important vantage point from which to grasp how migrants are governed beyond spatial confinement.

Migrants are confronted with temporal deadlines and compulsory time lapses also at the level of more daily basis procedures, which concern the access and use of services or forms of support. Importantly, the temporality of control does also include a certain discipline over time, which requests migrants to act and perform specific tasks. Together with their spatial fixation and restriction, a temporal discipline shapes migrants' lives on a daily basis, in particular those who are within the channels for the asylum system. Temporality of control was at the heart of the Hotspot approach launched by the European Commission in May 2015 in the European Migration Agenda and implemented in Greece and in Italy the same year: the Hotspot Approach consists in fact not just of infrastructures for detention but in specific modalities and temporalities of migration management. First, European agencies (Easo, Frontex and Europol) are in charge of supervising and monitoring the work of the Greek and the Italian police concerning the obligation of identifying all migrants and share the data with the European database Eurodac. Second, such a spatial logistic of control is intertwined with a temporal one: in the hotspots, European and national actors should "swiftly identify, register and fingerprint incoming migrants".[7] However, the supposed speed and quick rhythm of control, which in part was implemented through the preventive illegalisation of migrants, does not involve a rapid "solution" or relocation for the same migrants who land and are swiftly fingerprinted. The thousands of migrants who have been stranded on the Greek islands for months, due to the geographical restrictions imposed by the EU-Turkey

Deal and the closure of the Balkan route, reveal the choke-points of the asylum regime and the protracted "stuckedness" that migrants experience. More broadly, the speed/slowness dichotomy does not really capture the temporality of migration control: if we want to grasp how temporal borders impact on migrant lives, this might be better done not through the lenses of velocity, rapidity or slowness, but by considering the split and heterogeneous temporalities of control which are at play.

Scholars have highlighted how the produced vulnerability engenders a temporal suspension and juridical limbo (see Mountz et al., 2002; Squire, 2018), as well as a condition of protracted and indefinite waiting (Hage, 2009; Khosravi, 2014), which generate uncertainty in migrants. Instead, what remains by far less explored are the injunctions and obligations to act – according to specific norms and times – that migrants are constantly targeted by, in order to get and keep their access to rights and support. That is, the temporality experienced by migrants as an outcome of their protracted vulnerability is not only one of indefinite and empty waiting; rather, migrants' forced waitinghood – waiting for the decision on the asylum claims, for a temporary authorisation to stay, for the decision of the court and so on – is often enmeshed with a series of deadlines, temporal borders and bureaucratic procedures to do in specific lapses of time. In this sense, the "stolen time" (Khosravi, 2018) of the illegalised migrants that Shahram Khosravi has cogently conceptualised, encapsulates both indefinite entrapment into the present – in the form of indefinite waiting but also compulsory temporal discipline and deadlines – and a sequestration of the future. Hence, the *making of migration* is formed by processes of undoing and unmaking, of subjectivities, spaces of liveability and, importantly, of migrants' futures.

To sum up, the opaque epistemologies of migration might result in an obfuscated knowledge about the effective numbers of migrants sent back to Italy. However, far from generating a space of exception or a space empty from state intervention, partial non-knowledge through non-recording has in fact enhanced channels of forced returns. How should we conceive practices of partial non-control and non-recording? On the one hand it is important to bring attention to incomplete and chaotic registration as mechanisms of governmentality that rely on the partial "illegibility" of the state (Das, 2004). On the other, we should caution against surreptitiously positing the state and governmental actors as the starting point for our analysis. In fact, the above-mentioned cases show that in part the states strategically do not record nor identify the migrants. Yet, such a view risks positing a sort of institutional established strategy by at the same time dismissing and taking out of the picture the incorrigibility of migrants and their troubling presence. That is, to some degree the opacity and chaotic implementation of migration policies correspond to a mode of governing through non-governing, which however far from producing an effective state retreat, forces migrants into specific (bureaucratic and administrative) channels by fundamentally restricting their autonomy of movement. Nevertheless, at the same time migrants' presence does also trigger states' frantic attempts to regain control over them. On this point, in order to undo what can be called the *methodological statism*, which consists of taking the state as the implicit epistemic referent of the analysis, I suggest starting from and bringing to the fore migrants' presence that could not be eradicated nor erased. The unpredictability of migration, in its composition, desires and numbers, makes full control and identification not only impossible but also undesirable.

Therefore, we can speak of an irreducible *ungovernability* that is constitutive of the ways in which states and non-state actors try to cope with migrants' presence – through practices of not-recording and non-registration. Ungovernability should not be confused, however, with more freedom and autonomy for the migrants. On the contrary, if practices of partial non-registration do in fact facilitate migrants' passage, they can also force migrants to enact convoluted geographies. Such a relative ungovernability can be to some degree the outcome of a multiplicity of frictions among different actors, as well as one of the heterogeneous ways through which migrants' incorrigible presence is managed through techniques of invisibilisation. Indeed, non-registration and non-recording contribute to put migrants out of sight, both in terms of digital traces left in databases and as subjects of rights.

Ungovernability is a term that conveys both a normative diagnosis and programmatic actions: indeed, as Claus Offe illustrates in his political genealogy of the notion, "ungovernability is a concept that has been used to describe conditions of institutional insufficiency with the potential of political crisis and subsequent institutional change" (2013: 1). Ungovernability designates a condition of relative state failure that concerns specific sectors, and requires special measures to be implemented but is distinguished from rogue states (Derrida, 2005). Hence, in order not to think of ungovernability in a normative sense, we have to think of it not in terms of states' insufficiency but as a political technology for coping with the incorrigible migrants' presence. In this sense, we can speak of partial ungovernability as the unstable outcome of a *will not to govern* as a political technology for handling migrants' presence. The term "ungovernability" has been widely used for corroborating the EU's narrative about an existing and threatening "refugee crisis" ("a specter is haunting Europe. It is the specter of ungovernability"[8]). Ungovernability encapsulates, in the EU's vocabulary, the destabilising effects of the economic backlash, in conjunction with the "refugee burden". The lexicon of ungovernability has been used by Giorgio Agamben who notably spoke about the ungovernable as what escapes the hold of the disseminated apparatus of control and that is ultimately linked also to the concept of inoperativity – conceived as "an operation that deactivates and renders works (of economy, of religion, of language, etc.) inoperative" (2014: 69). However, such an understanding of ungovernability is related to the image of a remainder that cannot be controlled nor transformed into bare life. Instead, from a different perspective, I am interested in pointing to the way in which ungovernability is produced and used as a mode for coping with migrants' presence – the will *not to govern too much* as a tactic for dealing with the incorrigibility of migration.

UNTRUTHFUL SUBJECTS

Disciplinary rules and moral techniques are constitutive of the daily management of asylum seekers (Pinelli, 2017). For instance, in Italy asylum seekers are not allowed to stay outside the reception centre for more than three days; in many centres they are requested to show their identification badge any time they go in and out; then local authorities as well as the cooperatives that run the reception centres can impose further arbitrary restrictions, such as allowing migrants to use prepaid cards only in some shops. Remarkably, these rules of conduct define the nexus between norms of spatial fixation, financial support and inclusion into the channels for asylum: migrants who disobey the three-day rule are excluded from the cash assistance and can be expelled from the hosting system. Once they are outside the official channels for hosting, the chances of them obtaining the international protection considerably decrease. The rules of conduct that are enforced in the hosting centres as well as in the hotspots do not (only) aim to exercise modes of direct control over the migrants.

Rather, the multiple obligations and restrictions that migrants have to comply with constitute a moral test repeated on a daily basis which turns out to be one of the conditions for being considered worthy of humanitarian protection. Even humanitarian measures inside reception centres are often deployed through disciplinary tactics. However, these latter aim less to correct or monitor unruly migrants than to create partitions and hierarchies among them and deny many their refugee status as well as economic support. Disciplinary techniques are not oriented in this framework towards maximising economic productivity and producing docile-utile bodies; rather, they establish a certain moral regime that produces and tests migrants' interiorisation of hierarchies of (non)citizenship. This is particularly evident in contexts where humanitarianism plays a central role in managing and differentiating migrants.

Through the rules of conduct, migrants are interpellated as subjects whose tolerated presence depends on their behaviour and conduct. That is, they contribute to make conditional migrants' claims (to asylum and to free mobility) and rights. Hence, an insight into the production and government of migrant singularities and multiplicities leads us to interrogate the very notion of discipline and the way in which this latter is articulated with other mechanisms of government.

Gilles Deleuze's text *Post-scriptum on the Societies of Control* has been a crucial reference for critical migration scholars who have questioned not only disciplinary power, as Deleuze does in the text, but also the paradigm of government, arguing that this latter is not adequate enough to account for the present modalities in which migrants as singularities and migration as flows are tackled. Such an argument has been pushed forward by Joshua Kurz who contends that the target of the state's regulation in the field of migration "is not primarily the subject, but is instead the regulation of a flow of mobile bodies" (Kurz, 2012: 31). He uses Deleuze's term "modulation" for describing this regulatory action upon migration flows, explaining that the logic that underpins modulation is different from that of "management": new control mechanisms "blur the interior/exterior dialectic into zones of indistinction, and […] require modulation rather than 'management' (Kurz, 2012: 34).

Following Kurz's analysis, "management" entails a direct engagement by state and non-state actors in channelling migrants, for instance dividing up "acceptable" mobility from the "bad" elements. In this regard, William Walters has pointed out that "any genealogy of state borders and their role in the governance of Western states would note how border control has moved closer and more fully towards functions of policing" (2006: 199). This partial shift entails a transformation in the way in which control itself is enacted and, relatedly, to a certain political technology, that is to a specific "hold" over migrants. In fact, as this chapter has shown it is not mainly through the direct monitoring and constant surveillance of migrant individual subjects that control is played out. The selective and regulative function of the borders does not replace nor marginalise the effects of subjection that bordering mechanisms produce over singular individuals. Importantly, control and discipline are not mutually exclusive political technologies – on the contrary, as Daniele Lorenzini argued, the two are fundamentally and historically articulated to each other (Lorenzini, 2017).

Within such a context, the migrant body appears as the surface of data extraction which becomes the source of an epidemic truth that cannot be discredited by the subject's speech. Yet, far from being fully legible, the migrant's body constantly deceives and actively withdraws from its readability and legibility. Such a tension between the displacement of the subject's speech and failures on the part of authorities to make the body legible has been notably illustrated by Frantz Fanon. In *Black Skin, White Mask* Fanon explains how the colonised subject constantly dodges and misfires the very possibility of a medical diagnosis: "The colonised Algerian proves to be an equally unsatisfactory patient […] the doctor has no hold on the patient" (Fanon, 1965: 128–129). It is at the level of the body and through it that the colonised resists becoming legible to the doctor.[9] Therefore, the colonised partially escapes the diagnostic gaze and hold of the doctor. This twofold refusal – physical and discursive – that the colonised engage shows the tension between, on the one hand, the injunction for the colonised subject to speak and to expose his own body readable and, on the other, the representation of the colonised as a subject of non-truth, that is conceived as incapable of telling the truth and, at the same time, as ultimately a liar.

Thus, the discourse required for the colonised subject turns out to be, as I have demonstrated elsewhere, a form of "confession without truth" (Tazzioli, 2015: 136); that is to say a mechanism of coerced knowledge extraction that is not predicated upon the injunction for the individual to tell the truth. Indeed, the asylum seeker is considered an untruthful subject – in the twofold sense of being deceitful and being incapable of truth – whose speech is partly assessed irrespective of its truthfulness. The obligation to speak, in Foucault's genealogical account of confession, is related to the injunction for the subject to decipher him- or herself. There is not something hidden to unveil about the story of the subject nor is the person asked to bind to his/her own discourse; rather, it is a question of scrutinising, up to the most minimal details, how and in which ways the asylum seeker does *not* match the criteria for being granted international protection. A sort of coerced discursivity is demanded of the asylum seeker, who is de facto subjected to an injunction to speak. Yet, such a coerced discursivity is partially disjoined from a game of veridicity, or better still the asylum seeker's discourse is requested to adhere to pre-established profiles and categories of refugeesness. The denial of refugee status that the majority of the asylum applicants receive[10] is the final outcome of interviews where migrants' speech is assessed not on the basis of their truthfulness as such but on the lack of coherence, even minor contradictions, detected in their narrative, and of the partial non-adherence to the multiple changing (and partially secret) criteria that migrants have to match. The asylum seekers are requested to engage in a confession without truth, unlike the confessional subjects who are demanded to tie themselves to their own discourse of truth (Foucault, 2018). In the case of the asylum seeker, the effect of subjection is produced precisely through the coercive discursivity associated with a fundamental distrust: that is, the subject is posited as unwilling and unable to tell the truth, but forced to speak anyway. What characterises migrants' obligation to speak is the twofold temporal dimension: they are questioned about their past but in order to determine the potential future threat to them if they go back to their country of origin. Such a future-oriented temporality of the panel decision is usually enacted by taking into consideration the level of insecurity for the migrants in their country of origin. Therefore, the future-oriented temporality of asylum assessment reinforces the territorial binding between the asylum seeker and their country of origin. The EU's attempt to introduce a harmonised list of safe countries actually goes in the direction of transforming the precautionary logics into a spatial trap determined by the "tyranny of the national" (Noiriel, 1991).

The *surplus of discursivity and self-narration* demanded of migrants, in particular during the interview to assess their asylum claim, is an act of *knowledge extraction*, more than a confession; such a knowledge extraction appears as necessary to the coloniser – in particular in front of a likewise resistant body – not for knowing the truth about the identity and the story of the colonised, but for inscribing the very self-narration of the colonised within a set of pre-established categories. The impossibility for the subject to tell the truth and the condition of being seen as fundamentally a "conduct of non-truth" (Lorenzini and Tazzioli, 2018) is daily experienced by migrants and asylum seekers. The injunction for asylum seekers to speak, and to do so for hours in front of the panel processing their asylum claim, is disjoined from the truth of their discourse as well as from the credibility of the subjects themselves. Ultimately, subjects are not supposed to produce a discourse with the goal of attaching them to their own discourse. Neither is the content of what they say assessed for checking that they are effectively corresponding to the factual reality of the lived experience. The speech of asylum seekers is put to the test by the internal contradictions that can emerge in the self-narration of their own journey and life. At the same time, the point is not to produce an effect of subjectivation on individuals by demanding that they bind themselves to their own discourse.

Nevertheless, the injunction for the migrants to speak is not narrowed down to the moment of the asylum interview. Migrants' coerced discursivity is a recursive aspect in the mechanisms of subjection and objectivation in migration governmentality, and it is deeply intertwined with techniques of governing at a distance and through digital tracking. The traceability of migrants' movements and the readable body of the migrant generated through the extraction of biometric traces are combined by state authorities with what the data in itself does or cannot say. That is, migrants' speech is repeatedly requested, although migrants' identity can be verified without such a coerced discursivity: apart from the asylum process, migrants' speech is needed for producing knowledge about their journeys, about the smuggling networks, about their migratory projects – both the economy of journeys and the subjective migrants' desires that migration agencies want to be aware of in order to govern them remain unknowable to the digital traces captured from the migrant body. The *hunters of migrant stories* in the hotspots, at the harbour or at the internal frontiers of Europe, wear different uniforms: UNHCR officers, IOM employees, Save the Children volunteers and Frontex's debriefing team.

Migrants are approached by these actors in the cities and more often in crucial border zones, like at the border crossing points along the Balkan route, or at the ports where migrants land. As I mentioned in Chapter 1, migrants at the harbour are interviewed by Frontex and sometimes even by the UNHCR and IOM as soon they disembark from the vessel, even before being identified by the police: "Which journey did you undertake?"; "How much did you pay in total and which smuggling networks did you use?"; "Could you tell us the names of some smugglers?"; "Through which cities did you pass, and where did you stop?" These are some of the questions asked of the migrants soon after landing but which are not used for obtaining in-depth knowledge of singular biographies. Individual stories are used and generalised for producing migration narratives about the routes used, as well as what cannot be captured by digital traces which could report only migrants' trajectories and the borders they crossed, that is to say, what happens to the migrants, how they act and how they manage to move. This does not mean, however, that their speeches receive more credibility. The question of the truth of migrants' testimonies is not contemplated from the beginning to the extent that agencies and international organisations like IOM do not interview migrants with the purpose of knowing and listening to individual stories of migration. Rather, interviews are based on preliminary fixed questionnaires that have been formulated on the basis of an oriented gaze.

In particular, the main focus that is at stake in these interviews is the smuggling economy, which nevertheless is not just narrowed down to the networks of smugglers used and the costs but includes also its geographies, the obstacles that migrants encountered and the fundamental dimensions of future destinations. Interviewed at specific borders, migrants are in fact interrogated for reconstructing in detail the spatial economy of their journeys, and simultaneously for gaining a sense of the *geographic fantasies* of future displacements, that are then translated by governmental actors as places of destination and linear routes. The future-oriented questions are asked not only on the basis of a preventative logics, which consists of anticipating migrants along their routes and blocking them, but also for crafting narratives and producing reports about migrants' final destinations. Thus, migrants' enacted geographies are spied on and studied by states by making migrants speak. Although migrants are seen and approached as "conducts of non-truth" (Fanon, 2011), irrespective of the veridicity of their discourses, they are constantly asked to speak to support the production of governmental narratives on migrations and anticipating future risk scenarios, while their speech is less and less determining for the result of the individual asylum process.

In *Politics and the Other Scene* Etienne Balibar contends that it is impossible to give a universal definition of "border", as this would require a "reduction of complexity" (2012: 76), ignoring the historical peculiarities of border functioning and the differentiations that they generate. A similar methodological move can be made concerning *the making of the subject*, as Foucault has repeatedly argued and demonstrated thorough his genealogies of the Western modern subject. Nevertheless, this chapter has shown that the very meaning of "subject" should be rethought in light not only of historical specificities but also of the differential ways in which people are targeted, governed and made the object of knowledge. To put it clearly, it is not only a matter of investigating the modes of subjectivation and individualisation in the present, but also of critically interrogating these categories. An in-depth analysis of the heterogeneous modes deployed for regaining control over unruly migration leads us to question the forms of individualisation that are actually at play.

As this chapter has illustrated, the scattered modes of control and of partial non-registration generate an amount of digital data – digital traces of migrants' passages. The latter, far from reproducing the image of a coherent subject, give rise, as I will show in the next chapter, to scattered digital subjectivities, that is to the dispersion and diffraction of the subject. The information collected is stored in many databases and it travels across sites, often without other biographical information about the subject. In this sense, we can speak of a partial de-individualisation as an outcome of processes of data-objectivation. The second aspect that this chapter has considered is about *the making of refugees*: as I have illustrated above, if on the one hand individual stories play a central role in asylum procedures, on the other we cannot speak of ways of governing through individualisation, but rather of a confession without truth that migrants are requested to do. Asylum seekers are posited at the same time as deceitful subjects and as subjects who are not able to tell the truth, while they are asked to fit into pre-established categories in order to obtain refugee status.

Building on Ann Laura Stoler, one can object that a central role has been played by the intimate as an object and a technique of government, both in the colonial spaces and in contemporary forms of control (Stoler, 2002). The intimate is in fact explained in these analyses not in terms of modes of individualisation but as a form of knowledge on the subjects that is exercised for getting a hold on them – through what Derek Gregory defines as "the intrusive intimacy of the biometrics" and the "claim to familiarity, understanding and even empathy [...] an intimate knowledge of adversary culture" (Gregory, 2008). However, while the intimate constitutes at the same time an object and a technology of government, the effects of individualisation are related also to a specific regime of truth,[11] and exercised through a constant hold over time.

CONCLUSION

This chapter has engaged with the production and governing of migrant singularities by focusing on four main interrelated aspects: subjectivities, control, objectivisation and discourses of truth. It has investigated modes of governing migration that are predicated on partial non-registering and arbitrary non-control, addressing at the same time the effects of violence and vulnerability that these generate on migrants' lives. A focus on migrant singularities has allowed us to engage in a twofold methodological move. First, it has been a question of interrogating and unpacking the figures of subjectivities that we usually mobilise to address migrants – e.g. "irregular migrants", "refugees", "vulnerable persons". Second, an insight into migrant singularities has enabled us to foreground the irreducibility of migrants' subjective drives and desires. In this sense, migration governmentality can be seen from the standpoint of modes of capitalisation acted upon migrants' desire to move. The economy of desire refers to the range of affects through which migration is regulated and that, at the same time, constantly interrupt the very possibility of disciplining migrants' subjectivities. As Scheel et al. (2015) have stated:

> the "management" of migration also involves the regulation of affects, emotions and desires as techniques of government. Yet, at the same time it is the multiplicity of subjective desires, hopes and aspirations that animate[s] the projects migrants pursue with their migrations, which is always in excess of their regulation by governmental regimes. (2014: 31)

The next chapter will develop the analysis of migrant singularities and collective formations by bringing attention to the production of datafied subjectivities – as a result of the extraction of biometric data from the migrants – and to the making of virtual multiplicities.

NOTES

1. Rey Chow criticises the exclusionary focus on subjectivities in post-structuralist philosophy, arguing that "nuanced reading of the subject as such also tends to downplay issues of structural control – of law, sovereignty and prohibition – that underlie the subject's relation with the collective" (2010: 58).
2. Interview with EASO, Athens, July 2018.
3. According to the 2013 Asylum Procedure Directive an "applicant in need of special procedural guarantees" is someone with a "reduced ability to benefit from the rights and comply with the obligations under the Directive due to individual circumstances". It does not include an exact list of "vulnerable persons" but it does refer to special guarantees that refer to age, gender, disability, mental disorder and "persons who have been subjected to torture, rape or other serious forms of psychological, physical or sexual violence, such as victims of female genital mutilation". https://eur-lex.europa.eu/legal-content/EN/TXT/PDF/?uri=CELEX:32013L0033&from=EN
4. www.msf.org/confinement-violence-and-chaos-how-european-refugee-camp-traumatising-people-lesbos
5. Interview with S, a citizen of Oulx, October 2018.
6. Activists who occupied a church in March and April 2018 to host the migrants who were trying to cross to France.
7. https://ec.europa.eu/home-affairs/sites/homeaffairs/files/what-we-do/policies/european-agenda-migration/background-information/docs/2_hotspots_en.pdf
8. www.theglobalist.com/europe-crisis-governance-integration-eu/
9. "The doctor rather quickly gave up the hope of obtaining information from the colonized patient [...] thinking that the body would be more eloquent. But the body proved to be equally rigid" (Fanon, 1965: 127).
10. On average, between 60 and 65 per cent of asylum seekers across Europe are "illegalised", that is their asylum claim is rejected.
11. In which the injunction for subjects to tell the truth about themselves is connected to the obligation for them to tie themselves to such a truth.

3

Digital Multiplicities and Singularities

(In)Visibility and Data Circuits

INTRODUCTION

At the Scientific Police Headquarters in Rome about five police officers update in real time the national fingerprint database (AFIS) where migrants' fingerprints and personal data are stored. From there, they can check EURODAC, the EU asylum fingerprint database,[1] where EU member states are obliged to store the fingerprints of migrants who enter "irregularly" and those who claimed asylum. In the AFIS database every file contains not only fingerprints but also a photo, the height and weight of the person, chromatic relevant data, age and nationality, as well as information about how the migrant entered the country and the reasons for such an entry. The somatic and (short) biographic narratives constitute part of the digital archive of migrants' histories recorded by states. These digital traces correspond to what the subject declares and what he/she looks like during the encounter with the police. Yet, the somatic and narrated stories of the subjects can be multiple since they might change over time and might tell different stories about themselves. Therefore, in order to check migrants' biometric identity the police use the Identification Unique Code (CUI) which corresponds to the fingerprints' digital trace.

The police check the fingerprints with the fingerprint records that are in the Italian system of fingerprint identification (AFIS): the system checks and finds possible matches, and then the police officer is in charge of deciding whether or not the fingerprints actually match the ones already stored in the database. This process normally takes a few minutes, and after that time the CUI is stored in the AFIS database. The same data are uploaded in the European database (EURODAC). The image of the migrant that is produced and circulated throughout the national police systems is an assemblage of scattered digital singularities and of a scanty narrated story about the migrant that, however, can take the form of a multiple biography – the multiple files associated with the fingerprints. This ordinary procedure of data collection and data storing involves direct border encounters and clashes between the migrant and the police officer and a series of mechanisms of data extraction that rely on the migrant's body as the source and, at once, the target of identification (Scheel, 2013). Data-collection activity at the border is also connected to a certain visualisation of the digital subjectivity: the digital traces immediately appear on the computer screen in front of the police officer and are shared on a national level. However, an analysis of biometric and identification techniques cannot be narrowed to the punctual moment of identification. In fact, through these digital captures, storing and visualisation of the data collected, new ways of thinking about migrant subjectivities emerge.

When we think about multiplicities and singularities we usually associate these, respectively, to actual groups of people that gather in a place and to individual subjects. In particular, as illustrated in Chapter 1, when associated with migration, the term "multiplicities" often refers to unruly migrant groups or to faceless bodies to be rescued at sea. The same migrants are also targeted by identification measures (e.g. the fingerprinting machine), detection tools (e.g. radars), face-to-face interviews and digital technologies that extract data from them: indeed, migrants' presence and passages are datafied, stored and categorised in multiple ways. The translation of the migrant into the data archive of the state is the digital outcome of the repeated encounter with the authorities. The data extracted from the migrant are used for multiplying profiles and categories, and are is assembled for generating what can be called "virtual multiplicities". These are multiplicities formed by data and digital information that are extracted from the individual and then combined to produce sub-groups or populations that do not correspond to actual persons and are used instead for labelling, dividing and classifying migrants. Virtual multiplicities that stem from data extraction, circulation and combination do not "merely constitute 'new' representations of "old" populations. The multiplication of assemblages also multiplies the object, the speciesbody" (Isin and Ruppert, 2019: 221). This chapter focuses on digital collective and individual subjectivities generated through data-extraction activities, and it asks: How are virtual migrant multiplicities produced? How are migrant subjectivities shaped by datafication processes? And to what extent are data circulated and not circulated?

The chapter starts with the section "Hit Without Interpellation?" which questions the role of discursivity in migrant identification procedures, showing how migrants are targeted by data-extraction activities without being directly addressed or interpellated as subjects, nor required to speak. Then the chapter moves on by retracing two fictional geographies of migration data circuits, taking as examples migrants who landed in Italy and in Greece, showing how different kinds of digital information extracted from the migrants are shared (and not shared) and how this affects migrants themselves. The third section, entitled "The Making of Humanitarian Datafied Identities", focuses on the performative character of digital technologies used by international actors such as the UNHCR for producing migrant identities. The following section investigates the articulation between financial and humanitarian interventions in the field of refugee governmentality, with a focus on the prepaid cards delivered to asylum seekers in refugee camps. The chapter concludes with an account of mechanisms of border control at a distance – monitoring tools and mapping activities oriented towards detecting migrants. The combination of close-up sight with modes of visibility at a distance determines how migrants are made the object of datafication (Gregory, 2011). The angle of digital technologies and data circuits is mobilised for investigating how some subjects are produced and made knowledgeable as "migrants". Indeed, the *making of migration* depends also on the daily use of digital tools for mapping, detecting and identifying "migrants".

In order for states and non-state actors to generate virtual multiplicities, the different data collected from the migrants should be stored, circulated and assembled. Digital technologies and modes of governing migration at a distance should be read in light of the modes of border enforcement that this entails. Indeed, Enrica Rigo and Serhat Karakayali have rightly observed that "virtual borders do not exist unless they are crossed" and, in turn, "the very possibility for them to be crossed by 'illegal' migrants implies that a boundary of difference between 'legal' and 'illegal' movement has already been traced" (Karakayali and Rigo, 2010: 126).

Throughout the chapter I use the expression "data circuits" to refer to data-circulation and data-exchange activity related to the digital information extracted from the migrants, both at a distance – e.g. through radars – and through direct border encounters – e.g. fingerprinting procedures. Data circuits do not involve a smooth logistics of circulation: on the contrary, data-sharing activities are characterised by choke-points, local resistances, technical jams and legal restrictions. By employing the expression "data circuits" I bring attention to a battlefield and a dimension of migration governmentality that remains fundamentally invisible by design but which still has tangible effects on migrant lives. More broadly, the chapter deals with different modes of migrant objectivation that are enacted through activities of data extraction and as a result of the knowledge production related to migration.

HIT WITHOUT INTERPELLATION?

The biometric trace encapsulates the history of multiple subject encounters and clashes with powers. Scholars have pointed to the transformations produced by the increasing use of biometric technologies for identifying migrants at borders (Amoore, 2006, 2013; Frowd, 2018; Scheel, 2013). The image of the body as a readable machine had been introduced to describe how biometrics has changed the conception of subjectivity and the relation between production of truth and processes of subjectivation. Biometric techniques contribute to shift away from a subject who is requested to speak, to tell the truth about himself and to narrate his own story towards a non-discursive truth extraction, also called epidermic truth: the injunction for the individual to tell the truth about himself is partially – although not fully– superseded by the extraction of *epidermic truth*, building on the evidence that "the body cannot lie" (Aas, 2005). In fact, a focus on data extraction from migrants bodies shows that the very meanings of identity and identification procedures are eminently connected to digital and non-discursive elements and traces. Together with the act of reading the body, biometric techniques of identification contribute to select what aspect of the subject is considered to be "of concern" to state authorities. However, descriptive and narrative elements provided by migrants themselves are not totally erased from the production of migrant identity: rather, the dactiloscopic file constitutes a field of tension with the multiple migrants' identities narrated to the police by the migrants themselves. From the fingerprinting operation onwards, migrants' journeys and the flow of their biometric traces fall apart. The Unique Identification Code mentioned at the beginning of this chapter constantly haunts at a distance the mobility and permanence of migrants in Europe. The biometric traces can be used as a sort of digital avatar of the person's identity, representing the only univocal and individualising data that make it possible to know the identity of the person which matters to the state, independently of the migrant's speech and changing bodily features.

Yet, the data can also be used as a digital check of migrants' changes in status and of their spatial position. In the first case, the fingerprints are associated with a person, proving at the same time their unicity. In the second case, the multiple reporting of fingerprint hits reveals something about a migrant's conduct – e.g. a migrant who entered illegally who then decides to claim asylum. This twofold process is part of what I call data-objectivation, or objectivation through datafication. Migrants are usually fingerprinted more than once, from the moment when they land in Europe, although only some of those digital hits are then put in wider circuits of data sharing, while others remain stored in the national databases. The circulation and elaboration of migration data also constitute the way in which migrants' subjectivities are materially codified by operations of datafication. Such a form of objectivation through datafication depends on technical devices, like the fingerprinting machines, that make data extraction possible. Importantly, data-capture activities constitute only one stage of the process: the data collected are then sent and stored into databases and shared among different actors.

In order to generate knowledge and value, data must circulate (De Goede, 2018). To be captured and stored in the database is both the entry into the national territory and the story of migrants' mobility. This is in part reconstructed by the European agency Frontex: both at the harbour where migrants are disembarked and inside the Italian and Greek hotspots, Frontex officers ask the migrants to provide information about their trajectories and the economy of crossing. Such a repository of migrant journeys is not used, however, for tracking and individualising purposes but, rather, for building a digital archive about the logistics and geographies of migration routes, which gives more concreteness to the abstract image of the "flows". Indeed, the flow in itself, as an abstraction of migrants' actual geographies, is considered insufficient by agencies like Frontex and IOM in order to anticipate and govern migration movements: an in-depth knowledge about migrant logistics and economy of crossing is in fact needed. To put it in spatial terms, a cartography of migration movements needs to be articulated with an in-depth knowledge of the materialities of migrant journeys – their temporalities, their economy and the infrastructures of mobility.

Nevertheless, it is important to undo the image of a total traceability of migrant journeys; rather, migration movements are the object of digital capture according to a temporal and spatial unevenness – corresponding to the moments when they are detected. The unevenness of migrant digital recording is not only the result of technical limits and of the impossibility of constantly tracing migrant erratic geographies. The digital mapping of migration movements is the outcome of the sites and the moments when migrants become visible, that is identified and monitored, and simultaneously reproduces a cartography of migration where subjects are seen as constantly striving to cross national borders. Migrants' digital traces are stored in different databases and concern both migrants' fragmented and convoluted geographies (e.g. multiple entries into a country, or multiple expulsions) as well as the migrants' changing status – visa applicant, asylum seeker, illegalised migrant or person returned to another member state on the basis of the Dublin Regulation. Hence, an overall visualisation of the datafication of migration movements would result in a map formed by dots – the places where migrants have been detected – that, if connected, give rise to routes of control more than to the effective migrant geographies. It follows that the object of datafication is not migrant mobility per se but the checkpoints for migration controls – transit, entry and crossing points where migrants' passage is registered, but where unmapped movements and erratic geography are erased and not considered as part of the migrant routes.

To sum up, the cartography that stems from these operations of data extraction is ultimately a point-based migration map, where migrant routes are artificially crafted by connecting dots and without taking into account what happens between one dot and another, in terms of immobility, forced internal displacements and circular movements. Thus, migrants' mobility is objectified into the specific points of capture where it is slowed down or blocked. The objectivation through data of migrant mobility hinges on singular migrants but then, starting from singularities, extends well beyond the bodies of the targeted migrants, as it concerns potential future migration flows, affecting in this way other singular migrants as part of abstract multiplicities. The increasing datafication of migrants' movements and the mechanisms of data extraction are telling of the ways in which migrants can be targeted, controlled and disciplined without being addressed, that is out of any modes of interpellation.

Interpellation, as I mentioned in Chapter 2, constitutes the enactment of the subject itself; that is, the way in which the individual is produced, addressed and transformed into a subject. As Louis Althusser notably defined it, interpellation is related to the making of the subjects: the transformation of "the individuals into subjects (it transforms them all) by that very precise operation which I have called *interpellation* or hailing, and which can be imagined along the lines of the most commonplace everyday police (or other) hailing: 'Hey, you there'" (Althusser, 1971). *Hit without interpellation* refers to a variety of processes of data extraction migrants are targeted by without being addressed, being asked to speak or to respond, and that still generate specific effects of subjectivation and subjection. Indeed, on the basis of data extraction and circulation migrants are identified and their biometric identity is secured and shared among different actors across Europe. At the same time, migrants' subjectivity turns out to be partially shaped by the awareness that, after being fingerprinted, their movements in Europe can be tracked at a distance, and that such a digital trace is stored independently of migrants' physical presence.

Related to that, *hit without interpellation* concerns how migrants are labelled and identified in a certain way, irrespective of their own speech, although as I have shown in Chapter 2 migrants' coerced discursivity is very often requested. The *hit without interpellation constitutes a way of governing that is not fully perceived as such by the subjects who are targeted by it* – that is not perceived as a mode of subjection and tends to be accepted as well as normalised as a technical procedure. The friction between the technological hit and the targeted body appears when migrants refuse to give their fingerprints and to be identified: although in most of the cases it is just a temporary mismatch, since the forced fingerprinting operation is repeated by the police officer, and the coerced hit spins freely. In a similar way, when migrants provide fake personal data, this cheating tactic can have implications for how digital technologies used in refugee governmentality work – for instance, as I show later in the chapter, with the debit cards delivered to asylum seekers in Greek refugee camps. In both cases, the hit without interpellation results in a visible friction, as long as it encounters the local resistance of the subject – who refuses such a process of data extraction for the spatial and legal implications this has for them.

A genealogical approach to the tactics and techniques for controlling and disciplining unruly mobility requires digging into the historical legacies of biometric technologies. The fingerprinting technique should be situated in a colonial genealogy and connected with procedures of branding that Simone Browne analyses for tracing the "links between contemporary biometric information technology and transatlantic slavery" (2015: 26). Browne remarks on the missing account of race in security studies scholarship, and proposes to rethink security and surveillance technologies in relation to the "archive of transatlantic slavery" (2015: 11). This enables displacing the focus from surveillance as such towards strategies of capture, branding, and racialisation mobilised not only for reproducing norms of whiteness and hierarchies of humanity, but also for producing knowledge of those targeted populations. Hence, a focus on migrant singularities requires taking into account the ambivalent target of these technologies – identifying and producing knowledge about individuals and also the *temporality of subjectivation*. By that I refer first to a future-oriented predictive logic; indeed, the reconstruction of the past mobility of the subject is articulated with a temporality of control centred around the notion of risk: body surveillance, as David Lyon has put it, "promises to offer not only detail about what happened in the past [...] but also of what will happen in the future" (2001: 306). Second, the temporality of subjectivation designates the multiple ways in which individual and collective subjects are crafted, and projected into the future, not only by identification technologies but also through the circulation of those digital traces.

GEOGRAPHIES OF DATA CIRCUITS

In this section I trace two fictional migrant geographies in order to show how migrants are differently targeted by a variety of bureaucratic, digital and police measures and how the heterogeneous data collected are stored in manifold databases. The two fictional migrant geographies that I have reconstructed here represent two trajectories – one of a migrant who landed in Italy, the other of a migrant who landed in Greece – which while they do not correspond to real stories retrace the main steps of what happens to most migrants who arrive in Europe by sea and then try to move on. These two fictional journeys do not intend to cover the heterogeneous routes, moments of blockage and strandedness, and the push-backs that migrants experience. Rather, in order to trace them I considered the physical and digital borders that most migrants encounter together with the most common trajectories that migrants who land in Greece and in Italy respectively undertake. Simultaneously, I have reconstructed these geographies on the basis of the main legal and identification steps that migrants are faced with, highlighting the crucial sites and moments when some kind of registration and data-collection activity is made by national authorities, European agencies or IGOs.

The first fictional migrant geography starts in June 2016, in the central Mediterranean sea, on board an Italian Navy vessel: S., the protagonist of this story, was rescued together with about one hundred migrants he was travelling with. On board, S. was asked by a Navy officer to give his name, surname and nationality. This information, together with the total number of migrants on board, had been communicated to the police at Pozzallo, where migrants had been disembarked two days later. Soon after landing, S. was subjected to a quick medical screening by the Red Cross. The police took a picture of him, which later would have been stored with the information provided during the proper identification procedure. On the deck of the harbour in Pozzallo, the first people that S. met after the quick medical screening had been one Frontex officer and one IOM officer, who asked him questions about the logistics and the costs of his journey. The information collected about the economy and logistics of S.'s journey is stored in Frontex's database and shared with the Italian authorities: for three months personal data can be accessed, after which time it will be anonymised, and what is kept is the history of the journey that S. gave to Frontex officers and that will be used to populate Frontex risk analyses. S. together with the other migrants saved at sea are counted both by the Navy and by the Italian police, respectively under the rubric of "rescued migrants" and "migrant arrivals": that is, S. becomes part of a numeric group, and is labelled with the number "110".

S. was transferred to the hotspot of Pozzallo, located a few hundred metres away from the harbour, where the identification procedure starts. There, his biometric fingerprint was taken for the first time in Europe, while the Italian police fingerprinted him, under the monitoring of Frontex officers, and the digital file was sent both to the Italian fingerprint database, AFIS, and to EURODAC. Therefore, in the span of a few hours, S.'s presence has been digitally captured by different actors and translated into different languages and codes: while the Italian police and EURODAC store S.'s biometric footprint (his fingerprints), together with his name, gender and nationality,[2] Frontex and IOM store the story told by S. about the logistics of his journey. If some suspicion arises about S., the European Police Office (Europol) can have access to the file sent by Frontex to the Italian police, although there cannot be a direct information exchange between Frontex and Europol without the mediation of the national authorities.

Biometric traces, identification forms with personal details (name, age, gender, nationality) and histories of journeys populate the multiple *migrant archives*. Some of these data and information will travel across space and be shared immediately with other actors, as is the case with the fingerprints taken during the identification procedure that the Italian police sends to EURODAC, where the data on average are displayed in about one hour. Although according to the EURODAC regulation migrants' irregular entry should be stored under Category 2 (irregular entry), and the fingerprints should be sent again to EURODAC under category 1 (asylum applicant), if the migrant claims asylum later, by praxis Italian authorities will refuse to duplicate the fingerprints transmitted to the European database: those migrants who declare their intention to apply for asylum are registered only once in EURODAC by Italy, under Category 1.[3] This was also the case with S.: thus, his entrance had been stored in EURODAC as an asylum seeker and not as an irregular entry. Importantly, the different data collected won't be used only for keeping track of S.: rather, some of this information will be used to update analyses and statistics about the daily number of migrant arrivals, and, on a long-term basis, by Frontex and by the Italian authorities for tracing current and future migration trends.

Methodologically, I start from the multiple chokepoints, local resistances and frictions of data circulation, and not from smooth channels and flows. While S.'s fingerprints were sent to EURODAC, this was not the case for many migrants who had arrived one year before, when the hotspot system was not implemented yet and when Italy used to dodge EURODAC obligations in order to avoid being responsible for their eventual asylum claims. After a couple of weeks, S. was transferred to a hosting centre in a small village in Northern Italy. There, he was taken to the police office to claim asylum: he was fingerprinted again, as part of the asylum procedure, and the biometric data were sent to the Italian ministry of the interior. The data related to his asylum application were inserted into the C3 form, which contains personal data, and this latter is shared only later, at the interview stage, with the UNHCR that is part of the asylum interview panels.

In September 2017, S. decided to escape to France, despite being aware of the spatial restrictions imposed by the Dublin Regulation. He went to the city of Ventimiglia, where he spent a few days in the transit centre run by the Red Cross: S. was asked to give his name and nationality, and his fingerprints were taken again: independently whether or not S. stated his real name, the file with personal data (name, surname) declared by him was associated with his fingerprint file. While he was trying to cross, he was pushed back twice by the French police. The first time, the policemen did not even register his passage, nor did they give him any notification of the push-back, and therefore his forced return was not recorded at all in the French database. Instead, the second time he was given a decree of expulsion, and the information he provided had been stored, together with a copy of the expulsion paper, by the French Police. After a few attempts, S. managed to cross and to reach Paris. However, after a few days there he was apprehended by the police who took his fingerprints and checked with EURODAC that he was already identified in Italy. Thus, France sent the request with S.'s data to Italy, to send him back on the basis of the Dublin Regulation, but the Italian authorities did not accept it, and the whole procedure was delayed.

The second fictional geography retraces the story of M., who travelled from Afghanistan to Greece. He landed on the Greek island of Lesvos on 23 June 2018, and his arrival was recorded by the Hellenic Police and by Frontex, on a vessel with 67 migrants on board. As part of the statistics, only numbers appear, while there is no reference to the nationality of the migrants. M. was transferred to the Moria hotspot on the island, where he was subjected to the identification procedure: the fingerprints were taken by an officer from the European Asylum Support Office (EASO) and the data were sent both to the Greek database and to EURODAC. Soon after that, he was registered as "vulnerable" by the doctors inside the hotspot. The medical form with personal data is stored by the Greek authorities only, and the EASO can also use it for producing analyses and statistics about migrant profiles and trends. Due to his recognised vulnerability, M.'s file was known also by the UNHCR, which is in charge of transferring "vulnerable cases" to the mainland. Once he arrived in Athens, the UNHCR stored M.'s case since, as an asylum seeker, he was entitled to get the monthly cash assistance managed by the UN agency. His personal data and information were taken from the Greek Asylum Service and stored in Progres 4, the UNHCR general database. Part of these data was shared with Cash Assist, another UNHCR database that includes information about the beneficiaries of debit cards (the Cash Assistance Programme).

The financial actor involved in the Cash Assistance Programme, Prepaid Financial Services, can access this database. In the Cash Assist database M. was registered not only as an individual beneficiary of the debit cards, but also as part of a temporary refugee population: in fact, in the database personal data were combined with the group that M. belonged to, according to the UNHCR, which divides between "catered" and "non-catered" groups, that is between those who received food and those who need to cook by themselves in the refugee camps. The updated information stored in Cash Assist can be accessed by the Greek authorities only on demand. In the meantime, after waiting for three months, M. was given accommodation by the Hellenic Red Cross. After a few months, M. managed to cross to Macedonia, and his disappearance was recorded at the UNHCR's monthly registration for the debit cards, as long as M. did not come. This absence was communicated to the Hellenic Police and to the Greek Asylum Service which suspended his asylum procedure. However, after spending some time in Macedonia without managing to move on, M. decided to come back to Greece where at least he had some contacts, and he temporary settled in Thessaloniki. In order to avoid being identified as an absconder, he has been trying to remain invisible to the police as well as to all humanitarian actors.

These fictional geographies show that the digital information extracted from the migrants is used not only for tracking migrants and storing their digital history of "illegal" passages and presence, but also for proactively generating and populating virtual multiplicities. Migrants are not only constantly made knowledgeable and "jabbed at" – as individuals whose digital traces show where they are or have been, what they have done, and so on; they are also a source of data extraction for potential and future data assemblages. Yet, the virtual multiplicities are never the outcome of mere technical data assemblages or sharing; rather, racialised criteria and epistemologies underpin the production of virtual migrant multiplicities. In other cases, individual data and information are used for grouping purposes; that is, for allocating individuals to collective categories and virtual sub-groups made by international organisations or states. For instance, in the UNHCR's database Cash Assist, which stores information about the beneficiaries of UNHCR's Cash Assistance Programmes, the data for those asylum seekers who are travelling with their parents, children or relatives are stored as part of the family group and the debit card that they receive is associated with the name of the father. Thus, far from being a random or neutral data assemblage, the artificial category to which individual migrants are allocated responds to a traditional patriarchal family model.

THE MAKING OF HUMANITARIAN DATAFIED IDENTITIES

The implementation of digital technologies in the field of migration governmentality has received a lot of attention in the scholarship, and in particular in critical security studies. This literature has mainly focused on the security-oriented use of technologies in relation to migration and borders (Broeders and Dijstelbloem, 2015; Jeandesboz, 2016). Jean Jeadesboz and Pierre Guittet (2010) have used the expression "security technology" to designate the functioning of technologies that have been implemented for strengthening and smartening border controls activities. Digital technologies have moved centre stage also in the field of refugee humanitarianism: in such a scholarship digital technologies are critically analysed as part of an ambivalent security-protection discourse (Abdelnour and Saed, 2014; Jacobsen, 2017). That is, digital technologies are used in the name of refugees' security and their protection. Both terms are, however, equivocal. Security is conceived at the same time as securing against potential refugees' identity frauds, and as human security – granting security to the refugees. Similarly, as Katja Jacobsen and Kristin Sandvik (2018) have noticed, the use of digital technologies is supposed to enhance the level of refugees' protection but in reality it introduces new risks for the refugees themselves. This chapter contributes to such a debate by using a slightly different angle, as it asks how the use of digital technologies and modes of control at a distance contributes to transform migrants into objects of knowledge, into transferrable data and sources of value extraction.

"Registration goes far beyond a mere head count":[4] the UNHCR's description of the registration process is telling of the proactive dimension of data-extraction mechanisms, since "counting is hungry for categories. Many of the categories we now use to describe people are by-products of the needs of enumeration" (Hacking, 1982). In fact, registration, identification and subjects' (digital) identity are mutually related: they go beyond head count, they also involve identifying who the person effectively is, irrespective of what she/he decides to say; in turn, identification is not only about verifying a migrant's "real" identity through biometric checks, it is also about giving an identity to her/him. That is, identification is conceived not only as data extracted *from* the migrants – against their will and beyond what they declare to be – but also as a process through which something is given *to* the migrants; that is, migrants would finally have a digital identity that would empower them as subjects.[5] Importantly, such a narrative on identification as an ambivalent process of *extraction from* (the migrants) and *equipping them* (with a digital identity) reveals a twofold mechanism of objectivisation and subjectivation. Indeed, migrants become objects of knowledge in a peculiar way, through processes of datafication and data extraction, while at the same time they are shaped as subjects empowered through identity documents. It is no small significance that the refracting of humanitarian discourses on identification is entangled with the World Bank's programmes on digital identity for unbanked populations.

First, the image of the refugee empowered by digital identity echoes the description of unbanked populations made in the World Bank's documents. Second, on a more practical level, the World Bank and the UNHCR are co-leading projects on digital identity that target both asylum seekers and "the poor". Third, the intertwining of financial and humanitarian actors is played out at the level of data-sharing activities. In 2017, the UNHCR announced the forthcoming launch of a joint data centre in collaboration with the World Bank "on forced displacement to greatly improve statistics on refugees, other displaced people and host communities".[6] This joint data centre will store data and information collected by the UN Refugee Agency (UNHCR) and the World Bank on refugee displacement situations. The UNHCR promotes the future joint data centre as a result of the effort to articulate development-based responses to displacement and humanitarian interventions, considering these latter as no longer sufficient for responding to the ongoing global "refugee crisis".

The "UNHCR strategy on digital inclusion and identity" states that "empowerment passes through digital inclusion: access to jobs, income and remittances, online learning and web-based economic activities will make a difference in the lives of people we care for".[7] Digital identity is presented as a *techno-humanitarian pathway towards refugees' dignified life*. In this way, we see that migrants become objects of knowledge both through datafication processes – of their body, presence and passages – disassembled into a multiplicity of data, and as *subjects to empower*. Thus, the asylum registration procedure which for the migrants is at the same time a necessary condition for accessing the asylum procedure and a moment of data extraction, is presented as a benefit for them, as a way of getting one's own digital identity. In this regard, Ian Hacking's theory of "dynamic nominalism" is quite helpful for addressing the interaction between the production of epistemic categories and labels on the one hand, and processes of subject formation on the other. According to Hacking, names and categories do not, however, merely enact subjects, which is the reason why he refuses to endorse a radical nominalist perspective; rather, he argues, "what I am deliberately doing depends on the possibilities of description [....] Hence if new modes of description come into being, new possibilities for action come into being" (2002: 108).

Nevertheless, this should not lead us to conclude that there is no room left for the subjects to alter, appropriate and disrupt the space crafted by those categories. On the contrary, a critical focus on modes of objectivation needs to grasp the leeway and discrepancies between how migrants' subjectivities are shaped by categorising labels and how subjects themselves tactically engage with those labels. In fact, migrants do often strategically appropriate, resist or twist the modes of objectivation that shape them.[8] In other cases, they also resist, subtract and desubjugate in front of the injunction to be an "autonomous empowered refugee" or to become a transferrable set of data. The protracted refusal to be identified and fingerprinted, or to tell one's own "true" identity, represents one among the many desubjugation tactics that migrants adopt. An insight into processes of migrant objectivation through datafication does not mean disregarding the modes of exploitation, violence and direct control exercised on the migrants: far from being "remainders" or the unintended side of technology-based migration measures, the *continuum of violence* acted upon the migrants' bodies and on their lives at large constitutes the backbone upon which the objectivation through data extraction can take place.

"PARA-CITIZENS" AND THE CIRCUITS OF FINANCIAL-HUMANITARIANISM

Greece has become a contentious political terrain due to the staging of the "refugee crisis" in simultaneity with the economic backlash; for this reason, in order to critically unpack the staging of the refugee crisis there is a need to analyse these multiple crises together (De Genova and Tazzioli, 2016; Kasparek, 2016; Mezzadra, 2018b). As Brett Neilson has advanced, in such a context migrants have become the actual currency in the political and economic negotiations between the EU and Greece (Neilson, 2018). Within such a framework, it is noticeable that Greece is the first European country where the EU has funded a Refugee Cash Assistance Programme, under the coordination of the UNHCR.[9] The Programme was launched in 2016 as a response to what European states were calling a "refugee crisis". It consists of prepaid debit cards delivered by the UNHCR to asylum seekers in refugee camps, hotspots and reception centres. All cards' "beneficiaries" – as the UNHCR call the asylum seekers entitled to the debit card – are topped up every month: in refugee camps and hotspots where the food is provided by the NGOs, asylum seekers receive 90 euros per month, while in the others they get 150 euros.

However, the circuits of financial-humanitarianism cannot be analysed disjoined from the constellation of technologies that asylum seekers are obliged to use and that actually constitute digital mediations, channels and obstacles between them and humanitarian actors or state authorities. For instance, in Greece migrants need to download and use Viber chats in order to communicate to the NGOs the technical problems they might have with the prepaid cards; and even before becoming asylum seekers, they will encounter technological obstructions, since in order to book an appointment for lodging the asylum claim they need to use a Skype system put into place by the Greek government in 2016. The difficulties that migrants experience depend also on the restricted time frames in which they might use those technologies for getting in touch with the humanitarian actors as well as the multiple changing rules they need to comply with. Overall, as long as technologies are compulsory steps and mediations to communicate with humanitarian actors or to gain access to the asylum, they end up as obstacles – digital disruptions – for the refugees.

The data collected at the moment of the asylum seekers' registration into the Cash Assistance Programme are stored in the UNHCR's central database ProGres – which includes personal data and the information to hand about each asylum seeker, including their legal status – and in the Cash Assist database. This latter, as in the case of ProGres, is owned and managed by the UNHCR and contains only data about asylum seekers as "beneficiaries" of cash assistance programmes: these include the registration date into the cash system; the transactions made by the beneficiaries; updated information about their eligibility; the amount of money received; and the name of the main family member. This second database constitutes a sort of digital interface between the UNHCR and the bank (PFS). In turn, PFS also has an autonomous database with the real-time transactions. PFS is not interested in tracking refugees' movements, nor in knowing if they are in the country legally or not: the Cash Assistance Programme is in fact conceived as a temporary measure by PFS, which is aware that a huge majority of beneficiaries will never become clients of a bank. Thus, asylum seekers are not subjectivised as (potential) customers but as temporary tenants of financial-humanitarianism. UNHCR's officers can have access in real time to asylum seekers' transactions, as well as to the exact location where the "beneficiaries" took cash from ATM machines or used the cards in shops. Hence, refugees' internal displacements might be tracked in real time but, in practice, the data collected are used to produce general surveys about refugees' purchases rather than to follow people's movements across the country.

However, most of the information contained in these reports is not the result of processes of datafication nor of the real-time tracking of refugee transactions but, rather, of the post-distribution monitoring system. In this sense, we can speak of "lateral data" that are not directly extracted from the cards and the real-time monitoring of transactions and that, rather, use the card as a sort of crystallised digital mediation to collect data. Indeed, the majority of the asylum seekers who hold the prepaid cards use these to take cash from the ATM machines and not to pay for purchases in shops. Therefore, even if refugees' financial transactions might be easily tracked, such digital traceability appears to be quite useless for producing knowledge about the mobile refugee population and their conducts and consumptions: refugees need to be interviewed and interpellated in order to understand how they have been using the cards, how often and where they are buying products. The circulation of the data extracted is actually characterised by a series of choke-points, local resistances and technical jams that are, however, not just "failures" of the system. Indeed, what appears as misfunctioning infrastructures of humanitarianism and of data circulation, does actually reveal the series of controversies among the actors involved; at the same time, repeated misfunctioning and chokepoints do underline the asylum system as such.

It is worth noticing that the actors involved in the project do admit the fundamental undecidability about how to use the data, even if they are able to collect a considerable amount. Hence, the objectivation of migrants through this specific kind of data extraction (use of digital technologies) does not generate stable virtual populations or neatly defined data-subjects. Overall, the use of digital technologies and data-extraction activities in the field of migration governmentality turns out to be partial, clumsy and non-working. Such a partial rudimentary and dysfunctional character is what makes migration an interesting lens for critically analysing digital technologies and investigating modes of governing through disjoint knowledge and disorientation – migrants being disoriented in front of the constantly changing rules and criteria. What emerges from the ways in which asylum seekers as card beneficiaries are interpellated, depicted and treated is that they are conceived neither as threats and risky subjects nor as mere victims and subjects to protect.

First, the use of digital and financial technologies contribute to foster the image of asylum seekers as *para-citizens* and *para-consumers* – that is, as subjects who are pushed would act *as if* they were citizens or consumers, regardless of the actual chances of becoming a refugee, and therefore eventually becoming in the future a citizen of the hosting country or an actual consumer. More precisely, temporariness characterises the programmes of digital and financial inclusion that (some) asylum seekers can benefit from. Indeed, if we take the Refugee Cash Assistance Programme in Greece, migrants have active debit cards only as long as they wait for the response about their asylum claim, which means while they are persons of UNHCR concern. After being temporarily included in the circuits of financial-humanitarianism and after getting the final response on their asylum claim, the asylum seekers are either illegalised as irregular migrants – if they are denied the international protection – or they obtain refugee status.[10] Furthermore, it is important to highlight that the migrants who are targeted by digital technologies in refugee camps, are in the meanwhile also subjected to a multiplicity of other techniques characterised by the intertwining of police and humanitarian logic (Pallister-Wilkins, 2015). More broadly, while migrants eventually receive the prepaid cards inside the hotspots, they are simultaneously subjected to protracted confinement on the islands and to the escalation of both visible and invisible violence in the camps.[11] An insight into the modes of subtle coercion and technological obstacles that migrants are affected by, shows that ultimately they are not portrayed neither in security nor in humanitarian terms. That is, they are not seen as pure threats and risky subjects nor as victims and subjects to protect. Rather, they are subjected to the injunction to be *temporarily autonomous humanitarian subjects* – and to act *as if* they were responsible consumers and citizens, although meanwhile constantly subjected to disciplinary restrictions and forced to comply with technological procedures. To some extent, asylum seekers are posited as sort of *citizen-proxies:* by that I refer to subjects who are supposed to act as if they were sort of best-by-date citizens, that is for a short time duration, and at the same time as subjects who need to comply with a multiplicity of restrictions and disciplinary rules. In fact, to what extent would debit cards enhance asylum seekers' autonomy? According to the World Food Programme (WFP) that co-founds the cash assistance for Syrians in Turkey, "it provides a sense of normality and dignity; it also restores a sense of being in control of their lives".[12] Thus, as this sentence stresses, what the cards are supposed to do is restore a sense of normality; that is, to make the beneficiaries *feel* that they are back to normal, and to make them act *as if* they were not in exceptional conditions.

This is a sort of *fictional normality*, since it does not necessarily correspond to an actual restoring of life beyond refugeesness and it is not future-oriented, as long as asylum seekers are not granted a form of protection, or the right to stay. Rather, they are seen as subjects who need to build their lives as potential citizens, while they wait to be denied refugee status and be deported, or while they hope to get international protection. Importantly, if we pander to asylum seekers as para-consumers, as debit card beneficiaries, we notice that, ultimately, they are not posited by NGOs and IGOs as productive subjects, as value producers; they are seen as sorts of connectors, transistors, between a multiplicity of economic interests (the UNHCR, hi-tech corporations and the bank). Such an idea of autonomy as a goal that asylum seekers are requested to reach – while they are within the channels for care and control of the asylum system – echoes the notion of self-reliance that has become widespread in the refugee policy vocabulary. Self-reliance ultimately refers to the individual's ability not to rely on external aids for economic and social needs; more precisely, the UNHCR defines it as 'the social and economic ability of an individual, a household or a community to meet essential needs in a sustainable manner".[13] Yet, I suggest that reading it through the lenses of self-reliance and neoliberalisation of humanitarianism tends to obfuscate two fundamental aspects: first, the high temporariness of migrant incorporation within the financial circuits and, second, the articulation between disciplinary control and dependency on the one hand, and compulsory technological procedures on the other.

The temporariness of programmes of digital and financial inclusion and the condition of protracted uncertainty of the asylum seekers go together. In particular, temporariness mainly depends on the length of the asylum application process – the more the migrants wait for a response about their asylum claim, the more they get their monthly financial support extended. Second, if we look at the temporality of the Cash Assistance Programme this is not future oriented: indeed, the prepaid cards that the asylum seekers receive are not connected to individual bank accounts but to a unique UNHCR digital wallet, and they stop being card-users when they receive their refugee status or, more frequently, when they get the denial of international protection. The protracted state of uncertainty that most of the migrants who land in Greece experience is bureaucratic, legal, economic, and more broadly concerns the level of life plans. During such an indefinite time of uncertainty, migrants, in particular on the islands, are often spatially confined. However this strandedness is not characterised by an empty waiting time: actually, migrants who get the prepaid cards and asylum seekers in general, are requested to comply with a series of deadlines, technical steps (e.g. to use Viber and Skype) and to learn how to navigate the system. Indeed, the techno-scientific assemblages which materially sustain the daily functioning of the asylum regime are characterised by a widespread bureaucratisation – what Roberto Beneduce and Simona Taliani define as a "bureaucratized social surgery" (2012: 243) made of "dispositives of the arbitrary" (p. 247) as political technologies for governing refugees.

Therefore, mechanisms of hit without interpellation are articulated with *lateral data extraction*, which requires the migrants to speak. This leads us to enquire about the forms of value produced in the field of migration governmentality. In particular, it requires supplementing research on the migration industry – which focuses on the economic profit made by states and private actors in migrant detention and border security sectors – with a study of modes of value extraction that centres on migrants' mobility and conducts. This entails, as Ruben Andersson argued, considering "forms of profiting and predating on people on the move" which rely on "the extraction – and generation – of value from human beings' vitality in the broadest sense" (2018: 414). It is in this specific sense that I propose to use the term *biopolitical value* to refer to the ways in which migrants' lives and mobility are the object of capitalisation and become a source of value on a twofold level: as individual conducts and as refugee populations. These modes of value extraction, which capitalise on refugees' mobility and conduct, supplement forms of value produced through direct exploitation of the migrant labour force or through the migrant detention industry.

THE ANTINOMIES OF FREEDOM AND AUTONOMY

Migrants who claim asylum are seen as subjects who should be available in giving away their freedom in exchange for protection. While such an account certainly clashes with the definition of the refugee enshrined in the Geneva Convention, asylum seekers are increasingly seen as the counterpart of the subject with rights. In this regard, some scholars have critically pointed to the fact that the refugee is coalesced into the figure of the victim (Ticktin, 2017). The victimisation of refugees should be situated as part of this antinomy between protection and freedom that affects those who claim asylum. However, the paradoxical opposition between freedom and protection that the state's narrative on asylum strengthens does not concern only those who are treated as victims but, rather, refugees as such. In a similar vein to discourses on protection, freedom of movement also disappears from the narrative on refugees' autonomy. In fact, autonomy has moved centre stage in UNHCR and NGO documents, as well as in development agencies' discourses.

Yet, autonomy is strikingly assumed as disjoined from freedom, as it is eminently conceived in economic terms, which corresponds to the capacity of managing oneself, or better as the possibility to choose the products to buy. In particular, it is in the field of refugee governmentality that autonomy has become a catchword mobilised by states and non-state actors to designate the new frontier of humanitarianism. If the intertwining of protection and autonomy could appear as an oxymoron, the redefinition of the former in light of the latter currently represents one of the tenets of refugee politics. In practice, according to the UNHCR discourse, refugees' autonomy is boosted through the implementation of financial tools and digital technologies. The partial autonomisation of asylum seekers from forms of humanitarian "care and control" (Pallister-Wilkins, 2015) ultimately consists of the possibility to select what to buy. In reality, the delivery of the debit cards fostered the dependence of asylum seekers on humanitarian actors and on the spatial disciplining that is imposed on them. In this regard, the subtle nexus between autonomy and vulnerability is noticeable in the odd terrain on which refugees' autonomy is itself predicated. Indeed, de facto those migrants who are deemed to be vulnerable by the Greek authorities and who remain inside the institutional channels of the asylum – e.g. living in refugee camps – are granted faster and smoother access than others to the cash assistance programme.

Thus, according to the humanitarian logics, what does it mean to strive for autonomy? What does refugee autonomy look like? In the end, autonomy is conceived as the possibility to behave *like a consumer* and *like a citizen* without in fact being either of these. Thus, autonomy appears as an apprenticeship to resilience that, paradoxically, refugees should forge by complying with disciplinary and spatial rules and technological obstacles that are protracted in time. For instance, asylum seekers who benefit from the cash assistance in Greece are subjected to spatial fixation, as they are not entitled to get the debit cards if they live in a squat, and they are excluded from the monthly financial assistance for misconduct.

Such a detour on the imbrication between financial tools and humanitarian logics enables highlighting the antinomies between freedom and autonomy that sustain the politics of asylum and that I have mentioned already concerning migrants' refusal to be fingerprinted. Indeed, despite the different steps at the level of migration governmentality procedures – the moment of the first identification on the one side, and the stage of the asylum procedure on the other – what these two snapshots reveal is the disjoining of freedom from the politics of asylum. The antinomies between autonomy and freedom have been clearly stated by Alexander Betts and Paul Collier who, in their book *Refuge*, have argued that states should build "safe havens" and not allow refugees to have freedom of movement: "there is nothing inherent to being a refugee that necessitates unrestricted global mobility or the ability to choose a destination country. The salient feature of being a refugee is the need of protection, not the need to migrate" (Betts and Collier, 2017). Through their project "Refugia", Robin Cohen and Nicholas Van Hear have pushed further the disjoining of autonomy from freedom: what they imagine is the establishment of an archipelago of cross-national entities, "a set of connections (*mise en relation*) between different sites developed through initiatives mainly taken by refugees and displaced people themselves, with some support from sympathizers" (Cohen and Van Hear, 2018: 498). These utopian spaces would be "self-governing and eventually self-supporting. The upshot is that refugees are no longer primarily the responsibility of the nation-state that 'hosts' them" (p. 498); they would not be dependent on humanitarian or state aid, but rather they would be in charge of their own self-maintenance. Thus, in these special interstitial zones refugees' autonomy would be not actualised through freedom of movement but, rather, through spatial confinement.

Therefore, autonomy is conceived by states and non-state actors paradoxically as disjoined from freedom. In the end, the antinomy between freedom and autonomy is part of the apparent opposition between freedom and security that is at the core of liberal discourses. In fact, as Carolina Moulin contends, in the field of refugee humanitarianism "security is thus equated with economic autonomy and political dependency" (Moulin, 2012: 59). This is certainly a significant tenet of the logic and functioning of the asylum regime. However, I suggest a more nuanced account of the intertwining of freedom and security. For instance, if we follow Foucault, this oppositional conceptualisation of the freedom–security nexus fails to account for the mutual support between the technologies (and ideologies) of freedom and the enactment of dispositives of security (Foucault, 2007). To be more precise, for Foucault freedom – of circulation of good and people – is the condition for the deployment of security mechanisms: no security, no technology of power, can be actualised without a certain infrastructure of enforced mobility. Moreover, the security–freedom nexus is not adequate enough to grasp the degrees of non-choice that asylum seekers are confronted with.

The non-negotiable exchange that asylum seekers are faced with ultimately does concern security. In fact, in the present European context, for a migrant getting a certain form of protection (refugee status, subsidiary protection, humanitarian protection) is de facto the condition and one of the few ways for remaining in the territory. That is, more than corresponding to being safe or being protected, being a refugee means having the (temporary) right to remain. If on the one hand even refugees are criminalised and unwanted in many places, on the other the racialised distinction between economic migrants and refugees makes the former less targeted than the former.

Autonomy is framed in relation to modes of spatial fixation or spatial restrictions that people seeking asylum should accept in exchange for protection: refugees are posited to become autonomous according to the terms established by the UNHCR. In this way, the hierarchies of lives, between saviours and saved subjects, and the unequal access to mobility that have been historically enforced by humanitarianism are not questioned at all (Salvatici, 2015). The financialisation of refugee humanitarianism and discourses around refugee autonomy represents a case in point for highlighting the extent to which freedom is not contemplated both in progressive and in liberal narratives on migrants in search of asylum.

The above case studies lead us to interrogate the limits of critique and to think what critical approach and critical knowledge production of migration might be articulated. The conundrums of critique emerge quite blatantly in relation to the financial and digital tools implemented in refugee humanitarianism that I engaged with by focusing on Greece. With the widespread use of digital tools for supporting and controlling asylum seekers, a critique that focuses on the pitfalls and failures of those technologies might end up in a reformist or normative approach. More broadly, if critique is conceived in terms of good/bad or from the standpoint of the effects of securitisation and control that these technologies eventually generate, we end up in a theoretical and political impasse. Instead, by paying attention to how migrants craft their claims and the kinds of struggles they engage in, we can grasp the forms of precarity and the modes of subjection that are connected to the constellation of technologies in refugee governmentality. For the purpose of a critical and non-normative analysis about the technologisation of humanitarianism, a comparative approach – between different migration contexts – would fall short. Indeed, while on the one hand through compulsory technological mediations (e.g. Viber and Skype in Greece) migrants are obstructed in accessing the asylum system or might be more controlled and tracked, on the other some of these digital technologies are helpful for the migrants – as is the case with the Cash Assistance Programme.

Yet, this is not to suggest that migrants consider the debit card system an adequate response nor that they accept its mis-functioning. On the contrary, for months the Refugee Cash Assistance Programme became a catalyst for migrant struggles. The difficulties in understanding how it works triggered a series of protests. In particular, one of these became a centripetal drive for other refugee claims and struggles in Athens.

8 August 2018: after meeting in a public garden in Athens to decide how to organise their protest against their protracted wait for getting the debit cards, about 120 asylum seekers decided to occupy the building used on a monthly basis by the UNHCR to deliver and top up the cards. The occupiers were women, children and men who had been waiting for months for the financial support they were entitled to. Their claim was simple and radical at the same time: "debit cards for all refugees". In fact, through their struggle and using such a claim they pointed on the one hand to the unjust exclusion of many asylum seekers, who matched the UNHCR's criteria to get the cards, from the cash assistance; on the other, they highlighted that all refugees, irrespective of their papers and of their

housing status, must have access to this financial support. The cards were not considered a solution per se but, rather, were seen as the minimal but important support they could get, while raising at the same time the condition of legal and economic destitution they were experiencing by being blocked in Greece.

Importantly, the occupation for the debit cards functioned as a catalyst for other related claims. First, in connection with the debit cards, refugees raised the point that many of them were not given accommodation and were forced to live in a squat. Second, they also seized the struggle for debit cards as an opportunity to carry on a protest against the technological barriers of the Greek asylum procedure. That is, they demanded the abolition of the Skype call system, which obliges migrants to firstly book their appointment for lodging the asylum claim via Skype. The occupation of the building went on for about a month and a half, when all the refugees received their cards. What is relevant about this struggle for the purpose of this chapter is that the migrants were not protesting against the risk of being tracked and controlled. Nor were they claiming that the debit card system was useless or bad. Instead, they highlighted the exclusion of many from the Programme, the repeated delays and the disciplinary rules and spatial fixations linked to it. In this way, they foregrounded the effects of subjection on their lives. Hence, if we pay attention to the claims and struggles of those people who are affected by techniques of humanitarian control and support, we can rethink critique out of a normative approach (between bad and good systems to improve) as well as beyond a security script (are the cards safe for refugees, or are they tracked?).

Actually, analytics of security/privacy and discrimination/sorting, if mobilised in an exclusive way, do have some limits, I contend, in capturing the operations of subjection and value extraction that are at stake in refugee humanitarianism. More broadly, I suggest that the focus of a critical analysis should not be technologies per se, nor the way in which these are used for controlling refugees (asking is it better or worse for them to be governed through digital tools?); instead, the partial and specific technologisation of migration governmentality might be situated in a wider account of the temporariness and conditionality that characterise migrants' access to financial support and digital technologies. The production of internal hierarchies based on nationality, and the restrictions in accessing the Cash Assistance Programme, are mechanisms that we find at stake in the asylum process as such; it is rather constitutive of the asylum system as such, which is historically predicated upon the multiplication of internal differences and changing mechanisms of exclusion. Indeed, from this point of view, digital and financial technologies rather reinforce those divisions and hierarchies that the asylum regime is grounded on. Instead, through this constellation of compulsory technological steps and procedures, asylum seekers are obstructed in laying the asylum claim and in getting access to the support that they are entitled to. This is what I call here the digital disruptions of asylum infrastructures.

Modes of subjection are not exercised only through direct coercion and control. Asylum seekers are increasingly incorporated and forced to cooperate in their own governmentality and required to become "autonomous" and "self-reliant". In fact, this striving for autonomy has been appropriated and twisted into a technology for governing migrants and refugees: the injunction for the migrants to be autonomous is de facto translated into the temporary use of financial tools, such as debit cards, and not fully relying on humanitarian assistance; that is, on becoming self-reliant. Related to that, refugees are increasingly requested to volunteer in projects for providing information and support to other refugees, which also involve monitoring their own peers, establishing in this a sort of peer-to-peer subjection. This latter consists of a horizontal system of mutual control that at the same time entails refugees' active participation. Importantly, peer-to-peer subjection is often predicated upon unpaid labour; that is, upon refugees volunteering to support and inform other refugees. Importantly, peer-to-peer subjection is often predicated upon unpaid labour; that is, upon refugees volunteering to support and inform other refugees. Simultaneously, far from grounding on equality, these mechanisms of peer-to-peer subjection recursively reinforce racialised hierarchies among the refugees themselves – e.g. producing a division between the "good" refugees involved in social work and who bring their contribution to the hosting society, and the wandering migrants.

Simultaneously, asylum seekers are disciplined through what might be called "participatory self-confinement" or "detention from below", meaning by that the cooptation of migrants in the the very mechanisms of governmentality, encouraging them to declare their needs, to participate in events and workshops concerning the improvement of hosting conditions, and to use digital apps in which they can share their journey experience. That is, the more and more central humanitarian discourse about giving migrants a voice and the possibility to express their needs, instead of imposing a top-down approach might obfuscate the asymmetric relationships and the conditions of forced confinement that migrants experience as a result of restrictive policies and laws. As a group of migrants stranded in the hotspot of Lesvos told me, "if someone asks me what can improve our situation, we respond 'give us freedom and let us move away'. We do not need tents, clothes or phones; we need these only because we are blocked here".

The coercive and active incorporation of the governed into the modes of control in the name of "let's help us to govern better" is ultimately not peculiar to the field of migration (Chamayou, 2018). Hence, together with the production of cramped space and the choking and obstruction of migrants' movements, there are also these apparently softer and more indirect mechanisms of subjection, which are predicated upon migrants' active participation and discourses on enhancing autonomy. It follows that notions such as autonomy, which have usually been mobilised in critical migration literature for describing collective migrants' resistances and subjectivities, constitute today a terrain of struggle that requires work on conceptual redefinition and political reappropriation.

"THIS IS NOT A MIGRANT": MAPPING SOFTWARES AND DIGITAL TRACES OF PASSAGES

In the control room of the Italian Navy at the headquarters in Rome about 40 Navy officers sit in front of computers attentively looking at the radar signals coming from the Navy vessels deployed in the central Mediterranean, both in Italian waters and in international waters. As one of them told me, "We can spot a migrant boat in distress with the radars that are situated on our patrolling vessels, or eventually with the coastal radar network. Other times we rely on migrants' phone calls." Indeed, if on the boat someone has a satellite phone, migrants are able to call also from international waters, and their exact location can be immediately found. "Indeed", the Navy officer pointed out "more and more migrants equip themselves with satellite phones for making SOS calls even when they are far away from the coast."

However, spotting a migrant vessel is not a smooth process: despite the Mediterranean being a highly monitored sea, many external factors might intervene to obfuscate the visibility of "technological eyes", such as the weather conditions or migrants' unregistered vessels. The computer screens in the control room display a multiplicity of green and yellow dots that need to be scrutinised by the Navy officers, to find out if a few of them correspond to an unauthorised migrant vessel. Due to the copious presence of commercial, military and civil vessels the Navy officers need to select what they want to spot on the real-time map of the radar signals in the Mediterranean. Indeed, without selection, the map becomes illegible: thus, the production of visibility through technologies – detecting vessels through radars – turns out to be fundamentally unintelligible. "The sight of migration" (Tazzioli and Walters, 2016) is constitutively ambivalent: being spotted at sea is the result of states spying on migrants and, at the same time, of migrants who try to become visible in order to be rescued. Therefore, visibility is not unidirectional, politically speaking: visibility is enacted by state authorities for spying on and controlling unauthorised migrants' movements; but becoming visible is also a weapon that migrants mobilise for calling the attention of the Coastguard and the Navy, against the left to die attitude that states often adopt. The constant reversibility of visibility and invisibility traces the coordinates of a dynamic battlefield between migrants, state authorities, NGOs deployed at sea and smugglers.

How are migrants visualised and represented on the screen? How are they objectified and seen? Migrants as such fade out from the scene: neither individual migrants nor migrants as indistinct multiplicities on the boat are represented. Rather, migrants' presence is visualised through the medium of the boat. In fact, it is the boat as such that is translated into an abstract image – the dot visualised on the digital map. Then, from the radar images, the Navy officers try to deduce the approximate number of migrants on board, in order to calibrate the rescue operation accordingly. No personal features of the migrants are displayed (e.g. gender or nationality). Therefore, while in the media migrants at sea are represented as shipwrecked bodies to rescue, the technical visibility generated by radars and satellites gives rise to a quite different image, where migrants are replaced with their means of transport. Ultimately, discerning individual migrants is not relevant to the purpose of rescuing or intercepting them: what matters is their exact location and an estimation of the size of the vessel and of migrant numbers. It follows that by being governed at a distance migrants are not objectified through modes of individualisation, and not even as part of groups. Rather, they are detected and visualised by the Navy as a "case", as an alert event. That is, migrants are not identified at this stage, they are instead incorporated into a governable case. In this respect, Dijstelbloem and colleagues speak of "operational vision" to account for the production of visibility through systems of control in the Mediterranean (2017: 227). Such an expression sheds light on the regime of visibility which underpins migration controls at a distance: visibility is less about seeing and identifying than about spotting and locating in order to intervene. By "regime of visibility" I mean the material and epistemic conditions that make some phenomena visible or invisible; the term "regime" highlights that both visibility and invisibility are in fact proactively generated and are not the outcome of gestures of obscuration or unveiling.

Migrant vessels are monitored simultaneously also by satellites that are managed at a European level by the EU Satellite Centre. At the same time, the European Maritime Safety Agency (EMSA) monitors the vessel traffic in the Mediterranean and, therefore, even when a vessel is spotted by national authorities, European actors are involved as well. How is this amount of data collected and visualised in (quasi)-real time stored and shared with other actors? The Navy has its own database where all information is stored. The most important data-sending and data-sharing activity on a European level is through the European External Border Surveillance System (EUROSUR) software, which I explain later in this section. In addition, since 2007, the Italian Navy has shared relevant data with the navies of other countries through the Virtual-Regional Maritime Traffic Centre (V-RMTC).[14] As part of that, a regional sub-group, named 5+5 Network, which includes the navies of eight Mediterranean countries (Algeria, France, Italy, Malta, Mauritania, Portugal, Spain and Tunisia), share information, via the V-RMTC Fusion Centre located at the Italian Navy Headquarters in Rome.[15] Importantly, this database contains information about ships' departures, movements and arrivals, and it has been devised not to monitor migrant vessels but commercial vessels. No data about the persons on board should be included. However, in the case of suspect or unauthorised vessels, the Navy can decide to send data that concern migrant boats as well. Yet, the data exchange in V-RTMC takes place on a voluntary basis only and in fact state actors often refuse to send the information gathered. On a national level, the data collected by the Navy are partially shared with the Coastguard, but also in this case both actors have the right to keep some information under a restricted access policy. Hence, the logistics of data circulation is far from being smooth and is actually underpinned by substantial disruptions, non-communication and delays. Yet, despite the proliferation of monitoring and mapping systems, the image of a fully and constantly watched sea with no shadow zones is deceptive in the face of high "patchy visibility" (Heller and Pezzani, 2014; Tazzioli, 2015) which is at play in the Mediterranean. Zones of opacity, undetected passages, ghost shipwrecks, disrupted data circulation and irregular monitoring all characterise the regime of visibility in the Mediterranean. Thus, the regime of visibility in the Mediterranean is also largely constituted by what is lacking – in the forms of the unseen, as well as of the active production of obfuscation and invisibility. Indeed, while in some cases the unseen is the outcome of technical glitches, in many others it is the product of a left to die state's (non-)intervention or of a dispute about whose responsibility it is to rescue the migrants.

Information about unauthorised entries in territorial waters, incidents and border crossing crimes gathered by the Navy should also be transmitted to the EUROSUR database. EUROSUR was launched by the EU in December 2013: conceived as "the system of the systems",[16] it has been presented as a tool for building a common pre-frontier intelligence picture of what happens at the external borders of Europe and as a mapping database elaborating information logged in different national and European monitoring devices and databases. Yet, the communication among the different actors involved in EUROSUR, and in particular between EUROSUR's national points and the single actors (the Coastguard, the Navy), is far from being smooth. In fact particular military actors, such as the Navy, are at times reluctant to share the information they have collected. What data are stored in EUROSUR and how is migration represented on the map? First of all, what the EUROSUR map visualises is neither migration movements – in the traditional migration mapping format of arrows oriented towards Europe – nor migrants. Rather, what appears on the EUROSUR screen is a map of coloured dots, each of them corresponding to a "migratory event", that is say to an irregular border crossing or a border-crossing crime. Therefore, the EUROSUR map does not "represent" migration, instead it structures the form and meaning of the event. In principle any migrant vessel that is detected at sea and is irregularly entering an EU member state is translated into an "event" and becomes of concern to EUROSUR (Tazzioli, 2018).Nevertheless, more than the dots signifying the single events, what characterises EUROSUR's map are the national coloured borders, whose colours depend on the "level of impact" factor associated with any frontier. It is not the number of migration events that have occurred at a certain border that determines if that frontier will be green (low risk), yellow (medium) or red (high risk) but their "impact". How is that impact measured? Even in this case the notion of operative vision is useful for grasping the governmental-oriented gaze: indeed, the impact is assessed on the basis of the level of governability of the event in question. However, if we interrogate what operability means in this case, we can notice a quite relevant difference in the way in which this is at stake in the Navy operations. In fact, while the radar and satellite images collected by the Navy are used (also) for intervening in real time to rescue or intercept migrants at sea, the operative dimension of EUROSUR is rather more future-oriented. Indeed, the data gathered are visualised on the map usually with a delay of a few hours, and are used for producing risk analyses about migration.

In order to fully grasp the functioning of EUROSUR the very register of the sight, as well as the action of seeing, need to be downplayed. In fact, EUROSUR's work does not consist of seeing the migrants but elaborating data collected by different actors in order to make the migration phenomenon governable. Indeed, as Gloria Gonzales Fuster, Rocco Bellanova and Rapheal Gellert aptly noticed, the association between control and surveillance with visibility has almost saturated the literature: "in/visibility implicitly affects the way in which scholars apprehend surveillance technologies and practices", while there is a need, they argue, to move beyond such a dyad (Fuster et al., 2015: 513). EUROSUR does not stare at, it does not exercise a gaze; it processes data about migrant detection that give rise to a map. Thus, the well-known motto "the map is not the territory" encapsulates well, I suggest, the functioning of EUROSUR: indeed, instead of providing snapshots of what is going on at the external frontiers of Europe, it codifies and translates migrants' presence into manageable events of concern. In this sense, the expression "technological eyes" is a bit misleading for describing modes of governing migrants at a distance, as long as the action of watching is secondary with respect to the laborious work of crafting maps of risk.

To sum up, the governing of migration at a distance through techniques of detection to some extent tends to dissolve migrant multiplicities and singularities: migrants' presence and passages are in fact translated into digitalised images that correspond to the boat. It follows that the boat per se is more than a means of transport as it corresponds to the materialisation of the "migratory event" – x number of migrants are detected at sea as long as they are all on board the same vessel. Relatedly, migrant multiplicities and singularities are recomposed within a field of human and non-human components, like the boat itself that moves centre stage in states targeting the migrants. In fact, as I illustrated above, what defines a migratory event is not the migrants' presence as such, nor the number of migrants. In fact, in order to assess the relevance of the event, the migrants' presence and number are situated within a configuration of power relations that include the capacity to manage the migrants in question, the predictability of the phenomenon and the amount of resources to deploy.

In the face of digital technologies and mapping softwares to detect migrants and at the same time to craft migratory events of concern, should we conclude, then, that migrants' struggles and subjective drives are erased? Actually digital technologies do not necessarily close up political spaces nor manage to fully monitor migrant movements. Quite the contrary, the implementation of digital technologies in the field of migration governmentality is seen here as part of states' capture strategies deployed for regaining control over unauthorised mobility (Mezzadra, 2011; Papadopoulos et al., 2008). Besides, if we look at a more local level how migrants engaged with their condition of being potentially monitored at any time, it is worth noticing that they have tactically appropriated the condition of being detected and visible. While most of the migrants in the past used to cross on the sly, trying to remain invisible to the state authorities, over the last few years, and in particular with the launch of the military-humanitarian operation Mare Nostrum, smugglers equip migrant vessels with satellite phones for making SOS calls. Nevertheless, the tactical use of the condition of being watched, and of technologies conceived for controlling and intercepting migrants, should not lead us to naively conclude that technology as such can be just twisted against the state. Instead, there is a need for complicating such a picture about symmetric uses of technologies – for the purpose of state control and for claiming to be rescued by the state – that ultimately overshadows questions about power and domination. In particular, the (geo)political Mediterranean context in which migrants act, using the technologies, needs to be analysed closely: first, a left to die politics has been increasingly enacted by the states, with a decrease in the number of rescue vessels deployed and the criminalisation of independent search and rescue organisations; second, the EU is currently enforcing a politics of migration containment that obstructs migrant departures; third, as far as migrants are concerned, unlike years ago, today the majority wants to claim asylum, and therefore they have no interest in arriving in Europe on the sly.

CONCLUSION

This chapter has taken into account the modes of objectivation that are at stake in governing migrants through the use of digital technologies, considering both techniques for controlling at a distance and the digital and financial tools used in the day-to-day relationship between migrants and NGOs. In the cases considered here, the crafting of migrants as objects of knowledge is mediated by processes of datafication and data circulation that open up contested spaces of governmentality. While there are technologies for detecting and then visualising migrants at a distance, like the radars or EUROSUR, the subjective component of the migrants is taken out of the picture and the very dimensions of individuality and multiplicity are superseded by the production of "migratory events". However, migrants' strategic appropriation and twisting of their condition of being detectable reveals well that reversibility of visibility: being visible is not only about being controlled but is also a possibility for the migrants to be rescued. The implementation of digital technologies in the daily life of asylum seekers in refugee camps is a quite different matter: the chapter has highlighted the effects of subjectivation and subjection that shape migrants as subjects who need to be temporarily autonomous without, however, being free to move.

NOTES

1. https://ec.europa.eu/home-affairs/what-we-do/policies/asylum/identification-of-applicants_en
2. Until 2013, EURODAC used to store the fingerprints only.
3. www.camera.it/_dati/leg17/lavori/documentiparlamentari/indiceetesti/022bis/008/intero.htm
4. www.unhcr.org/registration.html
5. www.unhcr.org/blogs/empowering-refugees-internally-displaced-persons-digital-identity/
6. www.unhcr.org/news/press/2017/10/59ea0f984/new-world-bank-unhcr-joint-data-centre-improve-global-statistics-forced.html
7. www.unhcr.org/blogs/wp-content/uploads/sites/48/2018/03/2018-02-Digital-Identity_02.pdf
8. The making of subjectivities from above is always confronted with "the vector of the autonomous behaviour of the person so labelled, which presses from below, creating a reality every expert must face" (Hacking, 2002: 111).
9. The Refugee Cash Assistance Programme is supported by the European Commission's Emergency Support to Integration and Accommodation (ESTIA) through the European Civil Protection Mechanism (ECHO).
10. In this second case, they become subjects with rights in Greece, but de facto they will struggle to build their lives in Greece – mainly due to the economic crisis.
11. www.doctorswithoutborders.ca/article/msf-pulse-suicide-attempts-and-self-harming-among-child-refugees-moria-greece
12. https://insight.wfp.org/eu-funded-cash-card-has-big-impact-on-syrian-refugees-in-turkey-8d51a83e8a13
13. www.unhcr.org/publications/operations/44bf40cc2/unhcr-handbook-self-reliance.html
14. www.marina.difesa.it/cosa-facciamo/cooperazione-internazionale/vrmtc/Pagine/default.aspx
15. www.marina.difesa.it/cosa-facciamo/cooperazione-internazionale/5piu5network/Pagine/Operationalagreement.aspx
16. "Examining the creation of a European Border Surveillance System", (MEMO/08/086). See also http://eur-lex.europa.eu/legal-content/IT/TXT/?uri=URISERV%3Al14579

4

"Keeping On the Move Without Letting Pass"

Dispersal and Mobility as Technology of Government

INTRODUCTION

Mobility has become a catchword that is used and studied across different disciplinary fields, from international relations to political theory, human geography and political sociology. Topics such as free European mobility, social mobility, urban mobility, mobile networks and mobile technology have moved centre stage in many analyses and in different academic debates, giving rise also to specific scholarships, such as mobility studies. In particular, the increasing mobility of social life as a result of global political processes has been widely tackled in the literature, de facto strengthening a progressive and teleological narrative that sees the present as characterised by an exponential increase in movements overall. However, social sciences are by far more reluctant in "appropriating" mobility as a method. By that, I refer to bringing in mobility as part of the analytics through which research objects are studied, approached and constructed. Indeed, taking mobility as a method, and not only as a research object, involves not just a questioning but also, more radically, a refusal of two implicit pillars of political thought: the methodological nationalism that tacitly underpins most of the analyses, and the sedentarist epistemology that presents mobility as a sort of surrogate of the citizen politics (Cresswell, 2010).

Positing mobility as a method for unsettling ways of thinking and framing problems and questions about borders, humanitarianism and govermentality enables us to "unhinge the epistemological and ontological foundations" (Huysmans and Nogueira, 2016: 301) of methodological state-centrism. In fact, this entails engaging in a theoretical and methodological stance that consists of politicising mobility while simultaneously mobilising politics. The latter refers to the need for putting politics on the move, undermining the citizen–state nexus that undergirds the ways of thinking politics. The former consists of refusing to take mobility as a merely descriptive term, and to consider it, instead, in light of the conditions and practices – in the plural, referring to the heterogeneous practices of mobility – that are highly shaped by specific power relations and situated within a certain field of struggle. Therefore, politicising mobility means also distinguishing it from movement and bringing to the fore the materiality of the struggles, the racialised policies and the mechanisms of exploitation that sustain and shape different practices of mobility, as well as the subjective side of it, that is the practices of mobility that women, men and children perform. Relatedly, politicising mobility also means avoiding empty and floating signifiers: thus, mobility cannot be taken as an ahistorical notion and should instead be analysed by retracing the historical and political genealogy of the different ways in which mobility has been regulated, enacted and problematised. However, what is the history to be told? Which genealogies do we want to retrace? There is not, in fact, something like a unique history of mobility to be reconstructed. A focus on migration enables shifting attention from "molar" histories about mobility towards minor genealogies of it.

This chapter focuses on the heterogeneous technologies of governing mobility through mobility; in so doing, it does not, however, repurpose binary oppositions such as between mobility and immobility or between control and freedom. Rather, through an analytical angle on mobility as a political technology of migration governmentality, this chapter aims to undo these binary oppositions, while, at the same time, engaging in what I call operations of disjoining, which consist of decoupling a taken-for-granted nexus such as freedom and mobility. Governing migrant mobility through mobility is far from resulting in a less violent borders for the migrants themselves, as it has tangible and dramatic consequences on their lives: being kept on the move and forced to undertake convoluted and diverted routes, migrants are worn out and their material and legal terrain, their spaces of life, are repeatedly undercut.

Taking mobility as a methodological starting point, and not simply as a research object, is not synonymous here with a romanticisation of mobility as such, nor does a focus on the practices and politics of mobility leave untouched the theoretical assumptions that orient the analytical gaze. That is to say it requires first of all a rethink of the categories and notions that populate political theory and political geography – the state, territory, borders, and so on. In particular, bringing mobility to the core and as the starting point of the analysis involves engaging with the edges and limits of what can be counted and mapped. As I will show, mobility conceived as a political technology for governing unruly mobility has historically been connected with measures of dispersal and ways of dividing populations. More broadly, mobility can be associated with a conceptual and semantic field that designates practices that are de facto hard to account for – such as dispersal, movement, displacement and rerouting. Not only are the focus and the categories of political theory and political geography predicated upon a sedentary epistemology; together with that, even the mechanisms of control and governing that are taken into account tend to be fundamentally static, territorialised and quite highly mappable. That is, when it comes to migration, modes of detention and confinement are put under scrutiny, while centrifugal spatial tactics enacted by states like dispersal and forced evictions are far less investigated. The same happens with migrant mobility, and with escapes and flights that take place on the sly, as long as mobility is taken as a lens and as an analytical starting point for rethinking key notions in political theory like territory and the state. As a final methodological point, it is worth noticing that dealing with mobility and taking it as an analytical lens means coming to grips with ephemeral spaces: in fact, the spaces of control and refuge that are the outcome of the clash between bordering mechanisms and migrants' struggles for movement are thoroughly precarious and subjected to an uneven temporality.

In this way, we might speak of an analytical sensibility that consists of undoing the boundaries between what is deemed political and what is dismissed as non-political subjects or actions. In fact, taking mobility seriously involves coming to grips with practices, spaces and subjects that are mobile, and therefore difficult to sediment or crystallise, as they are eminently fleeting. However, the fleeting and ephemeral spaces produced in the migration strugglefield are not political per se: taking mobility as a method for rethinking politics concerns the analytical sensibility through which we orient our attention towards certain subjects and phenomena and not others, which are instead immediately discredited as non-political or not sufficiently durable and stable to become political.

BIOPOLITICS OF/THROUGH MOBILITY

In *Security, Territory, Population*, Michel Foucault famously contended that since the eighteenth century the main governmental problem has been "a matter of organizing circulation, eliminating its dangerous elements, making a division between good and bad circulation, and maximizing the good circulation by diminishing the bad" (2007: 18). In that lecture series he links the emergence of biopower to dispositives of security that are apt at managing circulation. Literature on biopolitics has mainly focused on Foucault's famous formula "making live and letting die" (Foucault, 1998) and on the intertwining that exists between biopolitics, governmentality and population, as the functioning of biopolitical mechanisms in the eighteenth century should be analysed as part of a new governmental rationale – what he calls governmentality – that has "the population as its target, political economy as its major form of knowledge, and apparatuses of security as its essential technical instrument" (Foucault, 2007: 108). Surprisingly, far less attention has been paid by scholars to the constitutive nexus between biopolitics and circulation, apart from the quite famous quotation cited above, where Foucault speaks about the differentiation between bad and good circulation (although see Elden, 2007). One of the main theoretical arguments of this chapter is that in order to grasp how some subjects are racialised and governed as "migrants" we need to reconsider the nexus between biopolitics and mobility. It should be noticed, however, that to begin with Foucault himself did not expand on the circulation issue in his analysis on biopolitics and governmentality – instead centring his reflection on the population and on the shift from making die to making live. Also, it is worth noticing that in *Security, Territory, Population* Foucault speaks of "circulation" and not of "mobility". If we read the above cited passage, in which Foucault speaks about the "division between good and bad circulation" (Foucault, 2007: 18), in the broader context in which he takes into account circulation, we realise that this latter is assumed by him in quite hydraulic terms, conceiving of it mainly as a problem of infrastructures and logistics of circulation: "we can see that the problem was circulation, that is to say, for the town to be a perfect agent of circulation it had to have the form of a heart that ensures the circulation of blood" (Foucault, 2007: 17).

It is important to highlight this, in order not to conflate mobility with circulation: indeed, as this chapter illustrates, when it comes to the making of migration, there is a need for taking into account the hierarchical and racialised governing of mobility. In fact, circulation takes us in a straightforward way to the domain of economy and logistics (e.g. the circulation of goods and the supply chains economy). Relatedly, the term "circulation" recalls a quite smooth and to some extent enhanced movement of goods or first-class citizens. That said, the notion of circulation should not be erased from such an analysis on the politics of mobility. Indeed, circulation makes possible retaining a focus on the constitutive entanglements between migration and capitalism, pointing to the partial overlapping between migrant routes and the channels of economic exchanges, as well as to stress that migration itself is what states and non-state actors capitalise upon (see the smuggling economy, as well as the migration industry). However, the use of the term "circulation" in critical works on migration should not downplay the differences between mobility and circulation. "Mobility" is not just about making things or people circulate; it is also about the differential and racialised restrictions to the possibility to move that people experience, as a result of political, legal and economic mechanisms and it might involve conditions of being forced to move. Moreover, I suggest that the term "mobility", provided it is not taken as synonymous with movement, enables us to bring into the analysis the temporal dimension – which is formed also by protracted movements of immobility, is fundamentally uneven, and partially determined by the differential ways in which borders, laws and policies target people. Finally, the way in which I refer to mobility here is always in the sense of "practices" (practices of mobility) and not as an abstract descriptive category: thus, what can appear as a neutral term actually names a field of struggles, structured around conjectural power relations.

However, if we take into account the course *The Punitive Society* (1972–1973), Foucault has dealt with what in 1978 he left unaccounted for: that is, that "bad circulation" which dispositives of security, according to Foucault, would discard and marginalise. In fact, in *The Punitive Society* he draws attention to popular illegalism, that is conducts and practices of mobility that started to be criminalised in the seventeenth century: "illegalism takes the form of absenteeism, lateness, laziness, festivity, debauchery, nomadism, in short, everything that smacks of irregularity, of mobility in space" (Foucault, 2015a: 188). Thus, mobility is approached by Foucault not merely as movements in space but as those criminalised practices that were considered against the norms of (sedentary) societies – such as vagabondage – and that became the object of disciplinary controls. Although Foucault's first reference to biopolitics was in *Society Must be Defended*, we can speak of a sort of embryonic biopolitics *ante litteram* that is indirectly outlined by Foucault in the lecture series of 1973. This does not involve by any means backdating the moment of the emergence of biopolitical mechanisms. Rather, it is a question of shedding light on the nexus between the governing of/over life and the governing of mobility and its "bad elements" that is ultimately addressed by Foucault in *The Punitive Society*. Despite the absence of the object population and of the nation state as political referent, which Foucault puts at the core of *Security, Territory, Population*, what is salient in the 1973 lecture series is the historical articulation between unruly mobility, criminalised conduct and the dividing of potential collective subjects – not reducible to populations but that.

Thus, *The Punitive Society* enables our introducing a tangential approach to biopolitics that inscribes the question of life within an analysis of the criminalisation of marginal conducts and the "bad elements" of circulation. Such an insight into criminalised marginal mobilities equips us with the analytical tools for thinking about mobility not as mere movement but, rather, in terms of a struggle-field between subjective desires and enacted practices of freedom on the one hand, and disciplinary mechanisms on the other, which try to regain control over them. This is what distinguishes the perspective carried on in this chapter from the mobility studies literature that has put mobility at the core of the analyses (Adey, 2006; Cresswell, 2010; Sheller, 2017). While this latter stresses that mobilities are all different and that everything is on the move, although through a hierarchy of mobility and immobilities, my focus, via Foucault, rests instead on the practice of mobility insofar as, and precisely because these are at the core of mechanisms of governmentality today. This entails shifting the focus from the assumption that everything is on the move towards an analysis of the differential and racialised access to mobility, of the legal and material obstacles enacted by states, and, finally, of the tactics of "unruly" mobility played out by subjects to escape controls.

Why rethink biopolitics in light of mobility, as long as life (and the maximisation of life) has become the centre of power preoccupations? Ultimately, is not migration governmentality first and foremost a question of the "hold" over migrant lives? In order to grasp the specificity of the racialised power mechanisms that are at stake in the politics of migration, we need to undertake an in-depth analysis of how certain practices of mobility are hampered and posited as non-legitimate. More precisely, the near-exclusive focus in the scholarship on the Foucaultian formula "making live and letting die" to discuss the biopoliitcal mechanisms tends to narrow the analysis of the border regime to a question of life and death, by ultimately taking for granted the meaning of these terms. To put it more concretely, the current media and political debate in Europe around migrant death in the Mediterranean is centred around issues as to what extent and to what point European countries have the moral and legal obligation to rescue migrants.

The third point concerns the use of mobility as a political technology for governing unruly migration. If mobility is not only an object of government but also a mode for managing unruly migration – by keeping migrants on the move – life and mobility should be considered together as fundamental stakes in the politics of migration. Thus, biopolitical questions about how migrant lives are governed, by what power this "hold" is exercised over them, and what modes of making and letting die are at stake need to be supplemented with a reflection on how mobility is used as a disciplinary technique for managing migration and which hierarchies of lives are structured round it. Gesturing towards a biopolitics of/through mobility does not mean disregarding the politics of/over life, but instead grasping how these two modes of government play together for regaining control over unruly conducts and emergent collective subjects. It means scrutinising not only the modes of capture and government exercised over mobile bodies and populations – the biopolitics of mobility – but also the ways in which (forced) mobility is used to govern individuals and populations – biopolitics through mobility. Relatedly, this involves shifting the attention away from life as such, and the risk of ontologisation associated with the debate on bare life and productive life, towards the specific ways of governing people as long as they move and by making them move.

MOBILITY AS A POLITICAL TECHNOLOGY OF GOVERNMENT

Mobility is one of the words in the politics of migration lexicon that is characterised by a fundamental ambivalence: unruly mobility is "feared" and targeted by the states, and historically it should be seen as a tactics of flight that always exceeds border control. However, at the same time, mobility has been reappropriated by liberal discourse and "institutionalised" as one of the political values of the EU. The genealogy of the ways in which human mobility has been differentially subjected to control, restrictions and identification over time has been retraced by a rather huge scholarship (see, among others, Kotef, 2015; McKeown, 2008). Scholars have extensively analysed the mechanisms of border control and enforcement enacted to discipline migration movements, as well as the way in which migration has been securitised (Bigo, 2002; Geiger and Pecoud, 2013; Huysmans, 2006; Martin, 2010; Squire, 2010). Nevertheless, while mobility as an object of government and control has been widely studied, mobility as a political technology for governing unruly migration has received less attention by far and remains partially under-theorised. Indeed, mobility is also used as a technology for disciplining and regaining control over migrants, according to a wide range of modes of enforced movement. This includes deportations, removals and internal transfers from one detention centre to another, as well as the more indirect ways by which migrants are ultimately kept on the move and forced to undertake convoluted geographies, due to repeated police interventions or the restrictions and obstacles imposed by the Dublin Regulation.

Therefore, dealing with the politics of mobility involves more than considering mobility as a research object or as an object of government; it entails exploring on the one hand how mobility is differentially regulated, enforced and disciplined – and, thus, how some mobilities are racialised and labelled as "migration" – and on the other, it addresses the modes and the contexts when mobility is used as a political technology for governing unruly movements. On a methodological level, engaging in a politics of mobility entails shifting attention from a statist gaze on politics towards a mobility-centred approach. By that, I refer to an analytical perspective that refuses the methodological nationalism that underpins most of migration research and, more broadly, the statist gaze on politics that is ultimately at stake both in IR and in political theory literature. What does it mean to put mobility at the core of the analysis and, at the same time, to take it as the lens through which to look at the mutations of citizenship and of the state? How can we use mobility as an analytical angle in order not to operate "under the spectres of the state" (Basaran and Guild, 2016: 273)? In fact the risks associated with a mobility-centred analysis consist of overlooking both the racialised and hierarchical modes by which heterogeneous forms of mobility are governed, and, more broadly, the power relations and the field of struggles that shape the politics of mobility. This latter is formed not only by the series of policies, laws and technologies through which practices of mobility are differentially controlled and channelled, but also by the effects of subjectivation and subjection that these generate, as well as by the struggles over and refusals against the restrictions on free mobility.

In the field of carceral geography, the use of mobility as a strategy of government is tackled by bringing in the reality of forced movements; that is to say, these scholars highlight that (some) migrations are regulated through *forced* mobility. This literature mainly focuses on forced transfers of migrants between detention centres (Conlon et al., 2013; Hiemstra, 2013; Loyd and Mountz, 2014;

Martin and Mitchelson, 2009). In particular, Nick Gill mobilises the notion of "governmental mobility" to illustrate the "governmental effect of the mobility of the asylum seekers" (Gill, 2009a: 187; see also Gill, 2009b), referring to the forced transfers migrants are subjected to in the UK, when they are moved from one detention estate to another, with the result of preventing the consolidation of networks of support around them. Aila Spathopoulou has remarkably analysed how the ferry has been used in Greece as a sort of "mobile hotspot" to transfer migrants from the Greek islands to the mainland, and from one island to another (Spathopoulou, 2016). Yet, the migrants' erratic geographies that I discuss in this chapter are induced and forced by state authorities not only through official transfers from one detention centre to another, but also in a more indirect and informal way.

The governing of migration through mobility has been enacted through the entanglement of police and humanitarian interventions. Although the chapter deals with the present, it is important to engage in a genealogical perspective, retracing how some techniques of governmentality have been deployed and travelled over time for governing specific populations. That is, similar techniques of government have been used for policing marginal populations or "dangerous" collective subjects in the past. In so doing, on a methodological level we need to caution against the risk of stripping technologies of government out of the historical and political contexts in which these have been used. On this point it is in fact worth highlighting that a genealogical gaze aims at tracing similarities and differences, and at understanding the present, in its irreducible specificity, by looking at the historical conditions for the emergence of a certain "problem" or "fact" and, at the same time, foregrounding the conjectural moments and the power relations that are at stake in the present. The genealogical approach starts from "dispersal and from the hazard of the origin" (Revel, 2002: 37) whiteout but falls into empiricism; therefore it appears particularly suited for studying partially unmappable phenomena, like dispersal measures, as its main focus.

A COLONIAL GENEALOGY OF DISPERSAL

Dispersing migrants across the territory is one of the spatial strategies implemented for governing migrant mobility through mobility. Spatial dispersal is sometimes enacted by national authorities to distribute and channel asylum seekers across the country, to avoid big concentrations in the main urban centres. Such a spatial strategy for governing refugees by invisibilising their presence on the territory, relegating them to remote areas far from big cities, has been adopted by many European countries, which has inflected dispersal in different ways. For instance, since 2011 Italy has implemented a system of spread hosting which consists of prioritising the multiplication of small hosting centres, located in peripheral areas, to which asylum seekers are sent (Marchetti, 2014; Novak,

2019). In order to tackle the "Calais crisis", since 2015 France has started to manage asylum seekers' presence according to a logic of spatial dispersal that recalls Italy's system of spread hosting. In the UK a deliberate strategy for refugee dispersal has been adopted since the late nineties, which generates effects of destitution for asylum seekers (Darling, 2016a). As Jonathan Darling explains, the production of "enforced immobility of asylum seekers through dispersal" (Darling, 2016b: 236) is a central asset of the UK refugee governmentality and entails allocating asylum seekers to different cities across the country. In this sense, we can speak of state measures of (forced) internal relocation put into place in order to avoid big concentrations of asylum seekers in the main cities. Moreover, the UK dispersal policy essentially targets asylum seekers and thus consists of transferring and scattering across the country people who are inside the official and "legal" channels of the asylum system.

A spatial strategy that works by distributing and scattering asylum seekers' presence across the territory through institutional channels is not the only way in which dispersal is enacted. In fact, dispersal is also put into place in more indirect and unofficial ways that, however, do not have less of an impact on migrant lives. Dispersal can be, for instance, the outcome of police tactics aimed at demolishing migrants' spaces of life and informal encampments. Dispersal can also be the spatial outcome of administrative and police measures for emptying "critical" border zones. Strategies of migrant dispersal, taken in their heterogeneity, are widely used as one of the main modes, I contend, through which states try to regain control over migrants' unruly movements; and yet, dispersal remains quite unexplored in migration scholarship, in particular the more indirect strategies of dispersal that take place outside the institutional channels of the asylum. This is also due to the difficulty of mapping and coming to grips with dispersal, which is by definition quite elusive. In fact, to put it better, the elusiveness of dispersal as a phenomenon to study depends on the very effects that it triggers – namely, the invisibilisation and scattering of migrants' presence. Unlike other more spectacular forms of border enforcement, dispersal is played out at the thresholds of visibility and works precisely as long as it remains opaque and not fully accountable. Relatedly, at the level of public visibility, dispersal encapsulates a partial retreat from the staging of the border spectacle, dissuading and discouraging us to turn our gaze upon it.

Marc Bernardot has highlighted the police tactics for controlling migrants, and the dispersal measures that have been put in place in Calais since 2008 for "insecuritising, see hampering collective formations" – exercising in this way what he calls a specific "technique of hold" over migrants (Bernardot, 2009: 60). It is important to stress the partial continuity in the modes of governing "unauthorised" migrants' presence and of dividing migrants' temporary groups in critical border zones. In line with the methodological approach that I illustrated above – tracing a genealogy of political technologies – I avoid flattening the analysis onto the present, by reading instead the current widespread tactics of scattering migrants across spaces in light of a colonial genealogy of dispersal as a political technology for governing unruly mobility and populations. In fact, the politics of migrant dispersal is not a recent political technology: it can be traced back to urban plans and police measures for governing unruly colonised and formerly colonised populations (LeCour Grandmaison, 2005) and slaves. In the French colonies, gatherings of groups of slaves were forbidden by the Article 16 of the *Code Noir* (Black Code) (Dorlin, 2017).

Dispersal as a spatial strategy for the governmentality of former colonised populations had then been used in France for managing the presence of the Algerians in Paris: Françoise de Barros convincingly shows that in the fifties and sixties dispersal had been one of the main spatial measures for governing Algerians in French cities, in order to avoid concentrating them in the same neighbourhoods, as this could have provoked cohesion and political alliances against French authorities (De Barros, 2005; see also Blanchard, 2011). Scholars have explored, from a postcolonial perspective, modes of spatial segregation that have been adopted in European cities for confining people from ex-colonies. In particular, dispersal has historically been an ambivalent police tactic, as long as the produced partial invisibility connected to it was at the same time a weapon and a counter-strategic effect of dispersal: "the dispersion of the Algerians into the town also worried the police, because the near invisibility of this group [...] made control and monitoring operations difficult" (Blanchard, 2012: 6).

Indeed, dispersal was enforced by the French authorities in order to divide the Algerian population, preventing the formation of homogeneous collectivities that could represent potential social dangers, and to separate them from the rest of the French population. It is precisely due to and within such an ambivalent dimension of being scattered across the territory that people appropriated, twisted and seized dispersal as a double-edged sword to escape and to become more mobile. As some urban theorists have explained, in the French cities, dispersal was associated with house demolition programmes in the poor neighbourhoods. Or better, dispersal was at the same time a spatial strategy of urban governance, apt at dividing unruly populations, and the most immediate outcome of demolition programmes, a sort of side effect of it – in fact, demolition fostered undisciplined mobility (Lelevrier, 2010).

Dispersal strategies have also been adopted more recently, in response to the urban riots in the French banlieus in 2005 (Baudin and Genestier, 2006). Such a case is significant, I suggest, as it sheds light on the deeply political character of dispersal, and more precisely on the fear of the mob and of unruly collective formations. In other words, far from being a question of public order only, urban strategies of dispersal have been enforced for dividing, neutralising and disciplining potential or actual collective subjects. Therefore, far from being a political technology used for disciplining individual migrants or for allocating bodies in space only, dispersal should be analysed also in its function of mob division: indeed, through dispersal state authorities strive to fracture potential or actual collective formations, preventing the emergence of shared political claims as well as the actual physical proximity that can generate transversal alliances. If at the level of the subjects that are targeted by dispersal we should consider not only individual migrants but also collective formation and the fracturing of the mob, as far as the spatial effects are concerned it is worth noticing that dispersal has been historically enacted simultaneously with measures of spatial concentration.

Centripetal and centrifugal spatial strategies were used in Algeria by the French at the same time for controlling and dominating the colonised Algerian people: the grouping camps (*camps de regroupement*) that many Algerians had been transferred to were not an alternative to urban dispersal strategies but, rather, they were complementary to these (Sacriste, 2018). More broadly, a politicisation of the technique of migration governmentality involves situating these within the quite longstanding genealogy of tactics for disciplining colonial populations – in the colonies as well as in the metropolis. In his book *La Domination Policiere*, Mathieu Rigouste retraces the tactics of the French police for spatially segregating and disciplining the Algerian population in the French cities, both at the time of the colonisation of Algeria and soon after Algeria's independence. Since the thirties, and in a more blatant way since the sixties, police tactics paralleled urban planning strategies centred around the twofold spatial dynamic of concentration and dispersal of the Algerian population first, and of the popular classes at large later on. What must be highlighted here is the partial continuity between the spatial disciplining of former colonised populations and the biopolitical governing of migration in the French cities. These police urban tactics have been characterised by a hybridisation between "colonial police, political police and the police of the undesirable people" (Rigouste, 2012: 24). Yet, the urban politics of containment and dispersal cannot be analysed only in terms of spatial disciplining but necessitates being politicised by focusing on the attempts to neutralise emergent collective subjects and potential struggles: "this regime of segregation was at the same time in charge of hampering the free organisation of the bidonville as a territory of resistance and of autonomisation" (Rigouste, 2012: 25). Therefore, not only tactics of migrant dispersal should be policitised as measures apt at dividing and neutralising migrant multiplicities, as potential collective subjects, and situated within a colonial genealogy of urban policing; beyond that, attention should be paid to the partial continuity with a broader set of urban tactics that had been used initially to police formerly colonised populations, then the so-called "urban poor" – deploying counter-insurgent tactics – and thereafter illegalised migrants and, simultaneously, political uprisings. In such a way, (post)colonial urban policing works as a prism for analysing the spatial dynamics of concentration and dispersal that target migrant multiplicities. Taking the colonial genealogy of dispersal as an analytical angle sheds light on the racialised character of the spatial disciplining of migration. Indeed, an exclusive spatial approach is not sufficient for grasping the biopolitical effects – that is, how migrant lives are targeted, shaped and differentially managed – of strategies of dispersal.

The multiplication of refugee camps and migrant detention centres across Europe cannot be analysed in isolation from the less visible but no less violent modes of control by dispersal enacted in the cities and at the internal borders of Europe. At the crossroads between policing, urban politics and colonial measures for governing unruly populations, "dispersal" is an entry in the British Anti-Social Behaviour Act, enforced in 2003, and then revised as the Anti-Social Crime and Policing Act in 2014. According to the Act, "where a Police Superintendent or above has reasonable grounds for believing that members of the public have been intimidated, harassed, alarmed or distressed in public places in a specific area" he can "disperse groups of two or more people". What stands in the backlight of dispersal strategies however are collective formations that still tend to be disqualified or criminalised as non-political subjects. In fact, the main target of dispersal strategies is multiplicities. In other words, even if this appears as counter intuitive due to the effect of division generated by dispersal, looking at strategies of dispersal is a lens for focusing on how multiplicities that are not reducible to national populations are managed, neutralised and contrasted.

Across the literature, analyses about dispersal tend to focus on the policing techniques employed to discipline groups and potential mobs, as well as on questions around public order or urban planning. What is fundamentally left out of the picture are the very subjects over whom national authorities try to regain control and the ways in which these collective subjectivities exceed and recursively undo disciplinary tactics. Against this background, I retain and highlight here the politicalness of migrant dispersal by putting at the core the temporary multiplicities and the emergent collective formations that tactics of scattering and dispersal target, in order to neutralise and divide them. More precisely, I want to suggest that even more than the content of the analysis – focusing or not on the collective subjects that are objects of dispersal – it is at the level of the analytical angle and gaze that the politicalness of dispersal can be highlighted: migrant multiplicities are not merely the target of policing measures, but are also what both local and national authorities try to regain control over, and, at the same time, what they fear as potential subjects of collective struggles. A genealogy of dispersal has enabled situating the current widespread migrant dispersal strategies within a colonial historical context and simultaneously de-essentialising migration, shifting attention from migration taken almost as a sociological category towards police and urban strategies adopted for dividing potential mobs, for disciplining minorities or colonised populations and for neutralising "unruly" collective subjects. Relatedly, dispersal becomes a lens for analysing the governing of unruly mobility through mobility – that is, the effects of forced and convoluted mobility that dispersal engenders.

Without disregarding the differences with the past, it is worth noticing the colonial legacies of actors that currently collaborate with national authorities that displace asylum seekers across the country: in France, Adoma, a cooperative created in 1956 by the French Minister of the Interior under the name Sonacotral (then, Adoma since 2007) to solve the housing problem of the

Algerian workers and families, has become today one of the leading actors in the migration reception system in France. Sonacotral was born with the task of finding accommodation for the "French muslims originally from Algeria", and "as a public national instrument for displacing and controlling foreign populations of Magreb origin" (Bernardot, 1999: 40). Nevertheless, as Marc Bernardot has remarkably reconstructed, after the independence of Algeria in 1962 it was redesigned as an organisation in charge of managing the accommodation of both French and foreign workers (Bernardot, 2008). Then, since the late sixties, its main activities have largely been oriented towards foreign workers – thus, including not only the Algerians – rather than towards French citizens. Between the nineties and the early 2000s, the organisation became a leader in the management of accommodation centres for asylum seekers in France, and in 2007 its name changed to Adoma. Thus, the colonial legacy and the migration one are strictly interwoven as far as the management of the non-French-born population is concerned. Significantly, one of the main hosting policies towards Algerian families in France adopted by Adoma in the sixties and seventies was the politics of dispersal, which is currently employed to deal with the presence of migrants in the national territory. Indeed, while the temporary accommodation plans for migrant workers apparently consist of spatial strategies of concentration and segregation, in reality the moving of migrant workers into ad hoc spaces (the so-called sites of transit or foyers for migrants) in the premises of the city can be seen at the same time as a measure that engenders dispersal as well.

The spatial management of foreign populations through this twofold dynamic of concentration and dispersal led in France by Sonacotra has been part of a broader urban hygienist plan that aimed at imposing a certain moral economy and at socially disciplining the targeted populations. Nowadays, France and Italy are countries where strategies of dispersal have been adopted as main measures for regaining control over what the EU calls "secondary movements", a normative expression that implicitly subordinates intra-European migration movements to supposedly primary routes and movements – as linear displacements from a point A to a point B. Through dispersal migrants can be partially invisibilised, being transferred to remote areas, and potentially "dangerous" migrant concentrations can be avoided. At the same time, due to dispersal, for the migrants hosting can become synonymous with isolation and segregation: in fact, for those who are transferred to reception centres located far from cities and without public transport, being hosted means being in a humanitarian spatial trap.

INTERMEZZO ON "STRATEGIES" AND THE STATE

Dispersal, as the case above has shown, induces displacement but not necessarily protracted "fixation" or strandedness into a place, being instead followed by a permanent convoluted migrant mobility. By scattering migrants across the territory, state authorities render them more invisible, while at the same time they strive to exhaust migrants, generating in this way effects of deterrence. Seen from a spatial point of view, dispersal in made up of a series of centrifugal forces – from critical border zones and main urban contexts towards remote areas or less visibilised places. Yet, from the standpoint of migrants, dispersal is not only about being transferred away from these critical places but also means being forcibly and constantly on the move – being obstructed in the very material possibilities to stay. To put this in cartographic terms, if we follow the way in which dispersal is enacted by the police, we would end up drawing a map of hotspots corresponding to the border zones from where migrants are chased away. Instead, from the standpoint of migrants' experiences, dispersal results in a multiplication of convoluted routes (sometimes undertaken by migrants more than once), forced stops over time and diverted paths: dispersal measures disrupt not only migrant movements but also the temporality of their journeys.

However, how should we think of dispersal in terms of states' strategies? Is there a deliberate will to disperse migrants across places or is this more the result of a reactive attempt to invisibilise their presence and neutralise potential collective formations? Although I use the terms "strategies" and "tactics" throughout the chapter, I distance myself from analyses that frame the question in terms of deliberate or non-deliberate state strategies in two main ways. First, it would be misleading to look at the state as the only actor involved and to think of dispersal as the outcome of a univocal and smooth strategy. On the contrary, what can be broadly called the politics of migrant dispersal is characterised by a series of frictions between different governmental levels which actually produce a quite fragmented image of the state itself (Allen et al., 2018): local authorities and the municipalities; the prefectures; the national police and the home office; and the eventual pressure on the part of the EU.

By using the term "strategy" I refer here to a twofold aspect. On the one hand, building on Michel de Certeau's distinction between tactics and strategies, I consider the strategy as something that pertains to governmental subjects – although not necessarily to the state. Indeed, in Certeau's view, the strategy "assumes a place that can be circumscribed as proper (*propre*)", in opposition to the tactics that are characterised by the lack of a proper space, and "insinuates itself into the other's place" (Certeau, 1988: xix). From this perspective, it can be argued that as the strategy is a territorialising and bordering technique, which relies on a possessive relationship to the space (both legally and politically), there cannot be "migrant strategies" properly speaking, but only tactics. However, this does not entail erasing migrant subjectivities from the picture, nor downplaying the disruptive force of collective migrant struggles. Rather, I draw from Certeau the analytical distinction between tactics and strategies in order to illuminate the heterogeneous political terrain upon which migrants engage for resisting, troubling and interrupting mechanisms of bordering and capture enacted by states as well as by non-state actors. What characterises migrants' presence in critical border zones is in fact the partial absence of legal, material and existential terrain that is eroded and subtracted by governmental practices which demolish migrant spaces of life.

Therefore, more than asking the question "Is dispersal a planned strategy or an indirect outcome of police interventions?", it is worth shifting attention to, on the one hand, the frantic attempts by states – both at a national and a more local level – to regain control over an "unruly" migrant presence, and on the other, to the broader effects induced by dispersal on migrant routes and lives beyond the intentionality of those state authorities. Dispersal is a strategy that can be found in official police documents; in other cases it is more a reactive response to a "migration crisis" or a "humanitarian emergency". As the colonial genealogy of dispersal shows, what is important to highlight is the partial historical continuity with techniques of policing employed for disciplining "unruly" and racialised populations. Of course, techniques of policing can be reactivated in the present in very different political contexts and in articulation with other different disciplinary mechanisms. However, such an historical-colonial insight allows us not to flatten the present migration context into the present. Rather, it is important to look at the way in which similar tactics of policing are reactivated in the present, and in the case of dispersal, to consider how centrifugal and centripetal measures (dispersing and concentrating/segregating) have been at play in governing "unruly" populations.

DISPERSING MIGRANTS' MULTIPLICITIES IN CALAIS

What are the effects of dispersal on migrant lives and geographies? What does it mean for migrants to be kept on the move through dispersal? In fact, what characterises dispersal is spatial displacement and, together with that, forms of convoluted hyper-mobility. It is not only a question of being transferred from one place to another, nor of being forced, directly or indirectly, to leave that place, in an autonomous way: by speaking of dispersal I refer to the condition of being forced to repeatedly leave not only a specific place but most of the places where migrants try to stay.

> We have been chased away from here five times over the last two weeks. The police in Calais never stop harassing us; they patrol around the rail station, and if they find us, they take us to the police station and then to some detention centres. When you are there, you can be released after one or few days, or they can keep your passport, as it has been in our case, and force you to buy a ticket to Italy if you want your document back. Many of us went back and forth from Paris multiple times. It is so exhausting, but for the moment we don't give up. We will come back to Calais, anyway.

This testimony of a 22-year-old Afghan citizen who was in Calais in June 2017 is telling of the impact of dispersal on migrants' movements, presence and lives. Two months later, G.A., the Afghan migrant I met in Calais, ended up

Italy: he was forced to do what can be called a self-deportation, and go back to Italy, the EU country where he had been fingerprinted first and where he received international protection. The police kept his passport and his permit to circulate in Europe, justifying such an arbitrary sequestration of these documents with the fact that he could not prove that he had enough money to stay in the country, and obliged him to pay for his flight ticket to Italy. Hence, the legal status is not a guarantee against dispersal: irrespective of the legal subjectivities and of being considered a refugee under the law, it is the very presence of undisciplined mobility that is deemed unacceptable by the authorities.

In Calais, dispersal measures have been the object of local decrees to hamper the formation and crystallisation of migrant groups: on 6 July 2014, the municipality of Calais enforced an "anti-settlement and anti-gathering" decree which, without naming migrants directly, forbids the protracted permanence of groups of people in the urban area. Three years later, on 2 March 2017, the municipality of Calais enforced a new decree in which migrants are directly named and addressed as the effective "problem". In particular, more than migrants as such, it is the persistence of migrant groups in the urban area that was described as a cause of social tension and potential threat:

> Considering that migrant gatherings constantly trigger tensions and considering that the Dunes area [the place where migrants used to stay] is subjected to a municipality plan that forbids any gathering [...] it follows that it is necessary to impeach all gathering in the industrial zone of the Dunes.

However, what emerges after a close analysis of these texts is that, ultimately, migrants are not the only targets of municipal anti-gathering decrees; rather, what these anti-migrant groupings texts target are also emergent autonomous spaces of hosting and an independent infrastructure of support. In fact, a few days later, on 6 March 2017, the municipality of Calais amended the decree, widening the area where migrant gatherings are forbidden to the central square, D'Armes. The mayor of Calais, Natascha Bouchart, justified this by saying that "a regular presence of people who bring food to the migrants has been observed" and that this should be avoided in order to prevent the emergence of further migrant "fixation points" in the area. According to the municipality, the migrants are given food on a daily basis, and so there is no need to have a parallel system of support. Thus, the targets are not only migrants as collective formations, but also transversal alliances between migrants and citizens, as well as all independent solidarity networks. By spatially widening the anti-gathering area, local authorities wanted to neutralise the emergence of migrant collective subjects and undermine transversal solidarity alliances at the same time.

Such an insight into the politics of dispersal and the ways in which mobility is used as a political technology equips us with analytical tools for rethinking spaces in relation to migration governmentality. As long as migrant mobility is not only blocked but also forcibly boosted, as a way to exhaust migrants and hamper them from settling or moving autonomously, a representation of spaces predicated upon the binary opposition openness/closure is not adequate. What are the relationships between spaces and (governed, enforced, autonomous) mobility? Is migrant mobility contained only through spatial enclosure? William Walters and Barbara Luthi use the expression "cramped spaces" for addressing similar interrogations:

> Cramped spaces, operates at an oblique angle towards the axes which the social sciences typically use to think about space. It is not necessarily macro or micro, global or local, public or private. Instead, it registers degrees of deprivation, constriction and obstruction, but always and simultaneously a concern for the ways in which such limits operate to stimulate and incite movements of becoming and remaking. (Walters and Luthi, 2016: 3)

Hence, following their use of the term, to be obstructed and hampered in cramped spaces is not only movement but also permanence in a given place and liveability. In many contexts, migrants are not just chased or taken away: even if their presence is tolerated, they can be the object of police harassment, excluded from access to social services and rights, and deprived of what in Calais, where the police destroy informal encampments, migrants used to call "liveable places" ("*lieux de vie*").

The expression "cramped spaces" enables us to capture elements that concern not only the spatial dimension of containment but also the migrant condition of being "stifled", or subtracted of material and legal terrain. Thus, through violent evictions, by constantly making migrants move and by obstructing access to asylum and rights, state authorities take terrain away from the migrants. We can speak of choked mobility to give a sense of how migrant mobility is not only the object of restrictions, nor is it just spatially controlled; rather, control over mobility is intertwined with a certain governing of migrant lives. In this sense, it can be argued that all politics of mobility is always simultaneously a biopolitics of mobility. Choked mobility does in fact allow not restricting the meaning of mobility to its spatialised meaning – mobility as movement – and including the ways in which migrant lives and conducts are regulated, left to die or are deprived of material terrain. Ultimately, as Stuart Elden compellingly pointed out, "the aim of interrogating terrain is to make work on territory account more fully for this materiality" (2017: 208). This means, as Elden also explains, moving beyond flat surfaces and foregrounding the inscription of strategies – in this case, for obstructing migrants within the materiality of landscapes.

THE TRAPS OF HUMANITARIANISM

Until now, I have stressed the role of national authorities, and in particular the police, in enacting dispersal tactics to scatter migrants across space and divide migrant multiplicities. However, dispersal is not a police measure only. On the contrary the involvement of non-state actors and humanitarian organisations in operations of dispersal has been paramount. In some cases, NGOs have directly participated in actions of eviction and camp dismantling. In other cases they have been engaged in persuading and cheating migrants to move away from informal encampments and to eventually accept going to institutional hosting centres. This persuasive function has been crucial in carrying out "humanitarian evictions", as the French authorities call them. By humanitarian evictions – an expression that appears as to be an oxymoron – the French government refers to the forced dismantling of informal migrant camps, in particular in urban contexts, and to the consequent eviction and dispersal of migrants from those sites. By persuading migrants to move away, with the help of the NGOs that assure the migrants they won't be sent back to Italy on the basis of the Dublin Regulation, the French authorities could avoid a too blatant spectacularisation of police violence: evictions and migrant dispersal appear as an ordinary administrative measure, implemented for securitising public space on the one hand, and migrants on the other, accommodating them in institutional centres.

Traps of humanitarianism designate the ways in which humanitarian actors, discourses and interventions have been mobilised for convincing migrants to move from Calais and Paris to hosting centres, from where they are deported or returned by force to Italy, or to the first EU entry country, on the basis of the Dublin Regulation. More precisely, some humanitarian organisations – first of all France Terre d'Asile – have encouraged migrants to claim asylum in France, pushing them to give up their project of reaching the UK or discouraging them from their attempt to remain in France without being fingerprinted. In practice, migrants have been pushed to move from Paris and Calais towards reception centres for asylum seekers, named Centres of Hosting and Orientation (CAOs), which until the end of 2015 were called Centres of Rest ("Centres de Repit"). Such a state strategy falls under the rubric of *"mise à l'abri"* which literally means "putting (migrants) in a shelter". Ultimately, the dismantling of camps and forced evictions are equated in the French institutional lexicon with operations of *mise à l'abri*: in a document published by the Home Office 2017, to respond to the accusations made by NGOs and activists about the police use of pepper spray against migrants in Calais, the French authorities speak of "operations of dismantling of the encampments [...] that are more commonly named operations of *mise à l'abri*".

In reality, these operations of *mise à l'abri* turned out to be modes of spatial fixation: the vast majority of migrants who had been evicted from Calais and informal encampments in Paris had been forced to give their fingerprints in Italy or other European countries. Thus, on the basis of the Dublin Regulation, they risked being forcibly transferred to the first EU country they had entered. In other words, claiming asylum meant for many of them risking being removed from France. This became more blatant with the opening of new hosting centres, called PRADHA, in early 2017: these latter are used to host migrants who are in the Dublin Procedure, imposing on them restrictions in terms of freedom. The hosting system, the asylum procedure and identification mechanisms are strongly connected to each other: in order to get a place inside a CAO, migrants need to give their fingerprints as soon as they arrive, and within one month they have to decide on whether to make an asylum claim or leave the hosting centre. The multiplication of CAOs – there are currently more than 550 – responds to the need to take migrants away, although only temporarily, from big urban centres and critical migration zones, such as Calais, and not to enable them to settle in France as refugees. The French Asylum Office confirmed this declaring:

> we are aware that the most of the migrants who move to CAOs in the end won't stay here, since they will escape again. This is what can be called migrants' evaporation rate, which consists in the estimated percentage of migrants who disappear, as they escape before the asylum procedure comes to an end. In the end, if migrants decide to leave the hosting system it is their choice, we cannot force them to claim asylum in France.[1] (Containment through Mobility)

Como and Ventimiglia, two Italian cities located at the border with France and Switzerland, respectively, have become critical border zones for migrants in transit. Ventimiglia, an Italian outpost of the southern part of the French–Italian border, first became a racialised frontier in April 2011. At that time, France suspended the Schengen Agreement in order to impede the free crossing of thousands of Tunisian citizens who landed in Italy in the aftermath of the outbreak of the Tunisian revolution and who wanted to reach France. Thus, border controls have been reactivated for Tunisians only, and all migrants who have been racialised as "North Africans" or non-white persons. Between 2012 and 2014 migrant crossings did not stop, and the harnessing and push-back performed by the French police at the border continued, even if according to a desultory politics of control. The racialised border popped up again in 2015, when France suspended the Schengen Agreement for the second time, to prevent the crossing of migrants from different nationalities. On that occasion, in June migrants and activists organised a NoBorder space – a sort of free spot in opposition to the hotspot logic – in a pinewood next to the cliffs located about two hundred metres from the border line. The safe migrant zone resisted for three months, until 19 September, when the Italian police evicted the place by claiming it was necessary to "lighten the frontier" from the pressure of the migrants. In March 2016, the Prefecture of Imperia opened a "camp of transit" – Roja camp – where migrants can stay for one week to take a rest. If on the one hand the denomination of transit camp is telling of the Italian authorities' attitude to let migrants pass, in conflict with the French police, on the other hand most of the migrants who arrive in Ventimiglia refuse to go there, in order to avoid being fingerprinted and identified. Dozens of migrants have died along the motorway that connects Ventimiglia to Menton, the first French city. Meanwhile, in Ventimiglia locals and activists got organised: in 2016, the church in Le Gianchette opened to host families and migrant women. However, the municipality obliged the priest to stop the hosting activity at the end of 2017. Activists from across Italy constantly supported the migrants in transit, both logistically and through legal help. By increasingly criminalising solidarity practices, the municipality of Ventimiglia has been trying to disrupt the autonomous infrastructures of migrant support that function as a sort of counter-logistics of state-led humanitarianism.

The transformation of Como into a border zone is far more recent: despite its geographical location – being a frontier post close to Switzerland – Como had never been an effective border for migrants until the summer of 2016. Indeed, migrants who wanted to move to Germany used to board the train in Milan and cross directly to Switzerland without stopping in Como. Yet since the enforcement of border controls in late June 2016, Como has become a forced stopping point for migrants who then end up temporarily stranded in the city. In both cases, it is important to briefly retrace the history of those places as racialised borders for migrants and, at the same time, as spaces where locals have mobilised to support the migrants in transit. In fact, if on the one hand it is worth recognising the specificity and to some extent the exceptional dimension of border zones, on the other these latter should not be seen as spaces that suddenly spring up from nothing. Relatedly, the history of spaces as (unequal and racialised) frontiers is also, at the same time, a history of the local resistances, struggles and practices of solidarity that have shaped those places over time. As a matter of fact, forms of support, in friction with state authorities, have been historically mobilised in Ventimiglia, which constituted an important passage towards France for Italian partisans and Jews who escaped during the Second World War. In fact, a frontier is never exclusively a space of control: rather, what makes a given space a frontier is also the struggles, the individual and collective refusals and mobilisations that trouble the terrain for the intervention of state authorities.

The functioning of some spaces as border zones can be analysed by bringing attention to modes of governing mobility through (forced) mobility – thus shifting the focus from the government of mobility to government through mobility. Such an angle is helpful for understanding how states try to regain control over "unruly" mobility, that is on migration movements that "disobey" the spatial restrictions imposed by the Dublin Regulation and, more broadly, the tempos and the exclusionary restrictive legal channels of the visa system. This is what I call containment through (forced) mobility; that is to say, border tactics that consist of obstructing migrants' movements and presence, not by fully stopping migrants but instead by forcing them to undertake erratic geographies and to bounce across borders. These border tactics are predicated on a politics of dispersal of migrant multiplicities. In fact, migrants' presence on the territory is hindered and migrants' movements are disrupted, diverted and decelerated not only by putting migrants in detention but also by keeping them on the move. By focusing on (forced) mobility as a way of governing migration I look at the effects of containment beyond detention produced on migrant movements. These are the outcomes of border-enforcement practices at the internal frontiers of Europe and forced internal transfers that are not made for keeping migrants in detention but for producing effects of deterrence, decelerating and lengthening migrants' routes.

Speaking about containment through mobility could appear to be an oxymoron: to what extent can migrants' presence and movement be contained through mobility? Unlike detention, containment encompasses a series of strategies for limiting migrants' autonomous movements, not only by generating strandedness and immobility but also by keeping migrants on the move. Through (forced) mobility, containment illuminates a triple governmental withdrawal: not seeing, not dealing with and not protecting migrants in transit. Unlike hotspot centres located in Southern Italy – in Trapani, Lampedusa, Pozzallo and Taranto – Ventimiglia and Como are border zones in which the national authorities do not identify all migrants nor track their passage by storing digital traces (through fingerprinting). Or to put it better, fingerprints are irregularly taken, for instance by the police in Ventimiglia, from those migrants who ask to access the transit camp, but these are not sent to EURODAC, as officers of the local police informally declared. Moreover, at the internal borders there is no Europeanisation of controls that is at play in the hotspots – actualised through the presence of Frontex and EASO officers who monitor the Italian police checking all migrants. In fact, migrant transit points like Ventimiglia and Como are characterised instead by a politics of non-registration, or of partial registration. While for the French and Swiss authorities Ventimiglia and Como are critical border sites to monitor, which require the deployment of police patrols and even drones for spotting migrants trying to cross the border, for their Italian counterparts they are spaces of transit.

While official hotspots were opened in Italy and Greece, these anomalous spaces of containment and transit were being organised by the Prefectures in Italy and run by the Italian Red Cross. Unlike official hotspots, which all migrants are transferred to upon arrival to the country for the purposes of identification, admission to centres of transit in Como and in Ventimiglia is based on selective hosting criteria. In Ventimiglia, for example, only men can enter; women, minors and families are hosted in a church in the city centre and are therefore excluded from the hosting system. There is no individual identification in Ventimiglia but "only registration – what matters is to count how many migrants passed, not who they are", the manager of the camp explained to me. Conversely, in Como only pregnant women, under-aged persons and families are allowed to stay in the small paddock full of white containers, almost invisible from the street. From time to time, migrants are identified and even fingerprinted in Como. However, what is at play in informal hotspot-like spaces is neither a strategy of full identification, nor a politics of control conceived in terms of surveillance: indeed, only migrants who ask to be hosted in the centre are registered – filling in a form with their name and nationality – and only those who want to claim asylum are fingerprinted. Instead, the presence of others, who remain out of the camp, is not recorded. In spaces of transit, the traps of humanitarianism described above, directly affect migrants by impeding their journey and diverting their geographies. Similar to Calais, when migrants gather in groups or become too visible, they are dispersed and chased away: migrants who temporarily settle along the Roja river in Ventimiglia, and who refuse to go to the camp managed by the Red Cross, are constantly evicted from there, although the local authorities are aware of the uncontrollability of migration movements: "migrants' stubborn desire to cross the border and the unmanageability of the wide free spaces along the river", the Prefect of Imperia declared, "render the eviction of migrant camps quite useless".

The invisibilisation of migrants who pass through these border zones and are bounced many times from one side of the border to the other – being pushed back by the French and Swiss police – contrasts with the current images of huge numbers of migrants and asylum seekers that circulate in the media. According to the Italian Red Cross, around 9000 migrants transited through Ventimiglia since the opening of the camp and about 3000 passed through Como. At the same time, Swiss authorities reported that 17,500 migrants were pushed back from Switzerland to Italy from June 2016 until the end of the year. However, as Sunder Rajan points out, official statistics lead to "certain forms of blindness as a part of the rationality of a certain mode of seeing and accounting for the population" (Rajan, 2006: 99); for instance, migrants who are apprehended by the Swiss authorities at the border at night are taken back by force to Italy and dropped in Como without notifying their expulsion to the Italian authorities or the migrants. On both sides of the border, national authorities prevent any possible formation of collectives by dividing and scattering migrant multiplicities. The strategy of dispersal – which consists of scattering migrants across space – is combined with exclusionary criteria of access both to the camps and to the asylum procedure. The institutional channels for asylum are at the same time a humanitarian trap for migrants – as demanding protection entails leaving one's own digital trace and involves a spatial fixation – and what states try to restrict access to, preventively hampering some migrants from submitting an asylum claim. For instance, after the implementation of the hotspot system in Italy, some migrants have been denied the possibility of claiming asylum, and in this way had been illegalised on the spot.

In July 2016, the first forced transfers by bus of migrants from the French–Italian border to the hotspot in Taranto, 1200 km from Ventimiglia, took place. In September these internal forced transfers became a weekly routine, and the same measure was extended to Como: migrants who are pushed back from France and Switzerland are then taken by the Italian police to the south of Italy, not with the final goal of hindering their further movement through detention or abandonment but by lengthening and diverting their journeys. On the one hand, migrants are not kept inside the hotspot. After being fingerprinted and identified for the second time – after the registration inside the hotspot upon landing – they are released: both the humanitarian and the security "hold" over migrant lives are withdrawn. On the other hand, they are not abandoned, as this would require a prior state, where they were actually taken into account or protected. Though many of the pushed-back migrants return to Ventimiglia and Como in a matter of days, it is possible to understand their forced ongoing movement as a form of containment; their mobility is disrupted not by detaining them, but by keeping them on the move. The interventions conducted in informal hotspot-like spaces are not about control in terms of surveillance nor about detention. Rather, they consist of scattering migrants across spaces, generating containment through forced mobility and removing the "dangerous" conducts from the others: together with the migrants "bounced back" – to use the word employed by the Italian police – many times from the Swiss and the French side of the border, those who take part in visible protests are removed from the cities that have become frontiers. Thus, the government of mobility as a government through (forced) mobility brings to the fore the effects of containment generated beyond surveillance and detention, which force migrants to restart their journeys and undertake erratic geographies across Europe.

SCANTY MULTIPLICITIES AND (UN)COUNTED DISPERSAL

A focus on the politics of dispersal leads us to reflect on the question of numbers and, more precisely, on the "fear of small numbers" (Appadurai, 2006) in an ambivalent way: migrant multiplicities are dispersed in order to avoid the formation of huge numbers of migrants; and, in turn, the effect of dispersal consists of more and more tiny, scanty groups, or even single individuals, who are still no less targeted by repressive measures or racialised mechanisms. In fact, the politics of dispersal generates small numbers, as it divides and neutralises big concentrations. In this sense, the politics of dispersal can be seen as a sort of counter-measure against "big numbers". Are "small numbers" an appropriate expression to designate the effects of dispersal? It can be argued that the politics of dispersal contributes to strengthen the fear of what I call scanty multiplicities. By introducing such a notion I refer to tiny groupings of migrants who are still depicted as worrying presences and an unbearable burden – like the migrants in Ventimiglia. The expression "scanty multiplicities" enables us to avoid the trap of numbers, instead evaluating how the presence of a few migrants in a given place is considered a problem. On the contrary, by debating small or big numbers, we end up making statements on the actual numeric "size" of migrants. Indeed, two hundred migrants blocked in the city of Ventimiglia can certainly be considered a small number, but they are described in the media as a worryingly big number.

Thus, what (politically) counts are not numbers; rather, it is, to put it in Rancière's terms, what troubles and exceeds the geometric counting. Indeed, that geometric counting accounts for what is not there, what is not part of the political scene (Rancière, 1999). To be more precise, more than focusing attention on the part of subjects with no part, what matters is to highlight the pitfalls of disputing on small and big numbers and of mobilising arguments grounded in numbers – e.g. contending that what states consider big numbers of migrants are instead small numbers. As far as the politics of migrant dispersal is concerned, it is remarkable how this latter shifts the securitising gaze from big concentrations and the "border spectacle" (De Genova, 2013) towards scanty multiplicities and individuals. In fact, more than attenuating or defusing racist reactions or security-based discourses – by hampering massive concentrations of migrants – dispersal measures contribute to refocus the political attention away from visibilised and exposed migrant groupings towards the non-spectacularised and almost invisible presence of individuals and scanty multiplicities. At the same time, dispersal should be situated within an economy of power that aims at redistributing political visibility and in a certain way to redraw the geographies of grievability.

In May 2018, the French Home Office published a press release about the eviction that French authorities carried out on the same day of the so-called "Millénaire" informal migrant camp, which was located in the 19th arrondissement in Paris. Announcing the eviction, after 34 operations of dismantlement of informal camps enacted since 2015, the French Home Office mentioned that "in order to avoid that one more eviction is needed, the police services of the Prefecture will be fully mobilised to fight against the reinstallation of camps". The fear of informal camps popping up, together with migrant multiplicities, emerges in many state documents: "avoiding any restablishing of permanent installations (see camps)" appears as the main constant effort and goal pursued by the police in border zones like Calais and Dunkirk. Thus, far from assuming it as decisive measures, the French authorities are aware that the repeated evictions and the related effects of dispersal do not make the migrants disappear; rather, they make them temporarily invisible. Moreover, the return of the migrants in the evicted areas is assumed to be a constant factor. Importantly, the forced evacuation of the camp was described as an operation of *"mise à l'abri"* – that is as a police-humanitarian intervention aimed at relocating the migrants into official hosting centres.

The "Millénaire" was at that time the biggest migrant camp in Paris, in terms of migrant population, with about 2500 people temporarily living there. However, as is the case with most of the informal camps, there were no official statistics about the migrant population living there, even though the migrant turnover was quite high, with many of the people just in transit. Two days after the eviction, the French newspaper *Le Monde* published a temporal and quantitative graph with the number of migrants that have been evicted from informal encampments in Paris since 2015: about 30,000 is the approximate number, according to the temporal-quantitative map, of migrants displaced from the 39 informal encampments that had been evicted by the police. The graph visualises the data communicated by the French Minister of the Interior and it is an estimation of how many people were been living in the camps at the time of the evictions. Indeed, not only could the exact number of the migrants evicted be found, due to the hyper-mobility of the migrants and the many who were just in transit; beyond that, the wide margins of migrants' uncountability and unaccountability also depend on the state's disregard towards spurious migrant multiplicities. More than the state's willingness not to count, we have to speak of a generalised unwillingness to count nuanced with a disregard in counting autonomous migrants' spaces. In other words, the partial non-interest in counting on the part of the national authorities ultimately also works as a technique for governing unruly multiplicities.

First, the disregard in counting is in fact also a disregard in accounting for migrants' presences and lives – and thus, by not counting, state authorities discharge themselves from taking care of the migrants and from mobilising economic resources. Second, the whole range of miscounting measures – between partial not-counting and approximate counting – appears as one of main modes through which state authorities deal with spontaneous and heterogeneous migrant multiplicities. Should such an inaccuracy and disregard for counting be seen as part of a politics of (in)visibility? Is the attitude of partial non-counting related to the invisibilisation of migrants? Some scholars have rightly pointed to the nexus between specific spatial strategies for governing migrations and making migrants invisible. For instance, by speaking of the "enforcement archipelago" Alison Mountz has convincingly described the processes of "invisibilization through geographic distancing" that the detention of migrants on the island generates (2015: 184). More broadly the nexus between spatialities and spatial formations on the one hand and regimes of visibility on the other is recursively at play in border zones, and it is always inflected in different ways – e.g. the remote spatial confinement on the island tends to be associated with the invisibilisation of migrants' presences.

However, if we consider the evicted informal migrant camps and the related effect of migrant dispersal in the urban space to be at stake in the politics of partial non-counting there is more here than a question of visibility and invisibility. As discussed in Chapter 2, not fully knowing how many migrants are in a place, how many have been evicted, how many transit through a certain point, and so on, should not in fact be seen as the opposite pole of a politics of identification and registration. Nor does this mean that migrants are less subjected to control and identity checks. Rather, partial not-counting and inaccurate (undetailed) knowledge about migrant multiplicities constitute a way of governing through elusiveness: on the one hand, temporary collective formations are discredited as non-political; on the other hand, states strive to manage migrants' presences not by gaining direct control over them – that is, by monitoring movements and conducts – but by preventing them from pursuing their original journeys and migratory projects and by taking legal, material and terrain away from them.

A focus on the inaccurate counting leads us to consider dispersal and governing through partial non-knowledge as articulated to each other: measures of dispersal can be considered as the spatial strategies that complement and at the same time actualise processes of unaccountability. As I have explained above, migrants' unaccountability de facto means limited state responsibility in granting protection and rights to the migrants. Unaccountability is often enacted also through partial miscount, a non-count or inaccurate count of the migrants. In turn, this latter is in fact sustained by a wider politics of non-knowledge. Through spatial dispersal, both the accountability and the accuracy in counting migrant multiplicities are considerably reduced. Numeric inaccuracy is often coupled with the magnifying or, inversely, the cutting by subtraction of migrant multiplicities, depending if migrants are perceived as a troubling factor or if they are instead downplayed, in terms of numbers, for justifying eviction or dispersal measures. For instance, in the city of Ventimiglia the eviction of informal migrant encampments along the Roya river in January 2018 had been presented by the authorities and in the media as a question of "public safety" to protect citizens. Interestingly, the "public safety" justification is used at the same time also for protecting the migrants – taking them away against potential environmental disasters. Therefore, the eviction of the migrant is presented as functional to the protection of citizens from the potential public disorder that migrants could trigger and to protect migrants themselves from the risks of natural calamities, in this case against possible river floods. What are the effects of spatial dispersal and governing engendered through inaccuracy on migrant lives? Is an insight on spatial displacement sufficient to account for the modes of subjection and subjectivation that these tactics of governing generate? Actually, an exclusive spatial approach misses accounting for the biopolitical effects on migrant lives, which go beyond spatial displacement and mobility control. In fact, not only are migrants' routes diverted and migrants' geographies become convoluted, interrupted and decelerated; the governing of unruly mobility through forced mobility engenders effects on migrant lives, by exhausting them, wearing them out and stealing their time (Ansems de Vries and Guild, 2018; Khosravi, 2018): "disruptive practices such as expulsions and deportations produce existential conditions of precariousness, *restlessness* and *stuckness* at the same time" (Picozza, 2017: 237). As I have illustrated above, measures of dispersal – which also have an impact on singular migrant lives – should be read together with tactics for dividing migrant temporary multiplicities and groups. In other words, dispersal is enacted in many cases for neutralising and partitioning incipient political collective formations.

UNDOING THE MOBILITY–FREEDOM NEXUS

Insofar as mobility and dispersal are investigated as technologies of migration governmentality what emerges is the need to disjoin mobility and freedom. In other words, the fact that migrants are not only governed through blockages and detention but also by keeping them on the move entails challenging liberal understandings of mobility – which equate mobility with freedom – as well as analyses that oppose free mobility and forced mobility. In fact, as the above-mentioned migration contexts show, it is not a question of forced mobility in the sense of being transferred by force nor of being in a condition in which flight is the only solution. Rather, if in some cases mobility as a technique of governmentality consists of forced transfers made by the authorities, in many others it is about extenuating migrants – by making some spaces unliveable for them, by forcing them, also in an indirect way, to divert their routes or to make the same journey multiple times. This involves moving beyond the opposition between immobility and mobility, exploring instead how these two are differently and strategically played by migrants and by state authorities.

Mobility is ultimately one of the terms that have been fully appropriated by and incorporated into the EU neoliberal vocabulary: from the internal free mobility of European citizens to students' mobility and the Erasmus programmes, up to the mobility and circulation of goods. In this sense, rescuing mobility from its liberal inflection is not an easy task. The liberal conceptualisation of mobility also depends on the idea of freedom that is associated with it: in the EU vocabulary, freedom tends in fact to be equated with the freedom of doing or owning something. From such a perspective, freedom conceived in that way is inherently connected with a model of subjectivity that is fully autonomous and capable of self-governing. If we shift the attention from the model of subjectivity towards the political economy of free mobility, as Didier Bigo aptly noticed, "under liberal governmentality mobility is translated into a discourse of freedom of circulation" and, in turn, freedom is framed "as moving without being stopped" and "as speed" (Bigo, 2011: 31). Therefore, a twofold move is at stake here: the political economy of mobility is translated into a political economy of circulation – the channelling and moving of goods; and the framing of freedom as fastened circulation – freedom equated with non-obstruction and non-deceleration. With mobility flattened into circulation, to be left out of the picture are, first, the subjective dimension of migration – the struggles for movements as well what exceeds the economic and social determinations – and, second, the policies, racialising measures and laws through which human mobility is differently governed.

However, the fact that mobility has been appropriated by the EU's narrative does not mean that it cannot be politicised, nor that it is fully monopolised by the liberal discourse. On the contrary, it is precisely because of its ambivalent use and meaning that the notion of mobility opens up a productive terrain of struggle.

In fact, while historically mobility – conceived as flight, vagabondage or undisciplined movements – has been a weapon of resistance for people, in the sixteenth and seventeenth centuries, with the development of capitalism, mobility has become a problem to be managed and controlled and, at once, a fundamental economic resource (Anderson, 2013; Boutang, 1998; Mezzadra, 2010). A (re)politicisation of mobility means rescuing it from being a mere descriptive term as well as from a normative positive understanding that automatically connects mobility with freedom and freedom with a fast and smooth circulation. In the field of mobility studies, Nathaniel O'Grady has analytically distinguished circulation from mobility in the following way.

While circulation "captures the broad systems of flow that consolidate as normal over time", mobility "provides conceptual and critical purchase from which to name the conditions of possibility enabling, regulating, and making things move in specific ways" (O'Grady, 2016: 77). Politicisation of mobility requires looking at the history of the struggles around, through and against mobility that have shaped modern and contemporary capitalist societies. In other words, instead of framing mobility exclusively in terms of circulation, or as a mere spatial movement/displacement, mobility should be associated with the ongoing struggle between people's freedom and modes of exploitation and control that shape conducts, movements and labour forces. In this respect, the autonomy of migration literature equips us with a fruitful analytical grid to (re)politicise mobility, putting at the core the refusals, subtractions and flights that have been historically enacted by individuals against mechanisms of labour exploitation, in the factories as well as in the plantation system. By bringing in the struggles (for mobility) and the subjective experiences of migration, and by drawing attention to the specific mechanisms of capture and disciplining that are unequally exercised on the subjects, mobility would gain a certain autonomy in respect of the vocabulary of circulation. The politics of mobility and, relatedly, singular experiences and practices of mobility are by far not reducible to kinetic moments nor to the displacement and transfer from a point A to a point B. Rather, mobility – often neutralised as a term that refers to the act of moving or of being on the move – conveys a huge range of conditions, which can be more or less temporary, and that are part of the subjective experience of mobility: being stranded, being temporarily immobile, being forced to divert the journey, being forced to move; but also, escaping, dodging controls, striving to stay or to leave. If circulation always requires infrastructures in order to take place, mobility can certainly not dispense with that but, in addition to that, it is shaped by the encounters and the conflicts between subjectivities and modes of control, exploitation and capture.

CONCLUSION

The colonial genealogy of measures of dispersal as well as of the use of mobility as a technology of governmentality enables us not to flatten migration onto the present, and to challenge at the same time the register of the exception according to which migrants tend to be tackled in the scholarship and in the public debate. On the one hand, looking at the historical interweaving of the governing of migrants, and the spatial managing of colonised populations and its reactivation in the present, sheds light on the travelling, across spaces and times, of political technologies that have been implemented by states and non-state actors for disciplining unruly mobility and populations. In particular, the chapter has drawn attention to the way in which mobility is appropriated and twisted by states as a technique for regaining control over migration.

The use of mobility as a political technology of migration governmentality cannot be tackled in mere spatial terms; rather, this chapter has gestured towards a politicisation of mobility as a technique for neutralising and dividing emergent collective formations. As this chapter has illustrated, migrants are not just blocked or hampered in their mobility; more radically, they are obstructed and harassed as long as they try to build autonomous spaces and improve their conditions of liveability. In this regard, Brenna Bhandar's legal genealogy of eviction in the colonial context is particularly useful for grappling with spatial displacement: "eviction is the logical corollary of the right to exclude others from your property, and the right to possess your property exclusively" (2018: 193). If we broaden the definition of eviction beyond the legal domain, it is noticeable that the term is widely used for designating the forced and often violent displacement of migrants not only from occupied spaces but also from border zones and informal camps – as for instance from the Calais jungle – and public spaces. Eviction does in fact reveal the constant spatial displacement, and more precisely the potential constant displaceability of migrants from the territory – what I have defined throughout the book as tactics for taking terrain away, making it impossible for the migrants to stay and build spaces of life.

That is, migrants are repeatedly evicted in three different but mutually related ways: first, they are often cleared out from occupied buildings, that might be private properties or disused places; second, migrants are also evicted from public spaces – such as fields or squares – and their informal encampments are dismantled; third, migrants are protractedly obstructed from getting and keeping a place to stay. Thus, they face a condition of constant potential displaceability which involves violent operations, eviction from private property, eviction from public space and, more broadly, a subtraction of legal and material terrain. In fact, as the colonial genealogy of dispersal has shown, police tactics for scattering migrants across space and dividing migrant multiplicities are actually measures for hampering and neutralising any incipient collective political subject.

NOTE

1   Interview with the French Asylum Office, Paris, 6 June 2017.

5

Migrant Spatial Disobediences

Collective Subjectivities and the Memory of Struggles

INTRODUCTION

On 27 March 2019 about 108 migrants hijacked the merchant ship that had rescued them in the central Mediterranean, hampering the crew from taking them back to Libya. The Italian Minister of the Interior, Matteo Salvini, declared that they were not refugees but "pirates". Thus, people seeking asylum have been turned into pirates by European states. The Maltese authorities finally gained control of the vessel and allowed the migrants to disembark on the island. Three of the migrants on board were arrested by Malta for diverting the vessel and accused of terrorism. The heterogeneous group of migrants from different nationalities hijacked the merchant vessel to prevent being returned to Libya and being detained in prison and subjected to torture or blackmail. The hijacking of the vessel was also a way for the migrants to prevent any stand-off at sea; that is of being kidnapped for days on board a vessel while European member states did not allow them to disembark. Imprisonment, torture and blackmail in Libya or being taken hostage by EU member states at sea: migrants are currently being kidnapped in the Mediterranean Sea and at the frontiers of Europe. Notably, rescue has become a mode of capture. Therefore, the group of "pirates-migrants" engaged in a collective act of counter-kidnapping, refusing both to be taken back to the Libyan prisons and to be detained at sea for days. To some extent, they mutinied themselves in their role of shipwrecked subjects, and became agents of their own liberation.

This collective act of migrant counter-kidnapping was immediately criminalised as an act of piracy and terrorism. This episode shows that when migrants act, they are often turned into riotous subjects. This is the case in particular when migrants are deemed to be vulnerable subjects or bodies to be rescued, as is the case of migrants drowning in the Mediterranean, as well as when migrants protest not "just" by claiming rights but by directly preventing their own abuse and exploitation.

This chapter investigates *migrants' spatial disobediences*, that is migrants' refusals against the spatial restrictions imposed by the Dublin Regulation and the exclusionary geographies of the asylum regime, and it reflects on the emergence of migrant collective political subjectivities. As part of that, the chapter questions how to build a political memory and archive of migrant collective struggles, beyond punctual and visible moments of resistance. However, such an archive, the chapter argues, could not be homogeneous or complete; rather, it will necessarily be highly fragmented and partial, due to the elusiveness and fleeting character of migration. Spatial disobediences are constantly enacted by migrants, both individually and collectively, not only for dodging border controls but also insofar as migrants do not accept the restricted and exclusionary terms of hospitality and the politics of asylum. I focus here on the emergence of temporary multiplicities using this as an analytic for unsettling the methodological individualism that underpins migration literature and for rethinking collective political subjectivities beyond the categories that are usually mobilised in political theory to name collective formations – such as "populations", "multitudes", "assemblies" and "groups". Instead of transposing these latter into the field of migration, I suggest that looking at migration pushes us to reconceptualise categories and notions of political theory that pertain to the domain of collective subjectivities. In fact, the dimension of migrant multiplicities is quite underplayed and under-theorised in the literature, and this becomes a considerable limit when scholars speculate on migration and political subjectivities, or on migration and struggles.

The chapter starts by explaining the expression "migrants' spatial disobediences" and showing how this might be used as an analytical lens for questioning analyses of migrants' agency that rely on the image of the migrant as a proactive subject. The chapter moves on by engaging with some key texts in political theory that discuss and theorise collective subjects, arguing that we should not superimpose pre-existing categories of the political if we want to understand the specificity of migrant collective subjects. In the concluding section, the chapter interrogates how to keep the memory of the solidarity practices and migrant collective struggles that have shaped the European space.

MIGRANTS' SPATIAL DISOBEDIENCES

Learning not to be "seeing like a State" (Scott, 1998) is a difficult task: getting rid of the state as a standpoint and as an analytical lens means first of all undoing the taken for granted nexus between the terms "migration" and "government". Both in the academic scholarship and in the political arena, questions such as "How can we govern migrants better and in a fair way?", or "How could we solve the problem of the refugee crisis?" populate the debate, pushing people to endorse and perform the role of policy maker. In order not to see migration like a state, we need to interrogate what a critical approach to migration and borders might be; indeed, I suggest that critique should not be limited to the act of pointing to the violent functioning of the border regime. Rather, it should involve paying attention to the knowledge we generate about migration and the ways in which we frame research questions – around the nexus between migration and government. Taking for granted that (some) migration movements might constitute a problem to be managed involves reproducing a racialised gaze that considers the mobility of some people and their choice about where to stay as a non-right; that is, as non-legitimate acts that need to be authorised, restricted and controlled.

Not seeing like a state also involves not seeing migrants' struggles, refusals and tactics of mobility as a by-product of border controls: in fact, the subjective drive of migration is what states frantically try to regain control over and capitalise on. Thus, the border regime gets constantly readapted in order to capture and regain control over migration (Bojadžijev and Karakayali, 2010; Mitropoulos, 2007). However, foregrounding the reality of migrant struggles – both as struggles for movement and struggles for staying in a place – should not be confused with a romanticisation of acts of resistance and refusal that many among those who are racialised and governed as "migrants" engage in. Nor are migrants' struggles analysed here as exemplary expressions of political agency. Indeed, in critical migration literature there is a tendency to look at migrants as the paradigmatic figures of political subjectivity, acting as would-be citizens. In this sense, "the figure of the migrant" (Nail, 2015) is today often associated with the question, "Who is the subject of agency and resistance?"

In their introduction to *New Keywords: Migrations and Borders*, De Genova, Mezzadra and Pickles point towards the unsettling dynamism produced by migrants' struggles for movement (De Genova et al., 2015). Such an unsettling dynamism can be mobilised as an analytical tool for a renewed political epistemology of migration that draws attention to the collective dimension of resistances, agency and political subjectivities – something that remains undertheorised in political theory and migration scholarships. This book is informed by scholarly works that critically engage with the border regime from the standpoint of migrant struggles and the way in which these constantly exceed mechanisms of capture and control (De Genova, 2010; Mezzadra, 2010; Scheel, 2013). This scholarship also foregrounds the modes of exploitation that migrants are subjected to, contending that an analysis of migrants' struggles and political subjectivity requires an in-depth investigation of these latter (Andrjasevic, 2009; Mezzadra and Neilson, 2013). Yet I suggest that such an analytical gaze needs to be supplemented with an analytical gaze that accounts for the physical obstructions, the "cramped spaces" (Walters and Luhti, 2016), the legal hindering and the condition of *being choked without letting die* that many migrants face. Anne McNevin's conceptualisation of ambivalence as a constitutive dimension of migration captures migrants' condition of being choked and cramped, while struggling from within these obstructed spaces (McNevin, 2013). In fact, according to McNevin, "the notion of ambivalence provides a useful starting point for coming to terms with the transformative potential of claims [that] both resist and reinscribe the power relations associated with contemporary hierarchies of mobility" (McNevin, 2013: 183).

In *The Subject and Power* (1982) Foucault equips us with two key methodological points: first, resistance should be taken "as a chemical catalyst so as to bring to light power relations" (1982: 780); second, there is something like an ontological or essential freedom but "a reciprocal incitation and struggle" between freedoms and powers (p. 790). Thus, resistances constitute the actual fabric of power relations: according to Foucault every power relation ultimately entails "a strategy of struggle" (p. 794). In this way we see that both resistance and freedom are rethought in terms of struggle, and not as what stands at the opposite pole of power. The high heterogeneity of migrant struggles cannot be reduced to a single framework, nor can it fit into a specific category. By introducing the expression of spatial disobediences, I do not want to simplify such a heterogeneity but, rather, bring attention to migrants' subtractions and refusals against the spatial restrictions imposed on them by the states, as well as by European laws. A case in point is represented by the spatial disciplining of migrants enacted through the implementation of the Dublin Regulation that, as is well known, hampers migrants from applying for asylum in other member states than the first EU country of entry.

Over the last few years, with the temporary suspension of Schengen in some European countries and the implementation of the hotspot system, migrants' struggles against the spatial restrictions of the Dublin Regulation have been rife: many migrants, in particular those who arrived by sea and who had been identified in the hotspots, engaged in individual and collective refusals against the obligation of giving their fingerprints and, consequently, remaining entrapped in the first country of arrival. Thus, the fingerprinting procedure became a battlefield that also witnessed police brutality and violent techniques used by national authorities under pressure from the EU, to "convince" migrants to comply with the biometric identification. However, migrants' refusals to be fingerprinted and claim asylum in Italy or Greece, as well as unauthorised escapes from the hosting centres to sneak into other European states, cannot be narrowed to resistance against the spatial restrictions of Dublin. The spatial disobediences enacted by migrants to dodge the EU's disciplining of mobility actually reveal a stake beyond spatial boundaries: by unsettling the triple nexus between spatial fixation, compulsory identification and access to rights, migrants refused the very terms upon which asylum politics is predicated. Indeed, through their refusals and flights, they did not just dodge the spatial restrictions and police obligations, they also undermined the "moral economy" (Fassin, 2005) of the asylum and of a restricted or disciplined hospitality, by enacting the freedom to choose where to go and settle.

Hence, the "scandal" of migrants' spatial disobediences consists not (only) of the act of crossing the borders with no authorisation but, rather, on migrants' self-determination and stubbornness in staying or moving where they desire to. That is, the very fact that migrants do not accept the exclusionary and restricted conditions of hospitality and that they "even" want to decide themselves where to apply for asylum is deemed to be unbearable according to a statist perspective.

To put it otherwise, spatial disobediences reveal the untenable articulation between *freedom* (of choice and movement) and *asylum*. A focus on the spatial disobediences that migrants enact entails paying attention to what Bonnie Honig defined as a practice of taking rights, beyond any discursive claim (Honig, 2001). The question of freedom is fundamentally not contemplated in the political lexicon of protection: seeing migration like a state, to paraphrase John Scott's formula, means seeing the access to international protection as a sort of renunciation of freedom of choice and the right to mobility.

Ilker Atac, Kim Rygiel and Maurice Stierl have stressed how "over the past decade, we have witnessed an upsurge of political mobilization by refugees, irregularized migrants, and migrant solidarity activists […] With collective public actions that take on a variety of forms […] [These struggles can be] referred to as a 'new era of protest'" (Ataç et al., 2016: 527–8). In fact, the crisis of the EU border regime that states have narrated and presented as a "refugee crisis" has been characterised by a wave of collective and individual refusals, occupations of houses and public spaces, and marches and sit-ins to claim rights. In particular, we have witnessed the circulation of political claims. "We are not going back": the migrants in June 2015 chanted this motto on the cliffs of Ventimiglia and showed it on their banners. The strength of that motto lay in the fact that the claim was not in this case a demand, a request, but the reiteration of an ongoing struggle for movement: it does not matter how and for how long you will close the border, the argument goes, we won't give up on moving on. By chanting "we are not going back" and through their protracted presence on the cliffs, the migrants in Ventimiglia showed and embodied the sheer intractability of their struggle for movement.

The same year, on 17 December, a group of about two hundred migrants marched in the central streets of Lampedusa with the rallying crying "no fingerprints" and "we want to move out of the camp". After the march, they continued the protest by organising a three-day sit-in in front of the city's main church. The protest was the most visible moment of a protracted collective refusal that a group of migrants detained in the hotspot of Lampedusa started in November against the obligation to give their fingerprints. They were aware of the implications of the Dublin Regulation, and therefore they did not want to leave their fingerprints in Italy, as they wanted to move to other European countries. After one month of protest, the migrant group had been divided: in the span of a few weeks they had all been fingerprinted by force, and they had been transferred to the mainland in small groups of ten. "I want to choose where I want to live, it is not up to the European leaders to decide about my life, about where I want to work and stay": the words uttered by a Senegalese man at the protest foregrounded the unbearable claims of the migrants' resistance against the Dublin Regulation. Indeed, as I mentioned above, through their refusal of being fingerprinted the migrants blatantly posited as unacceptable the spatial restrictions imposed on them and at the same time they took their freedom to choose where to stay.

Together with these visible and mediatised migrants' protests, even more silent and invisible migrant struggles have taken place in Europe: migrants' refusals have multiplied across the European space, and should be considered part of a submerged archive of Europe's migrant history. Indeed, the multiplicity of migrant struggles that have shaped Europe's border zones are not considered part of Europe's history. For this reason, building a political memory of migrant struggles and of the solidarity networks between migrants and citizens would enable the retention of a political memory of these fleeting collective subjects and transversal alliances. Nevertheless, thinking about an archive of migrants' spaces and struggles does not mean considering this as a linear counter-narrative of Europe's history. On the contrary, such an archive is a constitutively heterogeneous and fragmented one, characterised by a "piecemeal partiality" (Stoler, 2010: 43); this is because of migrants' elusive dimension and partial invisibility on the one hand, and because of the constant repressions and evictions migrants are subjected to on the other, which results in the erasure of many spaces of struggle from the map. From such a perspective, the pursuit of such an archive responds to a specific analytical sensibility that tackles migration from the standpoint of minor history. As Ann Laura Stoler aptly defined it, this latter is conceived here as "critical space: it attends to structures of feeling and force that in major history might be otherwise displaced [...] a symptomatic space in the craft of governance" (2010: 7). That is to say, the political memory of migrants' spaces of struggles and control could be seen as part of a minor history not in the sense that it provides an overwhelming counter-map of the official history of Europe, or that it enables the unveiling of some hidden truth. Rather, it might show the constituent force and dimension of migrants' contested presence in the remaking of Europe, highlighting at the same time the constitutive fragmentariness and precariousness of those migrants' spaces. Indeed, coming to grips with the precarious and fleeting character of migrants' spaces is not in contradiction to an analysis that accounts for the constituent force of migrants' movements in shaping Europe's legal and political geographies: ultimately, "the unity and continuity of the European legal and political space may only be reconstructed through migrants' experience of its borders" (Karakayali and Rigo, 2010: 127).

THE PROXY MIGRANT-CITIZEN

Migrants are often depicted as the proxies of the active citizen, and as the bearer of agency. As Filippo Furri has suggested, "Can the migrants act?" is one of the principal questions asked by researchers insofar as migrants are posited either as agential subjects par excellence or as those who are unable to act at all as victimised subjects (Furri, 2016). As if "migrant" per se would constitute a sociological category and as if, simultaneously, this could be considered as inherently political or not. By hypostatising the migrant as an agent and resistant subject, these analyses corroborate a liberal model of political subjectivity predicated upon a proactive and direct clash between subjects and powers, between individuals and norms to be subverted. Relatedly, migrants do appear as subjects who cannot but speak, that is who can take their rights by speaking up and claiming (Lazzarato, 2014).[1] For instance, the widespread use of the term "protest" to designate migrant struggles immediately conveys the idea of a direct confrontation that migrants would engage in with state authorities and border policies. In fact, speaking about protest corroborates the image of individuals or groups that challenge the border regime, its deadly/violent functioning, and capitalism's exploitative mechanisms.

Such a view on migrant struggles transposes the figure of the activists onto the figure of the migrants, positing these latter as resistant subjects who want to contest and defy borders. Of course, as the struggle on the cliffs of Ventimiglia shows, on many occasions migrants also organise visible protests with banners, in a similar way to other demonstrations. Very often, locals act in solidarity with the struggles for movement of the migrants. Nevertheless, even in Ventimiglia, the motto "we are not going back" could not be contained within the codes of the "protest", as it is more than this and less than this at the same time. Indeed, it cannot be described as a challenge against the border regime, nor as a demand, but instead as a sort of claim in action, an embodied claim that asserts and reinforces migrants' actual condition and will – the stubbornness of not going back anyway. More silent and invisible struggles for movement – as when migrants try to cross the border on the sly or when they try not to be fingerprinted – fit even less into the category of "protest", insofar as their goal is to move on or to stay without being deported.

The question of the collective dimension emerges in a quite peculiar way here, as even when there are migrant groups laying political claims or organising a struggle, it is noticeable that these groups are not only temporary but that they do also change very quickly at the level of their composition. Indeed, in many squats or informal camps, there is a huge migrant turnover due to migrants' autonomous or forced mobility – that is migrants who managed to move on or are deported.

Similarly, the notion of "agency" that is widely used in migration scholarship to designate migrants' political claims and their direct engagement in struggles needs to be subjected to a critical investigation. In this regard, the feminist literature equips us with useful analytical tools, I suggest, for critically coming to grips with the notion of agency, that is the limits and the criticisms raised by some feminist scholars towards the use of "agency" to name the capacity of the subjects to act against mechanisms of domination, exploration and subjection. Feminist literature helps us to question the model of the "active subject" that is predicated upon a liberal conceptualisation of subjectivity. Saba Mahmood's critical approach to "agency" represents a fundamental contribution to grasp the limits of the uses of such a notion that tends to be used in an unquestioned way. Mahmood questions the liberal conception of agency, conceived exclusively "as a synonym for resistance to relations of domination" (Mahmood, 2011: 6), since this restricts a view on agency to political modes that involve a sheer and deliberate confrontation between subjects and powers. In this way, to be discredited as non-political are those practices that are not "encumbered by the binary terms of resistance and subordination" and to "motivations, desires, and goals that are not necessarily captured by these terms" (Mahmood, 2011: 38). By the same token, she critically engages with Judith Butler's use of the term "agency" by arguing that if on the one hand Butler radically challenges a liberal and progressive model of subjectivity, on the other her definition of agency builds upon the subversion of the norms.

Questioning agency through such an analytical angle enables us, I contend, to foreground struggles for movement and the freedom to stay that do not consist of openly clashing with the state, nor in attempts to challenge migration policies. In this sense, agency as a notion might be conceptualised by taking migration as a privileged terrain and, at once, as a lens, to rethink it beyond the image of a "sovereign agent" (McNay, 2000; see also Revel, 2015). In their book *Vulnerability in Resistance*, Butler, Gambetti and Sabsay question the taken-for-granted binary opposition formed by agency and being active on the one side, and vulnerability and being passive on the other: against the "foreclosing or devaluing modes of collective resistance among designated as vulnerable", they gesture towards "modes of vulnerability that inform practices of resistance" and "forms of political agency developed under conditions of duress" (Butler et al., 2016: 6). Their stress on duress, as a condition lived by many as the outcome of mechanisms of subjection and exploitation, and the rethinking of agency via duress, is of particular relevance when we bring attention to migration. In fact, legal status and material conditions highly shape the ways in which subjects can and do resist, as well as the modes of action they mobilise.

By rethinking agency in duress and practices of resistance from within cramped spaces we avoid producing degrees of agency that depend on the subject's capacity to act against powers. Practices of escape and wandering, underground collective refusals and temporary occupations, are common struggles that migrants engage in and that rely on what De Certeau defined as the non-autonomous terrain of action (De Certeau, 1988). In fact, if we take vulnerability and the condition of being cramped as the daily experience of many subjects, and not as a deviation from the norm of political subjectivity, agency itself can be revised from the point of view of heterogeneous modes of desubjugation and depart from agonistic models. These do not necessarily entail a direct confrontation with state authorities, nor a deliberate challenge to migration policies, nor, finally, visible struggles driven by declared political claims. Even if these visible struggles that reproduce a citizen-agency model are also at play, they do not encapsulate the range of heterogeneous tactics of desubjugation that migrants engage in, which can consist in more silent struggles.

Actually, as postcolonial feminist analyses have pushed it further, delinking agency from resistance to the norms enables attention to be brought to struggles that consist in partially inhabiting and negotiating norms and restrictions, as well as conditions of dependence (Abu-Lughod, 1990; Mahmood, 2011). Once again, this is particularly helpful when we take into account migrants' struggles: considering migrants as subjects who automatically oppose relations of dependence – for instance who reject humanitarian control and support – means disregarding the specific relations of power where they find themselves and that push many to negotiate the norms, restrictions and modes of subordination. As Lila Abu-Lughod aptly stated, everyday practices of resistance should not be taken as a marker of the agential capacity of the subjects to challenge and openly confront with power but, rather, we should let these practices "teach us about the complex interworkings of historically changing structures of power" (1990: 53). Nevertheless, what is partially missing in these critical approaches to agency is a deeper reflection on the collective dimension of struggles and modes of agency. Indeed, the starting point for all these analyses is in fact the individual subject, and how to rethink political subjectivity in light of a diverse subject status. Questions around which and how collective dimensions are at play in struggles remain under-theorised in comparison with enquiries about the (individual) subject of agency.

THE MAKING OF TRANSVERSAL ALLIANCES

In which ways is the collective dimension at stake in migrant struggles? And what do we mean by collectivities or by collective subjects as far as migrant multiplicities are concerned? These questions are eluded in analyses that focus on migration governmentality and that investigate how border controls and disciplinary power affect migrants. Indeed, methodological individualism surreptitiously undergirds theories on migration, and bordering mechanisms are in fact studies by taking as a unit of referent and as a target individual subjects. Such an elision of the collective dimension is likewise glaring as far as migrants' struggles and agency are concerned. To be more precise, the collective dimension is not absent from that literature: many scholars have in fact focused on rights' claims made by migrant groups, on organised protests as well as on the alliances between activist networks and migrants. However, instead of interrogating what are the peculiarities of these collective formations and what the political collective dimension consists of, these analyses tend to mobilise taken-for-granted notions of collectivities. As I illustrated in Chapter 1, temporariness and unevenness characterise migrant multiplicities. Moreover, when it comes to questions of political claims and struggles, notions that convey a certain homogeneity or stability – like "the precariat" or "the class" – turn out to be inadequate for designating temporary multiplicities, formed by people in transit.

Actually, analyses about emergent political collective subjects that cannot be described in terms of class or through traditional sociological categories had been rife in political theory. Just to mention a few of them: Toni Negri and Michael Hardt have notably used the notion of "the multitude" to rethink contemporary collective subjects. Guy Standing has introduced the term "the precariat" to name the collective subject that would emerge from the alliances between precarious workers, while Judith Butler has focused on the notion of "assembly". Another stream of literature has instead engaged in revising the notion of "the people" in light of the current social and political transformations, and in particular of the increasing precarisation of lives (Badiou et al., 2016). For instance, Alain Badiou argues that the term "the people" "gets a positive meaning only provided that it is connected to a potential non-existence of the State" (2016: 31), adding that migrants, as the new proletarians per excellence, embody the essence of a people that is not recognised as such by the state. In this way, he posits migrants as the emergent evolutionary subjects around which other political figures, like the precariat, should coalesce.

There is no similar debate with respect to migrations. Rather, all the above-mentioned notions are eventually used by scholars for naming migrant multiplicities and, in particular, migrant collective struggles, without questioning the differences and the specificities of collective formations constituted by migrants. In order to problematise migrant collective formations, I proceed by first taking into account Butler's conceptualisation of "assembly" and the way in which Negri and Hardt have also used it in their book *Assembly*. This is because the term "assembly" is the one that encapsulates most the heterogeneity of subjectivities that coexist and build alliances in contemporary urban contexts. However, as I will show, even such a notion does not allow us to grasp the specificities of temporary collective formations and how these latter push us to rethink traditional sociological categories such as "the people" or "social movements". Butler's reflections on assembly interestingly stem from an analysis of the Arab uprisings protest movement, with particular attention given to Tahir square in Cairo, and, jointly, of the Occupy movement in the US. Neither case fits in with the notion of class nor the traditional categories for social movements. Butler's theoretical operation is situated at the crossroads between the attempt at "renewing what we can mean by the people" (Butler, 2015: 6) and a focus on subjects stripped of rights who are deemed non-political. The notion of "the people" is exclusionary by design: by naming the people, as broad as the definition could be, we implicitly or implicitly trace boundaries that set who counts as "the people", and consequently who is excluded from it and remains uncounted. The homogeneity and, together, the exclusionary character of the people are encapsulated in Kant's definition in which the outside of the people are presented as the outcome of a sort of self-mutiny: "by the term 'the people' (populous) we mean a mass of men who gather together in a land insofar as they constitute a whole [...] the part which exclude itself from these laws (the undisciplined element of the people) is called 'the plebs' (vulgar); when it unites against the laws it is the revolt (agree per turban)" (Kant, 1798 in Balibar, 1997). For this reason, Butler gestures towards the notion of assembly, conceiving this in terms of "embodied and plural performativity" (2015: 8) that would unsettle the boundaries and the composition of the people, or more precisely what constantly exceeds it. Such an understanding of assembly is particularly useful for developing a political-analytical sensibility towards collective and individual subjects who are unaccounted or non-recognised in the public space.

However, Butler's theory of assembly remains partially wedded to an image of politics predicated upon recognition. This emerges even more clearly when she articulates the notion of "assembly" in terms of bodies in alliance, as "bodies that come together to make a claim in public space" (2015: 70). Far from having a pre-established space of appearance, bodies in alliances struggle to become visible in the space, and to produce that terrain. Such a move also captures well the difficulty for many migrants who struggle in groups to be recognised as political subjects and even to become visible. In fact, the terrain of struggles, the visibility that these struggles acquire and claims to political recognition are strictly intertwined with each other. Yet, in order to rethink migrant collective formations, I suggest that the claims for visibility in the public space encapsulate only a few of the struggles that migrants engage in. If we consider informal encampments set in the peripheries of many towns in Europe, migrants' struggle for staying might be seen as a "politics of presence" (Darling, 2017) more than as their attempt to be visible in the public space. Temporary migrant multiplicities often constitute what is irreducible and, at once, not containable, within the space of appearance. Therefore, if on the one hand the notion of assembly enables accounting for collectivities that are both temporary and heterogeneous in their composition, on the other it implicitly presupposes a sphere of political visibility and recognition that the assembly would look for.

It is worth noticing that the term "assembly" has three main interrelated meanings. First, assembly refers to "a group of people gathered together in one place for a common purpose". Second, it contains an electoral meaning as long as it refers to parliamentary assemblies. Third, it names the act of putting together the components of a machine or a given object. Hence, to be enshrined in the notion of assembly is both a constituent drive – gathering for a common goal – and an ordered (material) assemblage and (political) gathering. In other words, assembly conveys at the same time the image of a heterogeneous and spontaneous gathering, and the idea of an organised composition. Michael Hardt and Toni Negri have centred their work on a rethink of political collectivities. Assembly, according to them, "is meant to grasp the power of coming together and acting politically in concert" (Hardt and Negri, 2017: xxi). Similar to Butler, assemblies are conceived by Hardt and Negri not just as the gathering of heterogeneous subjects with diverse claims but, rather, as movements with converging goals that are carried out in concert without erasing everyone's differences: far from the need to "spontaneously form together" it requires "a political project to organize" (Negri and Hardt, 2017: 69). Notably, Jacques Rancière has remarked on the pitfalls of the notion of the multitude, pointing to the denial of any divisive element that it entails. On the contrary, according to Rancière, the conceit of a multiplicity formed by singularities fails to capture what cannot be subsumed in the multitude (Rancière, 2010). Such a criticism should be situated in the quest for politics as the space of production for a disagreement that is unbridgeable according to an arithmetic logic – "politics exists wherever the count of parts and parties of society is disturbed by the inscription of a part of those who have no part" (Rancière, 1999: 123).

To recap, for Butler, assemblies refer to people who rally for "an equally livable life" and who "struggle for an egalitarian social and political order" (2015: 69). Hardt and Negri do not speak of a liveable life and bring in the theme of the common: "one key struggle on the terrain of social production plays out over the uses, management, and appropriation of the common […] The common is increasingly today both the foundation and primary result of social production" (2017: xvi). Unlike Butler, Hardt and Negri do not downplay the dimension of antagonism and of social conflict that for them is ultimately at the core of any assembly. In other words, the making of assemblies cannot be disjoined from the dimension of the struggles for it. In *Assembly* Hardt and Negri replicate the image of the migrants as potential political vanguards, as subjects who are highly precarious and, at the same time, as people who "have the potential to undermine fixed identities and destabilize the material constitutions of the global order" (2017: 60). Instead, this book does not consider migrants as revolutionary subjects nor as the exemplary figures of political agency but, rather, pays attention to the ways in which migrants unsettle the ordinary or common collective subjectivities. Migrants and migrant collective formations are certainly not isolated from other emerging political subjectivities: the politicalising of migrations and their potential to disrupt the "national order of things" (Malkki, 1995) mainly hinge on the transversal alliances of solidarity put into place between migrants, locals and activists. Nevertheless, the very presence of migrants – most of whom are in transit, or have been "illegalised" – in these collectives, and their claims, which often cannot be recuperated with a citizen-centred struggle, require us to radically rethink what we mean by collective subjects.

Therefore, migrant collective formations refer both to temporary multiplicities formed by migrants only and broader coalitions in solidarity with migrant struggles or where migrants are involved – e.g. struggles for housing. Both in Butler and in Hardt and Negri, the multiplicities of singularities are posited to be in alliance, to struggle against increasing precarity and for the production of common spaces. The image of transversal alliances enables de-essentialising migration as a supposedly self-standing terrain of struggle or sociological field. At the same time, a focus on the making of multiplicities enables us to capture the politicalness of movements which tend to be uncounted and unaccountable as political subjects. Thus, interrogating collective subjectivities in the light of migration enables us, first, to avoid any reification of migration as a separate and bordered field and, second, to draw attention to transversal collective formations and alliances formed by migrants and non-migrants. Such an analytical move consists of twisting the gaze from an exclusive focus on migration towards transversal struggles against precarity and for claiming rights – to education, work and housing, but also, building on migrants' experiences, to move and stay. This contributes, to de-exceptionalise migrants' presence and struggles through "an ethnographic focus on the similarities between politicized subjects that are often taxonomically separated by means of the categories of migrants, religious or ethnic minorities, the (working) poor, and ordinary" citizens" (van Baar, 2017: 226); at the same time, it allows questioning narratives of the "refugee crisis" that reproduce a racialised image of migrants and that posit migration as a self-standing terrain of analysis.

Through use of the notion of the "motley crowd", Peter Linebaugh and Marcus Rediker have started from the irreducible heterogeneity of subjectivities exploring how, historically, they formed alliances. Historically, the motley crowd corresponds to the crews of the slave ships that sailed in the Atlantic – to "a mob of sailors" and slaves from different national origins that engaged in rebellions and mutinies (Linebaugh and Rediker, 2013: 211). What qualifies a motley crowd is, according to Linebaugh and Rediker, its interracial composition and "subversion of power" as the main shared goal (p. 28). They show that in the eighteenth century the motley crowd was a revolutionary subject, as it played a crucial role in urban and slave revolts. Although it would be misleading to transpose historical examples into the present to discuss collective migrant formations, Linebaugh and Rediker's reflections on the motley crowd equip us with the appropriate analytical tools for coming to grips with migrant temporary multiplicities.

While the term "assembly" is on the one hand helpful to account for the temporary alliances among migrants, as well as between migrants and citizens, between migrants and other precarious subjectivities, on the other it still partly presupposes subjects acting in concert and in an ordered way. Also, the term "assembly" entails a quite stable ground (the possibility to stay and lay claim in a given place) and a presence that is quite protracted in time. Therefore, I suggest that such an image cannot fully capture the peculiarities of collective formations, although in part it certainly does. However, this does not mean at all inclining towards an anarchic vision of collectivities. Linebaugh and Rediker's genealogy of the motley crowd allows for supplementing analyses about assemblies with, first, a deep postcolonial take on multiplicities – which brings in questions of racialised subjectivities – and, second, a different conception of heterogeneity. The adjective "motley" foregrounds the undecidability of the outcomes of temporary alliances and, at once, the criminalisation and discrediting of these collectivities, considered as non-political mobs. Hence, we can speak of the motley formations that we see at play in many border zones in Europe, as migrant multiplicities that struggle to stay in a place, occupying squares or buildings, or that struggle for moving on. In fact, the making of migration refers not only to the legal, political and economic mechanisms through which some people are subjectified and governed as "migrants" but also to the production of temporary collective subjects. Indeed, these need to be investigated in the specificity of their making, paying attention to claims and practices that cannot be codified through pre-established categories.

WHAT MAKES A MIGRANT (COLLECTIVE SUBJECTIVITY)?

A wide scholarship has explored how the institution of citizenship is recursively unsettled by migrant struggles and acts that are excluded from the scene of political space. In particular, citizenship studies literature has drawn attention to the disruptive effects of migrants who claim rights, despite being "illegal", and who appropriate their own condition of being without a status (Isin, 2009; McNevin, 2009, 2016; Nyers, 2010). Notably, Engin Isin has coined the expression "acts of citizenship" to conceptualise a non-legal meaning of citizenship, and to show how, through rights claims protests, undocumented migrants have opened up new ways of being political, undermining the exclusionary boundaries of citizenship. In this regard, Anne McNevin cautions against a normative approach to migrants' acts of refusal, resistance and escape, suggesting to ground the analysis within the material fabric of the struggles as what anticipate "without necessarily naming) the dissonance between what may be emerging as thinkable and possible on the one hand and the limits of existing analytics" (McNevin, 2013: 187). McNevin's contention helps gesturing migrants' struggles from the standpoint of the constituent subjectivities and spaces, however temporary and precarious these could be, that are generated beyond their ephemeral existence.

Overall, this literature enables elaboration on migration as an analytical lens for conceptualising and disrupting the borders of the political. That is, as these authors show, migrants' struggles and claims cannot be fully grasped as part of the pre-existing order of citizenship – for instance, by considering the migrant as the figure of the empowered citizen. On the contrary, migrant struggles should be tackled by foregrounding what disrupts and cannot be accommodated within the actual exclusionary space of citizenship. However, such a disruptive move should not be seen in opposition to operations of *constituent desubjugation*; that is, practices of resistance that consist of transformative struggles and give rise to "constituent spaces" (Mezzadra in Garelli et al., 2018). In fact, racialised subjects are often entrapped in demands for recognition but at the same time through strategic desubjectification they twist these latter into "struggles for freedom on their own terms" (Coulthard, 2014: 43).

Citizenship studies have bridged analyses of individual struggles with considerations of collective movements and the emergence of collective political subjectivities. While in most migration literature there is quite a lot of emphasis on individual migrant agency, and in this way methodological individualism is reinforced, these analyses have paid attention to the formation of collective subjectivities that exceed the people and the population (Isin, 2018), and that are "characterised by their ambiguous grounding in mobility" (Andrijasevic et al., 2012: 412). As a third point, such an insight into the political subjectivities that emerge out of collective or individual migrant struggles for rights, enables circumventing the discourse on migrants as mere lives to be rescued, as bodies to be saved. The notion of spatial disobedience draws in part from those analytical insights – in particular by highlighting the emergence of migrant collective formations, as well as individual refusals that consist of the non-acceptance of the spatial and freedom restrictions imposed by the border regime.

Nonetheless, the analysis carried out here partly differs from such a conceptual framework, as it points to the pitfalls of a citizen gaze on migration. More precisely, instead of focusing on visible and deliberate protests, I am interested in exploring more fleeting and unruly migrant struggles. That is, the empirical examples given by the citizenship studies scholar reproduce an image of citizenry politics, although from the position of those who are formally excluded from it. On the contrary, I aim at interrogating and grasping the politicalness of migration collective formations and individual refusals that cannot be fully translated into the language and spaces of citizenship. Another salient element to consider in relation to migrants' spatial disobediences concerns the temporality of the struggles. Indeed, the notion of "act", as it is conceived in the idea of acts of citizenship, is related to a certain disruptive moment, as clearly explained by Engin Isin: acts, he argues, "create a scene, which means both performance and disturbance. Acts are ruptures or beginnings" (2009: 379).

Acts, and the concrete examples of acts of citizenship reported in the literature, are often associated with punctual moments. Although the temporal dimension of borders, and their irreducibility to a spatial one, is remarked by authors – see, for instance, Nyers (2010) – the temporality of (migrant) struggles is not likewise analysed in depth nor something that these works account for. The focus on "moments" (Johnson, 2012) of migrant irruption onto the public space overshadows both fleeting spaces opened up by migrant struggles and enduring conditions of struggle, where the disruptive effect cannot be easily captured. Indeed, the politicalness of migrant collective formations cannot be grasped only through the lens of punctual disruptions. In some contexts, it is precisely the persistent and unauthorised presence of a migrant group that generates unsettling changes or that eventually disrupts, even if temporarily, the actual hierarchies of subjects in a given space. Therefore, both the persistence in time of some unauthorised migrant collective formations and, in a specular way, the fleeting character of many spaces opened up by migrant movements make of temporality a fundamental issue for dealing with migrant struggles.

The description of punctual moments of migrants' agency and of their irruption into the political scene is ultimately related to a specific politics of visibility, which pivots around the hyper-visibilisation of acts of protest and those occasions when migrants break the silence. However, such a *script of struggle* does not capture the wide heterogeneity of modes through which migrants strategically deal with visibility and invisibility. In particular, migrants' struggles for movement – that is when these concern the right to mobility – are often carried out by the migrants themselves by trying not to be too visible, or not being visible at all. "We are not going back": the slogan chanted and written on the banners by the migrants blocked in Ventimiglia in 2015 was in fact the most visible moment of a struggle for movement that was enacted on the sly. Visible and more opaque modes of struggling to cross borders have not been mutually exclusive of each other. Nor does such a focus on the nuances of (in)visibility mean mythologising the dimension of the ephemeral or the imperceptible.

On this point, Papadopolous and Tsianos have questioned what they call "the 2R axiom" (2008: 3) of rights and representation, showing that these two terms do not encapsulate the multiplicity of migrant struggle, most of which resists being framed in terms of rights as such. In particular, they cogently notice that the condition for an inclusive dimension of rights and representation to take place is the exclusion of some – that can be many – from it. In the same wake, they have pointed out the limits of an analysis exclusively centred on visibility, remarking that imperceptibility is the condition in which many migrants find themselves or sometimes also strive for. Nevertheless, they tend to emphasise migrants being under the threshold of visibility as a desirable condition or as something that they are looking for. Instead, I caution here against any praise for the ephemeral and the invisible, suggesting that an analytical and political distinction should be traced between tactics of invisibility – or conditions of forced invisibility – on the one hand, and the will to remain politically and socially invisible on the other.

Migrant collective formations might be absent on the political scene even if they are physically there – as long as their claims are not heard by anyone, or if their presence in space is just ignored. The argument that I push forward here is that we should move away from binary oppositions – such as viability vs invisibility, struggles for mobility vs claims to stay, migrant agency versus migrants as victims.

First, methodologically this involves refusing to fit subjects into identity categories, like the citizen, the foreigner and, to some extent, the refugee. In fact, more than assuming that "the language of citizenship is still that which best encapsulates the language of political subjectivity" (Nyers and Rygiel, 2012: 11), I instead start from disarticulating connections between subjectivities and their institutional representation. Second, it entails assuming as non-mutually exclusive those that are posited as binary oppositions. For instance, as far as the diptych visibility/invisibility is concerned, it is worth noticing how migrants tactically deal with visibility and with the condition of becoming or being invisible, without taking this as a permanent status, or as something that they identify with or strive for.

Up to now I have reflected upon migrant spatial disobediences and temporary collective migrant formations, analysing which political subjectivities emerge and, reversely, how categories like "agency" and "political subjectivity" should be rethought in light of migrant struggles for movement. Yet migration is not a self-standing object or phenomenon. Nor should the image of the enclosed community be replicated in order to think of temporary migrant multiplicities: the risk behind that is ultimately to corroborate a neat distinction between migrants (collectives) and non-migrants (mobilisations). In fact, the interrogation on migrant collective formations is also a question about the spaces, claims and composition of wider struggles – against precarity and for reappropriating the urban space. This is what in a slightly different way Balibar (2010) has defined as a movement for the democratisation of borders. These authors have explored how the exclusionary boundaries between citizens and non-citizens, as well as those of the democratic space itself, are unsettled by the presence and claims of unauthorised migrants, and by the transversal alliances with citizens. Here, I draw attention to the way in which some struggles have reshaped and opened up political spaces. Rutvica Andrijasevic and Bridget Anderson assert that "the reading of movements of migration in terms of collective migrant subjectivity" involves grappling with "its real political dynamics and on the ruptures it produces within the existing order" (2009: 634).

MIGRANT SHARED GEOGRAPHIES AND THE POLITICAL MEMORY OF STRUGGLES

How have migrant collective formations redrawn the historical geographies of Europe? What traces and political legacies have migrants' spatial disobediences left, beyond the punctual moment of refusals? Many of the temporary migrant multiplicities that carried on their struggle for movement or for staying, in different European border zones, "vanished" after weeks or months of protest, as they were evicted or because they managed to cross the border or find a temporary solution in the country. Indeed, the conundrums of migrant spatial disobediences rely in part on the difficulties of retaining the memory of those collective experiences and movements. To put it differently, there is a partial or total absence in the archives and political memory of Europe of migrant collective struggles and experiences that reshaped many European spaces, with their claims and presence. Grappling with those migrant collective experiences and spaces of struggle, it is worth asking what are their political legacies and what is left, beyond their fleeting and ephemeral character. The re-activation of a shared memory of collective struggles and solidarity practices is ultimately what political theorists has left unaddressed.

Therefore, far from emphasising the temporariness and elusiveness per se, I ask what has been sedimented over time about those struggles, at the level of political memory and spatial inscription. Raising such a question involves moving beyond a containerisation of migration; that is, avoiding taking migration and migrant struggles as something that happens disconnected from the social context and modes of political activism where it takes place. The Alpine migrant passage that I briefly described in Chapter 2 is a case in point: the transnational migrant solidarity networks that have been built across the two sides of the Alps constituted a crucial mobile infrastructure of support for the migrants who were trying to cross from Italy to France. That citizen mobilisation – in a political moment when both in France and in Italy the right-wing, populist and racist parties gained centre stage – was partly sustained on a local level by some municipalities (Briancon in France, Bardonecchia and Oulx in Italy) and was enacted without much clamour or media visibility. Although the channels of support across the Alps were not totally clandestine, they were not even under the spotlight of the media; indeed, the goal was less to lay public claims about states' duty of hospitality than to facilitate migrants in passing and in demanding asylum.In the village of Claviere on the Alps, on the Italian side of the French–Italian border, in March 2019 a group of activists and locals occupied a room inside the church, renaming that place "Chez Jesus – occupied shelter". The strategic choice of the name depended on the opposition of the priest to the occupation but in solidarity with the migrants: in order not to be evicted, the activists defined the shelter as a sanctuary space. Inside that room, where the migrants in transit used to stop for one night or more, before trying to cross – or after being pushed back at the border – the activists showed a map to any group of migrants who reached the shelter. The mapping-orienting activity was for explaining to the migrants where and how to cross, which paths should be used and which ones were to be avoided, and so on; one hand-written map for migrants – with the main dangers and tips – and a traditional map of the mountain paths were used together for illustrating the doable crossing to them. The occupation of the church in Claviere and the counter-mapping activities conducted there – to dodge the cartography of police control – are examples of transversal alliances between migrants and citizens that unsettle the hierarchies and the top-down relationships that characterise humanitarian actions.

These mobile and temporary infrastructures of migrant solidarity across borders do not only travel through spaces but also over time. By that, I refer to the political memory of struggles that has been sedimented over the last few decades in the Alpine valleys and that recently has been reactive in support of the migrants. In particular on the Italian side of the frontier, the Susa Valley has been historically characterised by intensive and participated mobilisations against the building of a mortuary in the seventies, and against the construction of the high-speed train since the nineties (NoTav movement). Before that, the Susa Valley was well known in Italy for the resistance in the forties against the Germans occupiers during the Second World War. This retrieved political memory of solidarity practices speaks to the temporality of the struggle that, as I mentioned earlier in the chapter, tends to be overshadowed and under-theorised both in political theory and in migration scholarship.

The solidarity practices that have been transmitted over time have been intertwined with the practical knowledges shared among migrants about how to cross in that specific area; migrant spatial disobediences and the solidarity practices that have been reactivated in the present constitute to some extent a shared mobile political terrain which exists, as fleeting albeit as it could be, and even if no trace of it is left in the official archives (Tazzioli and Walters, 2019). In this sense, produced out of these fleeting experiences of crossing and solidarity with those in transit are forms of temporary mobile commoning (Linebaugh, 2009). By mobile commoning I refer here to a set of practical knowledges and sedimented experiences of struggle that shape some specific spaces in Europe and that meanwhile also travel to other spaces, being reactivated according to the specificity of the local contexts. I prefer to use the expression *unstable mobile commoning* instead of "mobile commons" (Trimikliniotis et al., 2014) in order to highlight the processual dimension – that is to say, it is constantly subjected to processes of making and unmaking. Unstable mobile commoning is not only at risk of vanishing – as its continuity over time is far from being granted. Moreover, its spatial dimension is fundamentally ambivalent: it is the result of spatially grounded experiences that shape a place over time; but at the same time it is spatially non-fixed, as it can be reactivated in other places, as a shared political memory of solidarity practices. The difficulty of retracing traces of what is left after the end of solidarity practices on the move is that they mainly concern migrants in transit, who are not there to stay and struggle in a given place, nor to lay claims on the public scene but, rather, to cross on the sly. In places like Claviere, we cannot even speak of collective formations – as migrants try to stop as little as possible – rather of migrant multiplicities on the move. Many experiences of solidarity with the migrants in transit come to an end as long as the frontier moves somewhere else; that is, when state authorities enforce border controls due to migrants' passages, and thus migrants try via another crossing point. A different case is represented by those migrant collective formations that define themselves in relation to a place, struggling in a visible way for a protracted time in a city. This is the case of Lampedusa in Berlin – a group of migrants from different African countries who fled Libya in 2012. They all reached Germany after landing in Italy, at different moments: thus, Lampedusa was the common spatial denominator of a shared geography that all of them undertook, and Berlin the space where they struggled to stay. The group camped in the Orianenplatz square in the centre of Berlin, which became the geographical signpost of their struggle. As Elena Fontanari has noticed in her ethnographic account of the Lampedusa in Berlin group, the term "Lampedusa" designated at the same time a shared geographical history – all migrants who fled the war in Libya and reached Europe to claim asylum – and the fact that "borders are not just on the island of Lampedusa, instead they are also within the European territory" (2016: 21). Therefore, Lampedusa represented at the same time the common gate into Europe and a border zone that migrants find everywhere in the European space. Since the outbreak of the Arab uprisings and the war in Libya, the Lampedusa in Hamburg (2012) and the Collective of Tunisians from Lampedusa in Paris (2011) have been two other temporary collective formations that named themselves on the basis of a *shared geographical history of migration*. In these cases, the names of these shared geographies circulated across Europe, constituting a political memory of the move by collective migrant struggles to find a space to stay. Therefore, drawing on Chandra Mohanty's work on solidarity across borders, traversal alliances – in the above-mentioned cases between migrants and non-migrants – are crafted not only on the basis of a politics of the governed but also by building on common differences (Mohanty, 2003).

A MAP ARCHIVE OF EUROPE'S MIGRANT SPACES

The geopolitical map of Europe is the main visual tool through which methodological nationalism is recursively reproduced in migration research. Yet, such a map is evidently not the map of the spaces criss-crossed and produced by the migrant: these latter can be defined as migrant spaces, in the twofold sense of spaces that are not fixed – at least for the migrants who move on or those who are displaced – and of spaces that pertain to migrants' experiences. In fact, migrant spatial disobediences often remain below the threshold of political visibility and the memory of their existence is usually lost, it not being part of the archives of Europe's history. However, despite their partial political invisibility, migrants' spatial disobediences are not mere ephemeral movements; they also produce spaces of liveability and collective struggles, and these experiences are sedimented over time, even if their actual existence is fleeting and brief. Similarly, those spaces of control and containment that are also the outcomes of border-enforcement measures leave some kind of trace on the territory; for instance, irrespective of migrants' current presence, places like Eidomeni – the Greek border zone at the frontier with Macedonia – Calais and Ventimiglia are carved out in the European history of migration and borders.

What I want to suggest is through a counter-mapping gaze the existence of ephemeral places of containment, movement and struggle can be brought to the fore. Such a counter-mapping approach is at the same time a cartographic experiment and a theoretical-epistemic perspective that foregrounds and keeps a memory of spaces that are invisibilised and whose traces get lost. This *counter-map of the European space* brings to the fore fleeting spaces that are not visible on the geopolitical cartography. Such a map would highlight unofficial encampments and migrant spaces that have been produced as an effect of migration and border policies (like Calais), as well as of migrants' practices of movement. Some of these spaces of transit (like the rail station in Milan) have then become places of containment (like Ventimiglia, after France's suspension of Schengen). Some of these are zones inside European cities that have been both spaces-refuge for the migrants in transit and spaces of control. Others are self-managed places, like the Refugee City Plaza Hotel, or squares and public spaces that have been sites of migrant struggles for some time (like Orianenplatz in Berlin). Temporary encampments, practices of spatial occupation and the opening of collective spaces of livability counter to and resist the multiplication of hostile environments and forced evictions. These spatial struggles cannot be grasped through a geopolitical lens nor by keeping a focus on national borders and the tactics states adopted for controlling these latter. Rather, they require studying what Huub van Baar defined as processes of "evictability" (van Baar, 2017), local forms of expulsion and spatial tactics of deterrence.

Drawing attention to the traces left by these encampments and to the irregular pace of their emergence and disappearance it becomes possible to draw what I call a *minor cartography of vanishing refugee spaces*. Such a map would be a constitutively opaque and missing cartography, which would bring to the fore the spatial and temporal traces of heterogeneous encampments. By highlighting the fundamentally fleeting dimension of migrant spaces of refuge and confinement we should not conclude the impossibility of an archive of encampments nor the total disappearance of the memory and the existence of places that have been evicted or shut down. Spaces of refuge and transit often crystallise or remain alive in the collective memory due to a reiterated re-emergence of these spaces, upon eviction or, in the case of institutional camps, after being officially closed. Many of these places blur with the surrounding urban areas and cannot be approached through the lens of extraterritoriality. What I want to suggest is an ethnography of vanishing spaces, which brings attention to temporary migration sites where a certain historical memory of struggles has been sedimented and needs to be reactivated into the present. This echoes the idea of knowledges and practices that have been discredited, marginalised and overshadowed in the official historical archives (Foucault, 2003). Re-mapping Europe, as a space for migrants' and refugees' temporary spaces requires navigating the interstices of the produced opacity of migrant encampments, to grasp the persistence of camps' traces, as spatial landmarks in migrants' enacted geographies. Thus, it entails bringing into maps the dimension of temporality, accounting for and keeping alive the temporariness of these spaces. Yet, more than mapping official refugee camps or reception centres, the crafting of the refugees' European map involves research on unofficial spaces that have been produced as an effect of migration and border policies, as well as of migrants' practices of movements.

CONCLUSION

This chapter has highlighted that the unbearable character of migrants' spatial disobediences depends on migrants' refusal to comply with the spatial restrictions imposed on them, as well as with the impossibility of choosing where to stay. In a nutshell, it is the very nexus between (claim to) asylum and practices of freedom that appears untenable to the states (De Genova et al., 2018). However, spatial disobediences do not necessarily consist of struggles against border policies, nor are they narrowed to a rights claim frame. Spatial disobediences are enacted through performed geographies as well as through modes of active subtraction and withdrawal. Throughout the chapter the vocabulary about political subjectivities – resistance, struggle, agency – has been revisited and problematised in light of migrants' practices of spatial disobedience. A thorough analysis of migration policies and critical knowledge production around borders and mobility involves engaging in a subtle and nuanced diagnostic of power relations as well as their constant transformations. For instance, as the opening vignette about the migrants who hijacked the merchant ship illustrates, migrant multiplicities in the Mediterranean are currently subjected to kidnapping strategies enforced by the states to hamper them from disembarking in Europe. Kidnapping, in its multiple articulations, appears today as one of the main tactics used by states to contain and obstruct migration movements, transforming refugees into hostages of the EU politics and shipwrecked subjects into seditious individuals. In so doing, rescue as such has become a form of capture. Therefore, in order to disrupt the widespread *economy of migrant kidnapping* we need to interrogate how to connect these with the spaces *before crossing* and *after landing* where migrants remain entrapped. Paying attention to migrants' collective and active refusals, as the episode of the hijacked vessel shows, enables moving beyond a minimalistic biopolitics that is centred around the binary opposition between saving lives/letting people die.

NOTE

1   In *Signs and Machines* (2014) Maurizio Lazzarato writes a critique of contemporary poststructuralist philosophy, and in particular of authors such as Judith Butler, Paolo Virno, Jacques Ranciere and Ernesto Laclau, accusing them of "logocentrism", that is of considering language as the main vector of subjectivation and resistance.

Conclusion

The Algerian sociologist Abdelmalek Sayad famously argued that "thinking about immigration means thinking about the state" (2018: 166). The state-thought and the state-gaze on migration are surreptitiously replicated in most of the migration literature as well as in the "refugee crisis"¹ narrative. As this book has shown, some notions of the political theory lexicon, such as "collective subjects" and "individual", are similarly questioned insofar as they are approached by taking migration as an analytical lens. Hence, thinking about migration means thinking about the figures of subjectivity that populate the contemporary polis – the citizens, collective political subjectivities and individuals. Taking migration as a litmus paper for rethinking the lexicon of (political) subjectivities is connected to another methodological assumption that Sayad pushed forward: that is, migration "constitutes the limit of what constitutes the national state" (2018: 160). Therefore, rethinking political subjectivities via migration entails questioning the margins of the state and its constant reshuffling. This work has engaged in unsettling the notions of collective and individual subjectivities building on empirical material collected at different frontiers of Europe – at the French–Italian and Swiss–Italian borders, in Calais, in Paris, in Sicily and on the Greek islands. I did not carry out a comparative analysis of this multiplicity of sites, nor did I intend to provide an overarching overview of Europe's border regime. Rather, I have selected sites that are significant for the ways in which migrants are governed, as well as for the experiences of collective migrants' struggles. Although all of these sites have their own peculiarity, the book has engaged in putting these places into resonance, showing patterns of similarity among them in light of the political technologies deployed for containing unruly mobility and highlighting what each of them reveals about *the making of migration*. The *making of* retains a constitute duplicity, since migration is both the subject and the object of it: *making of* refers to the political, material and legal processes through which some subjects are racialised and governed as migrants; and, at the same time, migrants have been making and opening up spaces of liveability and struggle through their subjective drives and unauthorised presence. Throughout the book, I have used what can be called a chiasmatic structure; that is, I have investigated multiplicities and singularities by looking at processes of subjectivation and subjection on the one side, and at the twofold dynamic of objectivation–subjectivation on the other which shapes the individuals. Through such a focus on the making of migration, I did not aim at tracing a neat and bounded terrain of research sharply divided from others. On the contrary, in highlighting the political technologies by which some subjects are racialised and governed as migrants, or managed as unruly collectivities, it has engaged in de-fetishisng migration. In the remaining pages, and in the guise of a conclusion, I sketch out some of the main implications that stem from such a focus on multiplicities and singularities, by starting with the conundrums of critique; that is, by asking what a critical knowledge about migration governmentality could look like today.

A critical engagement with migrant multiplicities and singularities involves considering both the material and biopolitical mechanisms through which migrants are divided and controlled, and the level of discourses and representation – e.g. how migrants are criminalised and discredited as "mobs" or "swarms". Yet, a critical reflection on multiplicities and singularities should not be narrowed down to the political technologies deployed for governing migration only. The grouping and dividing of migrants is part of states' tactics for hampering the emergence of broader and transversal collective formations whose claims and spatial disobediences often cannot be contained within the conceptual coordinates of political theory. The violent forms of containment, the production of cramped spaces in which migrants are choked have proliferated, in a context that is characterised by the "disarticulation of the geographical coordinates of the process of the European integration" (Mezzadra, 2018b: 927). Simultaneously, an enquiry into migrants' subjectivities and mechanisms of objectivation that shape and target migrants individually enables our opening up a space to ask "Who is a migrant today in Europe?" Therefore, through a focus on the *making of migration*, the categories of multiplicities and singularities might be unpacked and put on the move looking at the materiality of the struggles, power relations and labelling processes by which some subjects are produced as migrants and collective formations are deemed as non-political.

MULTIPLICITIES AND CRITIQUE

Migration has been tackled here both as an object of study and as an analytical lens for rethinking subjectivities as well as collective formations that are not reducible to populations. However, in what way can such an analytical lens be used? How can we undo through that the predicaments of the "refugee crisis" narrative? In fact, the methodological gesture that consists in rethinking categories of political theory in the light of migration helps, I suggest, in reopening the space of critique not framed – exclusively – in terms of bringing evidence. What does it mean to produce a critical knowledge about migration governmentality, in a context that is saturated by the media exposure of border violence and in which states blatantly violate human rights and international law? What if, as Saidiya Hartman contended, the efficacy of violence depends at the same time on its opacity and transparency, while the exposure of the most horrific violence contributes to the foreclusion of the suffering of the other – in our case of the migrants (Hartman, 1997)?

What is the "diagnostic of the present" (Roitman, 2013: 4) through which we think critique? In the book *Anti-Crisis* Janet Roitman warns against the tendency to frame critique from within the taken-for-granted register of "the crisis". If we assume politics and the temporality of the crisis, the ways in which we conceive critique would be normative and functionalist-oriented without questioning the epistemic categories that underpin it: "when crisis is posited as an a priori, it obviates accounts of positive, pragmatic spaces of calculative possibility" (Roitman, 2013: 13). Thus, Roitman invites us to disjoin critique from crisis and to reopen spaces of political action and knowledge production that are not saturated by the narrative and the temporality of the crisis. The feminist historian Joan Scott has similarly engaged in an analysis about the pitfalls of critique, arguing that critique should not be confused with "an endorsement of objectivity" (Scott, 2007: 23): critique, she contends, consists of destabilising norms, retracing the historical and political conditions through which specific power dynamics become naturalised and unquestioned, in order to then engage in a transformative politics. In fact, according to Scott, critique is predicated upon an ethical engagement which consists of "staying open to the future", instead of fixing in advance the political outcomes and the evidence to provide proof. It is from such an analytical perspective that Scott cautions against the involuntary reproduction of the very terms the discourse or the object that we criticise is built upon. Roitman and Scott's insights help us in tailoring *the disquiets and limits of critique* that concern knowledge production about migration.

The hyper-visibilisation and blatant exposure of certain violences as well as human rights violations, together with the invisibilisation of others – such as the ghost migrant shipwrecks in the Mediterranean – lead us to rethink the critique and critical knowledge production on migration. This book does not provide answers to these interrogations around critique and critical knowledge, nor do I think that such an interrogation can be solved only from within academia. In fact, only building on the material fabric of struggles – for social justice and movement- knowledge production on migration – rethinks the meaning and the functioning of critique.

The current debate about migrants' border deaths is dominated by a discussion of sea-rescue operations in the Mediterranean, and about states' duties and responsibilities in saving migrants in distress. The escalation of border violence across Europe leads us to mobilise against states that let migrants die in the Mediterranean, and against the increasing criminalisation of refugees and of migrant solidarity networks. Through asymmetric cooperation with third countries, EU member states do not "just" let migrants die; they engage in an active politics of containment, preventing them from crossing the Mediterranean or, better, from becoming visible on the scene of rescue (Cassarino, 2018). In such a context, humanitarian actions at sea have become a terrain of struggle between states, established NGOs, independent actors and citizen organisations. However, the urgency of acting in front of states' violation of the duty to rescue people in distress at sea should not be disjoined from a critique of the geopolitical and biopolitical predicaments upon which the mobility of some is considered "illegitimate". The hierarchies of mobility across the world produced by the global visa regime are in fact at the core of *the making of migration,* that is of the discursive, legal and administrative mechanisms through which some subjects are racialised and governed as "migrants".

The high exposure of border violence in the media and its increasing normalisation have partly saturated the space of critique and intervention. The monopolisation of the public and political debate on migrant deaths in the Mediterranean has twisted critical analyses towards a minimal biopolitical discourse about saving lives at sea vs letting them die. At the same time, the denunciation of deaths at sea is confronted with unequal *geographies of (un) greviability*: while there is uneven media attention paid to deadly shipwrecks that take place close to the European shores, ghost shipwrecks, violence in the Libyan detention centres and migrant deaths in the Sahara Desert are the object of invisbilisation and tend to be placed at a distance.

As I have sketched out in Chapter 2, a focus on migrants' forms of subjectivation and subjection is a crucial starting point for rethinking critique beyond the quest for objectivity and evidence on the one hand and denunciation on the other. In fact, rearticulating critique by building on migrants' claims and spatial disobediences helps to shed light on the specific effects of subjection that migrants are targeted by. Saying that means conceiving critique in connection with the production of the intolerable – or better of a shared intolerable, that builds on transversal mechanisms of prevarication and destitution that might affect citizens and non-citizens, according to different modes and degrees. Thus, the production of critique and ethical-political moves of desubjugation and refusal are mutually intertwined, although it is not a matter of a "heroic history of struggles, but of a fragile, a very fragile series of gestures" (Artieres, 2013: 347) that make something appear as intolerable.

Recalling Wendy Brown's argument, it is precisely when critique appears as anachronistic with respect the staged emergencies and crises that we need to rise again its salience and reinvent operations of critique – "to contest the very senses of time invoked to declare critique untimely" (2005: 4). Critique is not about being out of the present and out of time. On the contrary, "untimely critique insists on alternative possibilities and perspectives in a seemingly closed political and epistemological universe. It becomes a nonviolent mode of exploding the present" (2005: 15). As far as migration is concerned, this could involve undoing the biopolitical predicaments of the political debate about letting migrants die at sea or rescuing them. More broadly, conceived in this way, critique is connected to a methodological move that recursively disjoins migration from the conceptual and political framework of governmentality – that is, migration assumed as a problem and as a phenomenon that "we" should govern. The nexus between migration and governmentality is at the core of a series of epistemic and political articulations that are taken for granted when we speak about migration and that broadly concern the silent hierarchical racialisation of lives (De Genova, 2018). In order for critique not to remain an individual and isolated ethico-political gesture, it is fundamental to question the implicit collective subject or public of critique itself. Indeed, by whom is formed the "we" which is implicitly addressed and posited at the same time as object and subject of a critical analysis? In other words, in exposing and denouncing migrant deaths in the Mediterranean we should interrogate the virtual or actual collective subject that might be the public to whom the critical analysis is addressed and the "we" that articulates the critique. Hence, in the practice of critique the collective subject is questioned and produced at the same time. For instance, in the analyses about migrant deaths at sea, the European public appears as the subject which is implicitly assumed as the referent and the actor at the same time, while it might be an opportunity to rethink and enact other collective subjects.

COUNTER-GEOGRAPHIES OF TEMPORARY MULTIPLICITIES

The multiplication of border closures and the conditions of protracted confinement that migrants are subjected to across Europe and its external frontiers has reshaped migrants' "geographies of violence" (Doel, 2017). Calais, Lampedusa, Ventimiglia, Lesvos, Eidomeni, Marseille, Briancon, Berlin: the geographical signposts and hotspots of the so-called refugee crisis are in fact places of containment, control and protracted strandedness and, at the same time, places which have been reshaped by collective resistances, migrant struggles and transversal alliances.

Thus, the cartography of Europe's spaces of control should be confronted with a counter-geography of precarious mobile commons and a fragmented infrastructure of solidarity that oppose measures of migration containment and criminalisation by opening up safe spaces (Mitchell and Sparke, 2018). To be retained are precisely the sedimented practical knowledge of struggles for social justice that might be reactivated in the present. The attempt to build transversal alliances challenges the containerisation of critique into the discursive field of migration only. Instead of reproducing the asymmetrical division between rescuers and rescued subjects, it shifts the focus towards shared claims, between migrants and citizens, that bring together common needs and rights: such as the right to choose where to live, the right to a house and to mobility. In fact, a shift from an exclusive focus on migration assumed as a self-standing field towards the mechanisms of precarisation and the inequalities in getting access to education, to work and mobility and lack of rights, contributes to building transversal alliances that are not seen as struggles *of* and *for* the migrants only. An insight into the making of migration has enabled us to question the numeric dimension of collective subjects. On this, it is worth highlighting the discrepancy between the huge numbers of the so-called "refugee crisis" as part of the states' narrative on migration, and the scanty multiplicities of migrants that are often targeted at different border zones of Europe – for instance, in Calais, in Ventimiglia or in the Italian and Greek hotspots. Nevertheless, if on the one hand it is important to highlight such a numeric discrepancy – between the numbers of the "crisis" and the scanty multiplicities of migrants who gather at the borders – on the other it is likewise fundamental to deal with the ambiguities of numbers. A political genealogy of the mob has shown that the very unauthorised presence of migrants at some border zones as well as collective refusals of giving fingerprints appear to be "a problem" according to a "seeing like a state" (Scott, 1998) perspective. The political ambiguities of migrants' numbers should not be fully erased in favour of an analysis apt at proving evidence of "the few and not many" migrants who are in Europe. Indeed, as Claudia Aradau and Jef Huysmans have rightly pointed out in their political reading of the mob:

> mobility as democratic practice of the 'mob' introduces a numerical calculus of force into a political terrain that tends to be dominated by the primacy of legal reasoning [...] growing numbers of moving people also open a political terrain where the effects of global power structures need to be renegotiated. (Aradau and Huysmans, 2009: 599)

What is a multiplicity? Is it based on the actual number, or how the number is narrated politically, or how migrants' struggles and claims exceed the threshold of their tolerated presence? This book has engaged with the topic of multiplicities by bringing attention to the politicalness of migration; that is, to the battlefield that migrants' unauthorised and persistent presence opens up, between migrants and state authorities, as well as between different actors involved in containing migration. The analytical lens of migration makes it possible to deal with collective subjectivities without super imposing pre-established sociological categories. The temporariness, the heterogeneity and the "incorrigibility" (De Genova, 2010) of migrant multiplicities should lead us not only to destabilise but also to fully rethink collective subjectivities, unsettling the boundaries between what is deemed to be political and what is discredited and criminalised as non-political. Pushing this further, as Deleuze famously claimed, a minor literature is the one that is able to create certain revolutionary conditions and coefficients of deterritorialisation within a major literature; at the same time, a minor literature is the one "that becomes all the more collective" (Deleuze, 1986: 18). In fact, there are movements and subjectivities that escape the binary opposition between quantitative minority and majority, between inclusion and exclusion, as well we between agency and victimhood. These movements and unauthorised presences are not part of Europe's official archives and are deemed to be non-political, but they have actually contributed to shape Europe's space and its history of struggles. These are not only the archives of Europe but also the collective stories of the fleeting and temporary migrant multiplicities. In this sense, we should not stop asking "where could we find [...] the writings of the sans-papier, the place of those without a place, the claims of those without rights and the dignity of those without images? Where shall we find the archive of those we don't want to record and whose memory sometimes we want to kill?" (Didi-Huberman, 2012: 33). However, this is not just a story to be written. The incorrigible presence and the struggles of temporary migrant collective formations, with their visible, murmuring or concealed spatial disobediences, actively recraft the Mediterranean space.

The angle of migrant multiplicities pushes us to revisit and politicise the conceptual constellation of citizenry; indeed, a critical insight into Europe's borders involves engaging in a historical counter-geography of the political and physical spaces opened up by migrants and by the transversal alliances they established.

The making of migration, as multiplicities and singularities, sheds light on the making of mobile, contested and precarious spaces that have unsettled Europe's geography and collective political memory of struggles and transversal alliances.

References

Aas, K. F. (2005). 'Getting ahead of the game': Border technologies and the changing space of governance. In E. Zureik & M. B. Salter (eds) *Global Surveillance and Policing: Borders, Security, Identity*. Cullompton: Willan Publishing, 194–214.
Abdelnour, S. & Saeed, A. M. (2014). Technologizing humanitarian space: Darfur advocacy and the rape-stove panacea. *International Political Sociology*, 8(2): 145–163.
Abu-Lughod, L. (1990). The romance of resistance: Tracing transformations of power through Bedouin women. *American Ethnologist*, 17(1), 41–55.
Adey, P. (2006). If mobility is everything then it is nothing: Towards a relational politics of (im)mobilities. *Mobilities*, 1(1): 75–94.
Adey, P., Bissell, D., McCormack, D. & Merriman, P. (2012). Profiling the passenger. *Cultural Geographies*, 19(2): 169–193.
Agamben, G. (2014). What is a destituent power? *Environment and Planning D: Society and Space*, 32(1): 65–74.
Agier, M. (2011). *Managing the Undesirables*. New York: Polity Press.
Ajana, B. (2013). *Governing Through Biometrics: The Biopolitics of Identity*. Basingstoke: Palgrave Macmillan.
Allen, W., Anderson, B., Van Hear, N., Sumption, M., Düvell, F., Hough, J., Rose, L., Humphris, R. & Walker, S. (2018). Who counts in crises? The new geopolitics of international migration and refugee governance. *Geopolitics*, 23(1): 217–243.
Altenried, M., Bojadžijev, M., Höfler, L., Mezzadra, S. & Wallis, M. (2018). Logistical borderscapes: Politics and mediation of mobile labor in Germany after the "Summer of Migration". *South Atlantic Quarterly*, 117(2): 291–312.
Althusser, L. (1971). Ideological and repressive state apparatuses. *Lenin and Philosophy and Other Essays*. London: New Left Books.
Amoore, L. (2006). Biometric borders: Governing mobilities in the war on terror. *Political Geography*, 25(3): 336–351.
Amoore, L. (2013). *The Politics of Possibility: Risk and Security Beyond Probability*. Durham, NC: Duke University Press.
Anderson, B. (2013). *Us and Them? The Dangerous Politics of Immigration Control*. Oxford: Oxford University Press.
Anderson, B. (2017). Towards a new politics of migration? *Ethnic and Racial Studies*, 40(9): 1527–1537.
Andersson, R. (2018). Profits and predation in the human bioeconomy. *Public Culture*, 30(3): 413–439.
Andrijasevic, R., Aradau, C., Huysmans, J. & Squire, V. (2012). European citizenship unbound: Sex work, mobility, mobilisation. *Environment and Planning D: Society and Space*, 30(3): 497–514.

Andrijasevic, R. & Anderson, B. (2009). Conflicts of mobility: Migration, labour and political subjectivities. *Subjectivity*, 29(1): 363–366.

Ansems de Vries, L. & Guild, E. (2018). Seeking refuge in Europe: Spaces of transit and the violence of migration management. *Journal of Ethnic and Migration Studies*. DOI: 10.1080/1369183X.2018.1468308.

Appadurai, A. (2006). *Fear of Small Numbers: An Essay on the Geography of Anger*. Durham, NC: Duke University Press.

Aradau, C. (2004). The perverse politics of four-letter words: Risk and pity in the securitisation of human trafficking. *Millennium*, 33(2): 251–277.

Aradau, C. (2008). *Rethinking Trafficking in Women: Politics Out of Security*. New York: Springer.

Aradau, C. (2017a). Performative politics and International Relations. *New Perspectives*, 25(2): 2–7.

Aradau, C. (2017b). Assembling (non) knowledge: Security, law, and surveillance in a digital world. *International Political Sociology*, 11(4): 327–342.

Aradau, C. & Blanke, T. (2010). Governing circulation. Security and global governmentality: Globalization, governance and the state. In M. de Larrinaga & M. Doucet (eds) *Security and Global Governmentality: Globalization, Power and the State*. Basingstoke: Palgrave, 44–58.

Aradau, C. & Huysmans, J. (2009). Mobilising (global) democracy: A political reading of mobility between universal rights and the mob. *Millennium*, 37(3): 583–604.

Artières, P. (2013). *Intolérable: Groupe d'Information sur les prisons*. Paris: Gallimard.

Ataç, I., Rygiel, K. & Stierl, M. (2016). Introduction: The contentious politics of refugee and migrant protest and solidarity movements: Remaking citizenship from the margins. *Citizenship Studies*, 20(5): 527–544.

Atanasoski, N. & Vora, K. (2019). *Surrogate Humanity: Race, Robots, and the Politics of Technological Futures*. Durham, NC: Duke University Press.

Badiou, A., Didi-Huberman, G., Khiari, S., Rancière, J., Butler, J. & Bourdieu, P. (2016). *What Is a People?* New York: Columbia University Press.

Bagguley, P. and Hussain, Y. (2012). *Riotous Citizens: Ethnic Conflict in Multicultural Britain*. Burlington, VA: Ashgate.

Balibar, É. (1997). *La crainte des masses: Politique et philosophie avant et après Marx*. Paris: Galilee.

Balibar, É. (2003). The subject. *Umbr(a): Ignorance of the Law*, 1: 9–22.

Balibar, É. (2010). At the borders of citizenship: A democracy in translation? *European Journal of Social Theory*, 13(3): 315–322.

Balibar, É. (2012). *Politics and the Other Scene*. London: Verso.

Basaran, T. (2008). Security, law, borders: Spaces of exclusion. *International Political Sociology*, 2(4): 339–354.

Basaran, T. (2010). *Security, Law and Borders: At the Limits of Liberties*. Abingdon: Routledge.

Basaran, T. & Guild, E. (2016). Mobilities, ruptures, transitions. In T. Basaran, D. Bigo, E. P. Guittet & R. B. Walker (eds) *International Political Sociology: Transversal Lines*. Abingdon: Routledge, 272–275.

Baudin, G. & Genestier, P. (2006). Faut-il vraiment démolir les grands ensembles? *Espaces et sociétés*, 1: 207–222.

Beneduce, R. (2010). Archeologia del trauma. *Un'Antropologia del sottosuolo*. Bari: Laterza.
Beneduce, R. & Taliani, S. (2012). Les archives introuvables: Technologies de la citoyenneté, buréocratisation et migration. In B. Hibou (ed.) *La bureaucratisation du monde à l'ère néolibérale*. Paris: La découverte, 231–261.
Bernardot, M. (1999). Chronique d'une institution: la "sonacotra" (1956–1976). *Sociétés contemporaines*, *33*(1): 39–58.
Bernardot, M. (2008). *Camps d'étrangers*. Bellecombe-en-Bauges: Croquant.
Bernardot, M. (2009). Rafles et internement des étrangers: Les nouvelles guerres de capture. In Le Cour Grandmaison (ed.) *Douce France: Rafles, rétentions, expulsions*. Paris: Seuil, 40–65.
Betts, A. & Collier, P. (2017). *Refuge: Transforming a Broken Refugee System*. London: Penguin.
Bhandar, B. (2018). *Colonial Lives of Property: Law, Land, and Racial Regimes of Ownership*. Durham, DC: Duke University Press.
Biehl, J., Good, B. & Kleinman, A. (eds) (2007). *Subjectivity: Ethnographic Investigations*. Berkeley, CA: University of California Press.
Bigo, D. (2002). Security and immigration: Toward a critique of the governmentality of unease. *Alternatives: Global, Local, Political*, 27(1): 63–92.
Bigo, D. (2011). Freedom and speed in enlarged borderzones. In V. Squire (ed.) *The Contested Politics of Mobility: Borderzones and Irregularity*. New York: Routledge, 31–50.
Blanchard, E. (2011). *La police parisienne et les Algériens (1944–1962)*. Paris: Nouveau Monde Éditions.
Blanchard, E. (2012). Une émeute au cœur de la métropole coloniale: La Goutte d'Or, 30 juillet 1955. *Actes de la recherche en sciences sociales*, *195*: 97–111.
Bojadžijev, M. & Karakayali, S. (2010). Recuperating the sideshows of capitalism: The autonomy of migration today. *e-flux journal*, 17.
Bosteel, B. (2016). Introduction. In *What is a People?* New York: Columbia University Press, 1–19.
Boutang, Y. M. (1998). *De l'esclavage au salariat: économie historique du salariat bridé*. Paris: FeniXX.
Brighenti, A. M. (2014). *The Ambiguous Multiplicities: Materials, Episteme and Politics of Cluttered Social Formations*. London: Palgrave Macmillan.
Broeders, D. & Dijstelbloem, H. (2015). The datafication of mobility and migration management. In I. van der Ploeg & J. Pridmore (eds) *Digitizing Identities: Doing Identity in a Networked World*. New York: Routledge, 242–260.
Brown, W. (2005). *Edgework: Critical Essays on Knowledge and Politics*. Princeton, NJ: Princeton University Press.
Browne, S. (2015). *Dark Matters: On the Surveillance of Blackness*. Durham, NC: Duke University Press.
Butler, J. (2002). *Gender Trouble*. New York: Routledge.
Butler, J. (2015). *Notes Toward a Performative Theory of Assembly*. Cambridge, MA: Harvard University Press.
Butler, J., Gambetti, Z. & Sabsay, L. (eds) (2016). *Vulnerability in Resistance*. Durham, NC: Duke University Press.

Casas-Cortes, M., Cobarrubias, S. & Pickles, J. (2015). Riding routes and itinerant borders: Autonomy of migration and border externalization. *Antipode*, 47(4): 894–914.
Cassarino, J. P. (2018). Informalising EU readmission policy. In A. Ripoll Servent & F. Trauner (eds) *The Routledge Handbook of Justice and Home Affairs Research*. London: Routledge, 83–98.
Castel, R. (2000). The roads to disaffiliation: Insecure work and vulnerable relationships. *International Journal of Urban and Regional Research*, 24(3): 519–535.
Castel, R. (2003). *L'insécurité sociale: Qu'est-ce qu'être protégé*. Paris: Seuil.
Certeau, M. de (1988). *The Practice of Everyday Life*. Berkeley, CA: University of California Press.
Chamayou, G. (2018). *La société ingouvernable: Une généalogie du libéralisme autoritaire*. Paris: LaFabrique.
Chatterjee, P. (2004). *The Politics of the Governed: Reflections on Popular Politics in Most of the World*. New York: Columbia University Press.
Chow, R. (2010). *The Rey Chow Reader*. New York: Columbia University Press.
Closs-Stephens, A. (2018). National affects and the politics of knowledge: Notes from the funeral of Margaret Thatcher, unpublished paper.
Cohen, R. & Van Hear, N. (2017). Visions of Refugia: Territorial and transnational solutions to mass displacement. *Planning Theory & Practice*, 18(3), 494–504.
Conlon, D., Moran, D. & Gill, N. (eds) (2013). *Carceral Spaces: Mobility and Agency in Imprisonment and Migrant Detention*. Farnham: Ashgate.
Coulthard, G. (2014). *Red Skin, White Masks*. Minneapolis, MN: University of Minnesota Press.
Coutin, S. B. (2010). Confined within: National territories as zones of confinement. *Political Geography*, 29(4): 200–208.
Cremonesi, L., Irrera, O., Lorenzini, D. & Tazzioli, M. (2016). *Foucault and the Making of Subjects*. London: Rowman & Littlefield.
Cresswell, T. (2010). Towards a politics of mobility. *Environment and Planning D: Society and Space*, 28(1): 17–31.
Darling, J. (2016a). Asylum in austere times: Instability, privatization and experimentation within the UK asylum dispersal system. *Journal of Refugee Studies*, 29(4): 483–505.
Darling, J. (2016b). Privatising asylum: Neoliberalisation, depoliticisation and the governance of forced migration. *Transactions of the Institute of British Geographers*, 41(3): 230–243.
Darling, J. (2017). Forced migration and the city: Irregularity, informality, and the politics of presence. *Progress in Human Geography*, 41(2), 178–198.
Das, V. (2004). The signature of the state: The paradox of illegibility In V. Das, D. Poole, V. Das & D. Poole (eds) *Anthropology in the Margins of the State*. Santa Fe, NM: School of American Research Press, 225–252.
Das, V. (2006). *Life and Words: Violence and the Descent into the Ordinary*. Berkley, CA: University of California Press.
Davidson, A. I. (2004). *The Emergence of Sexuality: Historical Epistemology and the Formation of Concepts*. Cambridge, MA: Harvard University Press.
De Barros, F. (2005). Des "Français musulmans d'Algérie" aux "immigrés". *Actes de la recherche en sciences sociales*, 4: 26–53.
De Biasi, R. (1998). The policing of hooliganism in Italy. In D. Della Porta & H. R. Reiter (eds) *Policing Protest: The Control of Mass Demonstrations in Western Democracies*. Minneapolis, MN: University of Minnesota Press, 210–227.

De Genova, N. (2002). Migrant "illegality" and deportability in everyday life. *Annual Review of Anthropology*, 31: 419–447.
De Genova, N. (2010). The queer politics of migration: Reflections on "illegality" and incorrigibility. *Studies in Social Justice*, 4(2): 101–126.
De Genova, N. (2013). Spectacles of migrant "illegality": The scene of exclusion, the obscene of inclusion. *Ethnic and Racial Studies*, 36(7): 1180–1198.
De Genova, N. (2016). The European question: Migration, race, and postcoloniality in Europe. *Social Text*, 34(3): 75–102.
De Genova, N. (2018). The "migrant crisis" as racial crisis: Do Black lives matter in Europe? *Ethnic and Racial Studies*, 41(10): 1765–1782.
De Genova, N., Garelli, G. & Tazzioli, M. (2018). Autonomy of asylum? Undoing the refugee crisis script. *South Atlantic Quarterly*, 117(2): 239–265.
De Genova, N., Mezzadra, S. & Pickles, J. (2015). New keywords: Migration and borders. *Cultural Studies*, 29(1): 55–87.
De Genova, N. & Tazzioli, M. (eds) (2016). Europe/crisis: New keywords of "the crisis" in and of 'Europe'. *Near Futures Online*, 1: 1–45.
de Goede, M. (2018). The chain of security. *Review of International Studies*, 44(1), 24–42.
DeCerteau, M. (1988). *The Practice of Everyday Life*. Berkley, CA: University of California.
Deleuze, G. & Guattari, F. (1986). *Kafka: Toward a Minor Literature* (Vol. 30). Minneapolis, MN: University of Minnesota Press.
Deleuze, G. & Guattari, F. (1987). *A Thousand Plateaus*. Minneapolis, MN: University of Minnesota Press.
Della Porta, D. and Reiter, H. R. (eds) (1998). *Policing Protest: The Control of Mass Demonstrations in Western Democracies*. Minneapolis, MN: University of Minnesota Press.
Derrida, J. (2005). *Rogues: Two Essays on Reason*. Stanford, CA: Stanford University Press.
Desrosières, A. (1993) *La politique des grands nombres: histoire de la raison statistique*. Paris: La Découverte.
Didi-Huberman, G. (2012). *Peuples exposés, peuples figurants: l'œil de l'histoire, 4*. Paris: Éditions de Minuit.
Dijstelbloem, H., Van Reekum, R. & Schinkel, W. (2017). Surveillance at sea: The transactional politics of border control in the Aegean. *Security Dialogue*, 48(3): 224–240.
Doel, M. (2017). *Geographies of Violence: Killing Space, Killing Time*. London: Sage.
Dorlin, E. (2017). *Se défendre: une philosophie de la violence*. Paris: Zones.
DuBois, W. E. B. (1903). *The Souls of Black Folk*. Chicago, IL: AC McClurg.
Elden, S. (2007). Governmentality, calculation, territory. *Environment and Planning D: Society and Space*, 25(3), 562–580.
Elden, S. (2010). Land, terrain, territory. *Progress in Human Geography*, 34(6): 799–817.
Elden, S. (2017). Legal terrain: The political materiality of territory. *London Review of International Law*, 5(2): 199–224.
Engels, F. (2015). *The Peasant War in Germany*. Abingdon: Routledge.
Fanon, F. (1965). *Black Skin, White Masks*. New York: Grove.
Fanon, F. (2007). *The Wretched of the Earth*. New York: Grove/Atlantic.
Fanon, F. (2011). Condotte di confessione in Nord-Africa. In *Decolonizzare la follia*. Verona: OmbreCorte, 123–126.
Fassin, D. (2005). Compassion and repression: The moral economy of immigration policies in France. *Cultural Anthropology*, 20(3): 362–387.

Fassin, D. (2007). Humanitarianism as a politics of life. *Public Culture*, *19*(3): 499–520.
Fassin, D. (2011a). Policing borders, producing boundaries: The governmentality of immigration in dark times. *Annual Review of Anthropology*, *40*: 213–226.
Fassin, D. (2011b). *Humanitarian Reason: A Moral History of the Present*. Berkeley, CA: University of California Press.
Fassin, D. (2014). *Ripoliticizzare il mondo: Studi antropologici sulla vita, il corpo e la morale*. Verona: Ombre Corte.
Fontanari, E. (2016). Soggettività en transit: (im) mobilità dei rifugiati in Europa tra sistemi di controllo e pratiche quotidiane di attraversamento dei confini. *Mondi migranti*, *1*(1): 39–60.
Foucault, M. (1974). Émergence des équipements collectifs: État d'avancement des travaux. Available at: https://ici-et-ailleurs.org/contributions/politique-et-subjectivation/article/emergence-des-equipements (last accessed 22 December 2018).
Foucault, M. (1977). *Discipline and Punish*. New York: Vintage.
Foucault, M. (1981). Is it useless to revolt? *Philosophy & Social Criticism*, *8*: 2–4.
Foucault, M. (1982). The subject and power. *Critical Inquiry*, *8*(4): 777–795.
Foucault, M. (1984). "Foucault". *Dictionnaires des Philosophes*. Available at: https://foucault.info/documents/foucault.biography/ (last accessed 20 December 2018).
Foucault, M. (1986). Omnes et singulatim: Towards a critique of political reason. *Le debat*, *4*: 5–36.
Foucault, M. (1998). *The Will to Knowledge: The History of Sexuality*, Vol. I. Harmondsworth: Penguin.
Foucault, M. (2000a). Methodologie pour la connaissance du monde: comment se débarrasser du Marxisme. In *Dits et Ecrits*, II, Paris: Gallimard, 595–617.
Foucault, M. (2000b). Pouvoir et strategies. In *Dits et Ecrits, II*: Paris, Gallimard, 418–428.
Foucault, M. (2000c). Un problème m'intéresse depuis longtemps, c'est celui du système penal (1971). In *Dits et Ecrits, I*. Paris: Gallimard, 1073–1077.
Foucault, M. (2003). *Society Must Be Defended: Lectures at the Collège de France, 1975–1976*. Basingstoke: Palgrave Macmillan.
Foucault, M. (2007). *Security, Territory, Population: Lectures at the Collège de France, 1977–78*. New York: Springer.
Foucault, M. (2015a). *On the Punitive Society: Lectures at the Collège de France, 1972–1973*. New York: Springer.
Foucault, M. (2015b). *Théories et institutions pénales: Cours au Collège de France. 1971–1972*. Paris: Gallimard.
Foucault, M. (2018) *Les aveux de la chair*. Paris: Gallimard.
Frowd, P. M. (2018). *Security at the Borders: Transnational Practices and Technologies in West Africa*. Cambridge: Cambridge University Press.
Furri, F. (2016). "Can migrants act?": Presence, organization, visiblity in a precarious scape. *REMHU: Revista Interdisciplinar da Mobilidade Humana*, *24*(47): 11–26.
Garelli, G., Sciurba, A. & Tazzioli, M. (2018a). Mediterranean movements and constituent political spaces: An interview with Sandro Mezzadra and Toni Negri. *Antipode*, *50*(3): 673–684.
Garelli, G., Sciurba, A. & Tazzioli, M. (2018b). Mediterranean struggles for movement and the European government of bodies: An interview with Étienne Balibar and Nicholas De Genova. *Antipode*, *50*(3): 748–762.

Garelli, G. & Tazzioli, M. (2017). Choucha beyond the camp: Challenging the spatial and temporal boundaries of migration studies. In N. De Genova (ed.) *The Borders of Europe*. Durham, NC: Duke University Press, 122–143.

Garelli, G. & Tazzioli, M. (2018). The biopolitical warfare on migrants: EU Naval Force and NATO operations of migration government in the Mediterranean. *Critical Military Studies*, 4(2): 181–200.

Geiger, M. & Pécoud, A. (eds) (2013). *Disciplining the Transnational Mobility of People*. New York: Springer.

Gill, N. (2009a). Governmental mobility: The power effects of the movement of detained asylum seekers around Britain's detention estate. *Political Geography*, 28: 186–196.

Gill, N. (2009b). Longing for stillness: The forced movement of asylum seekers. *M/C Journal*, 12(1). Available at: http://journal.media-culture.org.au/index.php/mcjournal/article/view/123 (last accessed 3 December 2018).

Gilroy, P. (2013). *There Ain't No Black in the Union Jack*. London: Routledge.

Grandmaison, O. L. C. (2005). *Coloniser, exterminer: Sur la guerre et l'Etat colonial*. Paris: Fayard.

Gregory, D. (2008). "The rush to the intimate": Counterinsurgency and the cultural turn. *Radical Philosophy*, *150*. Available at: www.radicalphilosophy.com/article/the-rush-to-the-intimate (last accessed 20 December 2018).

Gregory, D. (2010). Seeing red: Baghdad and the event-ful city. *Political Geography*, 29(5): 266–279.

Gregory, D. (2011). From a view to a kill: Drones and late modern war. *Theory, Culture & Society*, 28(7–8): 188–215.

Guittet, E. P. & Jeandesboz, J. (2010). *Security Technologies: The Routledge Handbook of New Security Studies*. London: Routledge, 229–239.

Hacking, I. (1982). Biopower and the avalanche of printed numbers. Available at: http://digitalhistory.concordia.ca/courses/surveillance/wp-content/uploads/hacking_Biopower_and_the_Avalanche_of_Printed_Numbers.pdf (last accessed 20 December 2018).

Hacking, I. (2002). *Making Up People: In Historical Ontology*. Cambridge, MA: Harvard University Press, 99–114.

Hage, G. (2009). *Waiting*. Melbourne: Melbourne University Publishing.

Hannah, M. G. (2000). *Governmentality and the Mastery of Territory in Nineteenth-Century America*. Cambridge: Cambridge University Press.

Hardt, M. and Negri, A. (2017) *Assembly*. Oxford: Oxford University Press.

Hartman, S. V. (1997). *Scenes of Subjection: Terror, Slavery, and Self-making in Nineteenth-Century America*. Oxford: Oxford University Press.

Hayes, P. (1992) *The People and the Mob: The Ideology of Civil Conflict in Modern Europe*. Westport, CT: Praeger.

Heller, C. & Pezzani, L. (2014). Liquid traces: Investigating the deaths of migrants at the EU's maritime frontier. *Revue européenne des migrations internationales*, 30(3): 71–107.

Hess, S. (2012). De-naturalising transit migration: Theory and methods of an ethnographic regime analysis. *Population, Space and Place*, 18(4): 428–440.

Hiemstra, N. (2013). "You don't even know where you are": Chaotic geographies of US migrant detention and deportation. In D. Conlon, D. Moran & N. Gill (eds) *Carceral Spaces: Mobility and Agency in Imprisonment and Migrant Detention*. Farnham: Ashgate, i57–75.

Hindess, B. (2000). Citizenship in the international management of populations. *American Behavioral Scientist*, 43(9): 1486–1497.
Hobbes, T. (2008). *Thomas Hobbes: Leviathan*. New York: Routledge.
Honig, B. (2001). *Democracy and the Foreigner*. Princeton, NJ: Princeton University Press.
Honig, B. (2009). *Emergency Politics: Paradox, Law, Democracy*. Princeton, NJ: Princeton University Press.
Huysmans, J. (2006). *The Politics of Insecurity: Fear, Migration and Asylum in the EU*. Abingdon: Routledge.
Huysmans, J. & Pontes Nogueira, J. (2016). Ten years of IPS: Fracturing IR. *International Political Sociology*, 10(4): 299–319.
Isin, E. F. (2002). *Being Political: Genealogies of Citizenship*. Minneapolis, MN: University of Minnesota Press.
Isin, E. F. (2009). Citizenship in flux: The figure of the activist citizen. *Subjectivity*, 29(1): 367–388.
Isin, E. (2018). Mobile peoples: Transversal configurations. *Social Inclusion*, 6(1): 115–123.
Isin, E., & Ruppert, E. (2019). Data's empire: Postcolonial data politics. In D. Bigo, E. Isin & E. Ruppert (eds.) *Data Politics Worlds, Subjects, Rights*. London/New York: Routledge, 207–228.
Jacobsen, K. L. (2017). On humanitarian refugee biometrics and new forms of intervention. *Journal of Intervention and Statebuilding*, 11(4): 529–551.
Jacobsen, K. L. and Sandvik, K. B. (2018). UNHCR and the pursuit of international protection: Accountability through technology? *Third World Quarterly*, 39(8): 1508–1524.
Jeandesboz, J. (2016). Smartening border security in the European Union: An associational inquiry. *Security Dialogue*, 47(4): 292–309.
Jeandesboz, J. & Guittet, E. P. (2010). Security technologies. In J.P. Burgess (ed). *The Routledge Handbook of New Security Studies*. Routledge: New York, 229–239.
Johnson, H. (2012). Moments of solidarity, migrant activism and (non) citizens at global borders: Political agency at Tanzanian refugee camps, Australian detention centres and European borders. In P. Nyers & K. Rygiel (eds) *Citizenship, Migrant Activism and the Politics of Movement*. Abingdon: Routledge, 121–140.
Karakayali, S., & Rigo, E. (2010). Mapping the European space of circulation. In N. De Genova & N. Peutz (eds) *The Deportation Regime: Sovereignty, Space, and the Freedom of Movement*. Durham, DC: Duke University Press, 123–144.
Kasparek, B. (2016). Routes, corridors, and spaces of exception: Governing migration and Europe. *Near Futures Online*, 1(1). Available at: http://nearfuturesonline.org/routes-corridors-and-spaces-of-exception-governing-migration-and-europe/ (last accessed 6 June 2019).
Keith, M. (1993). *Race, Riots and Policing: Lore and Disorder in a Multi-Racist Society*. London: UCL Press.
Khosravi, S. (2014). Waiting. *Migration: The COMPAS Anthology*, 74–5.
Khosravi, S. (2018). Stolen time. *Radical Philosophy*, 2(3). Available at: www.radicalphilosophy.com/article/stolen-time (last accessed 21 December 2018).
Kofman, E. (2018). Gendered mobilities and vulnerabilities: Refugee journeys to and in Europe. *Journal of Ethnic and Migration Studies*.DOI: 10.1080/1369183X.2018.1468330.
Kotef, H. (2015). *Movement and the Ordering of Freedom: On Liberal Governances of Mobility*. Durham, NC: Duke University Press.

Kurz, J. J. (2012). (Dis) locating control: Transmigration, precarity and the governmentality of control. *BEHEMOTH – A Journal on Civilisation*, 2(1): 30–51.
Lazzarato, M. (2014). *Signs and Machines: Capitalism and the Production of Subjectivity*. Los Angeles, CA: Semiotext (e).
Legg, S. (2005). Foucault's population geographies: Classifications, biopolitics and governmental spaces. *Population, Space, Place*, 11(3): 137–156.
Lelevrier, C. (2010). La mixité dans la rénovation urbaine: dispersion ou re-concentration ?, *Espaces et Sociétés*, 1(140): 59–74.
Linebaugh, P. (1975). The Tyburn riot against the surgeons. In D.P. Hay, J.G. Linebaugh, E.P. Rule, C. Thompson & C. Winslow. (eds.) *Albion's Fatal Tree: Crime and Society in Eighteenth Century England*. New York: Pantheon Books: 65–117.
Linebaugh, P. (2003). *The London Hanged: Crime and Civil Society in the Eighteenth Century*. London: Verso.
Linebaugh, P. (2009). *The Magna Carta Manifesto: Liberties and Commons for All*. Berkeley, CA: University of California Press.
Linebaugh, P. & Rediker, M. (2013). *The Many-Headed Hydra: Sailors, Slaves, Commoners, and the Hidden History of the Revolutionary Atlantic*. Boston, MA: Beacon Press.
Lisle, D. (2016). Waiting for international political sociology: A field guide to living in-between. *International Political Sociology*, 10(4): 417–433.
Lorenzini, D. (2017). La société disciplinaire: généalogie d'un concept. In D. Lorenzini & I. Fouchard (eds) *Sociétés Carcerales: Relecture(s) de Surveiller et Punir*. Paris: Mare & Martin, 21–30.
Lorenzini, D. & Tazzioli, M. (2018). Confessional subjects and conducts of non-truth: Foucault, Fanon, and the making of the subject. *Theory, Culture & Society*, 35(1): 71–90.
Lowe, L. (2015). *The Intimacies of Four Continents*. Durham, NC: Duke University Press.
Loyd, J. M. and Mountz, A. (2014). Managing migration, scaling sovereignty on islands. *Island Studies Journal*, 9(1): 23–42.
Lyon, D. (2001). Under my skin: From identification papers to body surveillance. In J. Caplan & J. C. Torpey (eds) *Documenting Individual Identity: The Development of State Practices in the Modern World*. Princeton: Princeton University Press: 291–310.
Macherey, P. (2009). *De Canguilhem à Foucault, la force des normes*. Paris: La Fabrique Éditions.
Macherey, P. (2014). *Le sujet des normes*. Paris: Éditions Amsterdam.
Macherey, P. (2015). The productive subject. *Viewpoint Magazine*. Available at: www.viewpointmag.com/2015/10/31/the-productive-subject/ (last accessed 20 December 2018).
Mahmood, S. (2011). *Politics of Piety: The Islamic Revival and the Feminist Subject*. Princeton, NJ: Princeton University Press.
Malkki L. H. (1995). Refugees and exile: From "Refugee studies" to the national order of things. *Annual Review of Anthropology*, 24(1): 495–523.
Malkki, L. H. (1996). Speechless emissaries: Refugees, humanitarianism, and dehistoricization. *Cultural Anthropology*, 11(3): 377–404.
Marchetti, C. (2014). Rifugiati e migranti forzati in Italia: Il pendolo tra 'emergenza'e 'sistema'. *REMHU-Revista Interdisciplinar da Mobilidade Humana*, 22(43): 53–70.
Martin, L. L. (2010). Bombs, bodies, and biopolitics: Securitizing the subject at the airport security checkpoint. *Social & Cultural Geography*, 11(1): 17–34.
Martin, L. L. & Mitchelson, M. L. (2009). Geographies of detention and imprisonment: Interrogating spatial practices of confinement, discipline, law, and state power. *Geography Compass*, 3(1): 459–477.

Mbembe, A. (2017). *Critique of Black Reason*. Durham, NC: Duke University Press.
Mbembe, J. A. (2003). Necropolitics. *Public Culture*, *15*(1), 11–40.
McKeown, A. M. (2008). *Melancholy Order: Asian Migration and the Globalization of Borders*. New York: Columbia University Press.
McNay, L. (2000). *Gender and Agency: Reconfiguring the Subject in Feminist and Social Theory*. Cambridge: Polity Press.
McNevin, A. (2009). Contesting citizenship: Irregular migrants and strategic possibilities for political belonging. *New Political Science*, *31*(2): 163–181.
McNevin, A. (2013). Ambivalence and citizenship: Theorising the political claims of irregular migrants. *Millennium*, *41*(2): 182–200.
Mezzadra, S. (2010). The gaze of autonomy: Capitalism, migration and social struggles. In V. Squire (ed.) *The Contested Politics of Mobility*. Abingdon: Routledge, 141–162.
Mezzadra, S. (2016). MLC 2015 Keynote: What's at stake in the mobility of labour? Borders, migration, contemporary capitalism. *Migration, Mobility, & Displacement*, *2*(1).
Mezzadra, S. (2018a). *In the Marxian Workshops: Producing Subjects*. London: Rowman & Littlefield.
Mezzadra, S. (2018b). In the wake of the Greek spring and the summer of migration. *South Atlantic Quarterly*, *117*(4): 925–933.
Mezzadra, S. & Neilson, B. (2013). *Border as Method, or, the Multiplication of Labor*. Durham, NC: Duke University Press.
Mezzadra, S. & Neilson, B. (2014). Geography is not enough. *Dialogues in Human Geography*, *3*(3): 332–335.
Minca, C. (2015). Geographies of the camp. *Political Geography*, *49*: 74–83.
Mitchell, K., & Sparke, M. (2018). Hotspot geopolitics versus geosocial solidarity: Contending constructions of safe space for migrants in Europe. *Environment & Planning D*. Available at: https://doi.org/10.1177%2F0263775818793647.
Mitropoulos, A. (2007). Autonomy, recognition, movement. In S. Shukaitis, D. E. Graeber & E. Biddle (eds), *Constituent Imagination: Militant Investigations, Collective Theorization*. Oakland: AK Press, 127–136.
Mohanty, C. T. (2003). *Feminism Without Borders: Decolonizing Theory, Practicing Solidarity*. Durham, NC: Duke University Press.
Moulin, C. (2012). Ungrateful subjects? Refugee protests and the logic of gratitude. In P. Nyers & K. Rygiel (eds) *Citizenship, Migrant Activism and the Politics of Movement*. Abingdon: Routledge. (66–84).
Mountz, A. (2015). In/visibility and the securitization of migration: Shaping publics through border enforcement on islands. *Cultural Politics*, *11*(2): 184–200.
Mountz, A., Coddington, K., Catania, R. T. & Loyd, J. M. (2013). Conceptualizing detention: Mobility, containment, bordering, and exclusion. *Progress in Human Geography*, *37*(4): 522–541.
Mountz, A., Wright, R., Miyares, I. & Bailey, A. J. (2002). Lives in limbo: Temporary protected status and immigrant identities. *Global Networks*, *2*(4): 335–356.
Nail, T. (2015) *The Figure of the Migrant*. Stanford, CA: Stanford University Press.
Neilson, B. (2018). The currency of migration. *South Atlantic Quarterly*, *117*(2): 375–392.
Ngai, S. (2005). *Ugly Feelings* (Vol. 6). Cambridge, MA: Harvard University Press.
Nieuwenhuis, M. (2015). Atemwende, or how to breathe differently. *Dialogues in Human Geography*, *5*(1): 90–94.

Noiriel, G. (1991). *La tyrannie du national: le droit d'asile en Europe (1793–1993)*. Paris: Calmann-Lévy.
Novak, P. (2019) The neoliberal location of asylum. *Political Geography*, (70): 1–13.
Nyers, P. (2010). No one is illegal between city and nation. *Studies in Social Justice*, 4(2): 127–143.
Nyers, P. & Rygiel, K. (eds) (2012). *Citizenship, Migrant Activism and the Politics of Movement*. Abingdon: Routledge.
O'Grady, N. (2016). Mobility, circulation, and homeomorphism: Data becoming risk information. In M. Leese & S. Wittendorp (eds) *Security/Mobility: Politics of Movement*. Manchester: Manchester University Press, 74–92.
Offe, C. (2013). Ungovernability. In *Fragile Stabilität–stabile Fragilität*. Wiesbaden: Springer VS, 77–87.
Ogilvie, B. (2012). *L'Homme jetable: Essai sur l'exterminisme et la violence eextreme*. Paris: Éditions Amsterdam.
Pallister-Wilkins, P. (2015). The humanitarian politics of European border policing: Frontex and border police in Evros. *International Political Sociology*, 9(1): 53–69.
Papadopoulos, D., Stephenson, N. & Tsianos, V. (2008). *Escape Routes: Control and Subversion in the Twenty-First Century*. London: Pluto Press.
Papadopoulos, D. & Tsianos, V. (2007). The autonomy of migration: The animals of undocumented mobility. In A. Hickey-Moody & P. Malins (eds) *Deleuzian encounters: Studies in Contemporary Social Issues*. London: Palgrave Macmillan: 222–235.
Papastergiadis, N. (2000). *The Turbulence of Migration*. Cambridge: Polity Press.
Parvan, O. (2017). Unruly lives: Subverting "surplus" existence in Tunisia. *Metamute*. Available at: www.metamute.org/editorial/articles/unruly-life-subverting-'surplus'-existence-tunisia (last accessed 20 December 2018).
Picozza, F. (2017). Dubliners: Unthinking displacement, illegality and refugeeness within Europe's geographies of asylum. In N. DeGenova (ed.) *The Borders of "Europe": Autonomy of Migration, Bordering Tactics*. Durham, NC: Duke University Press, 233–254.
Pinelli, B. (2015). After the landing: Moral control and surveillance in Italy's asylum seeker camps. *Anthropology Today*, 31(2): 12–14.
Pinelli, B. (2017). Borders, politics and subjects: Introductory notes on refugee research in Europe. *Etnografia Ricerca Qualitativa*, 1: 5–24.
Puar, J.K. (2017). *The Right to Maim: Debility, Capacity, Disability*. Durham, NC: Duke University Press.
Rajan, K. S. (2006). *Biocapital: The Constitution of Postgenomic Life*. Durham, NC: Duke University Press.
Rajaram, P. K. & Grundy-Warr, C. (2004). The irregular migrant as homo sacer: Migration and detention in Australia, Malaysia, and Thailand. *International Migration*, 42(1): 33–64.
Rancière, J. (1999). *Disagreement: Politics and Philosophy*. Minneapolis, MN: University of Minnesota Press.
Rancière, J. (2010). The people or the multitudes? In J. Rancière, *Dissensus: On Politics and Aesthetics*. London: Bloomsbury, 84–90.
Rediker, M. (2014). *Outlaws of the Atlantic: Sailors, Pirates, and Motley Crews in the Age of Sail*. New York: Beacon Press.

Revel, J. (2002). *Le vocabulaire de Foucault*. Paris: Ellipses.
Revel, J. (2004). *Fare moltitudine*. Rome: Rubbettino Editore.
Revel, J. (2015). In the meshes of power: Dispositives, strategies, agency. *Darkmatter Journal*. Available at: www.darkmatter101.org/site/2015/10/05/in-the-meshes-of-power-dispositives-strategies-agency (last accessed 20 December 2018).
Rigouste, M. (2012). *La domination policière: Une violence industrielle*. Paris: La Fabrique Éditions.
Roitman, J. (2013). *Anti-crisis*. Durham, NC: Duke University Press.
Rozakou, K. (2017). Nonrecording the "European refugee crisis" in Greece: Navigating through irregular bureaucracy. *Focaal*, *2017*(77): 36–49.
Sacriste, F. (2018). Les "regroupements" de la guerre d'Algérie, des "villages stratégiques"? *Critique Internationale*, 2: 25–43.
Salvatici, S. (2015). *Nel nome degli altri: storia dell'umanitarismo internazionale*. Milano: Il mulino.
Sayad, A. (2018). *The Suffering of the Immigrant*. Chichester: John Wiley & Sons.
Scheel, S. (2013). Autonomy of migration despite its securitisation? Facing the terms and conditions of biometric rebordering. *Millennium*, *41*(3), 575–600.
Scheel, S., De Genova, N., Garelli, G., Tazzioli, M., Grappi, G. & Peano, I. (2015). "Subjectivity": New keywords: migration and borders, *Cultural Studies Journal*, *29*(1): 83–85.
Schlesinger, A. M. (1955). Political mobs and the American Revolution, 1765–1776. *Proceedings of the American Philosophical Society*, *99*(4), 244–250.
Sciurba, A. (2016). Hotspot system as a new device of clandestinisation: View from Sicily, OpenDemocracy. Available at: www.opendemocracy.net/can-europe-make-it/alessandra-sciurba/hotspot-system-as-a-new-device-of-clandestinisation-view-from-si/ (last accessed 21 December 2018).
Scott, J. C. (1998). *Seeing Like a State: How Certain Schemes to Improve the Human Condition Have Failed*. New Haven, CT: Yale University Press.
Scott, J. C. (2010). *The Art of Not Being Governed: An Anarchist History of Upland Southeast Asia*. Singapore: NUS Press.
Scott, J. W. (2007). History-writing as critique. In *Manifestos for History*. London: Routledge, 31–50.
Sharma, N. (2013). Migrants and indigenous nationalism. In S. J. Gold & S. J. Nawyn (eds) *Routledge International Handbook of Migration Studies*. London: Routledge, 225–236.
Sheller, M. (2017). From spatial turn to mobilities turn. *Current Sociology*, *65*(4): 623–639.
Shoemaker, R. (2007). *The London Mob: Violence and Disorder in Eighteenth-Century England*. London: A&C Black.
Sibertin-Blanc, G. (2009). Deleuze et les minorités: Quelle "politique"? *Cités*, 4: 39–57.
Sibertin-Blanc, G. (2013). Du simulacre démocratique à la fabulation du peuple: Le populisme minoritaire. *Actuel Marx*, 2: 71–85.
Spathopoulou, A. (2016). The ferry as a mobile hotspot: Migrants at the uneasy borderlands of Greece. *Society & Space*. Available at: http://societyandspace.org/2016/12/15/the-ferry-as-a-mobile-hotspot-migrants-at-the-uneasy-borderlands-of-greece/ (last accessed 21 December 2018).
Squire, V. (ed.) (2010). *The Contested Politics of Mobility: Borderzones and Irregularity*. Abingdon: Routledge.

Squire, V. (2017). Unauthorised migration beyond structure/agency? Acts, interventions, effects. *Politics*, 37(3): 254–272.

Squire, V. (2018). Mobile solidarities and precariousness at city plaza: Beyond vulnerable and disposable lives. *Studies in Social Justice*, 12(1): 111–132.

Stierl, M. (2018). *Migrant Resistance in Contemporary Europe*. Abingdon: Routledge.

Stoler, A. L. (2002). Colonial archives and the arts of governance. *Archival Science*, 2(1–2): 87–109.

Stoler, A. L. (2010). *Along the Archival Grain: Epistemic Anxieties and Colonial Common Sense*. Princeton, NJ: Princeton University Press.

Sunder, R. K. (2003). *Biocapital: The Constitution of Post-genomic Life*. Durham, NC: Duke University Press.

Tazzioli, M. (2015). *Spaces of Governmentality: Autonomous Migration and the Arab Uprisings*. Lanham, MD: Rowman & Littlefield.

Tazzioli, M. (2016). The migrant mob: The production and government of multiplicities in border zones. *European Journal of Social Theory*, 20(4): 473–490.

Tazzioli, M. (2017). Calais after the jungle: Migrant dispersal and the expulsions of humanitarianism. OpenDemocracy, www.opendemocracy.net/beyondslavery/martina-tazzioli/calais-after-jungle-migrant-dispersal-and-expulsion-of-humanitarianis (last accessed 20 December 2018).

Tazzioli, M. (2018). Spy, track and archive: The temporality of visibility in Eurosur and Jora. *Security Dialogue*, 49 (4): 272–288.

Tazzioli, M. & Walters, W. (2016). The sight of migration: Governmentality, visibility and Europe's contested borders. *Global Society*, 30(3): 445–464.

Tazzioli, M. & Walters, W. (2019). Migration, solidarity and the limits of Europe. *Global Discourse*, 9(1): 175–190.

Thoburn, N. (2002). Difference in Marx: The lumpenproletariat and the proletarian unnamable. *Economy and Society*, 31(3): 434–460.

Thompson, E. P. (1963). *The Making of the English Working Class*. London: Gollancz.

Ticktin, M. (2008). Sexual violence as the language of border control: Where French feminist and anti-immigrant rhetoric meet. *Signs: Journal of Women in Culture and Society*, 33(4): 863–889.

Ticktin, M. (2017). A world without innocence. *American Ethnologist*, 44(4): 577–590.

Trimikliniotis, N., Parsanoglou, D. & Tsianos, V. (2014). *Mobile Commons, Migrant Digitalities and the Right to the City*. New York: Springer.

Tsianos, V. & Karakayali, S. (2010). Transnational migration and the emergence of the European border regime: An ethnographic analysis. *European Journal of Social Theory*, 13(3): 373–387.

Tsing, A. L. (2005). *Friction: An Ethnography of Global Connection*. Princeton, NJ: Princeton University Press.

Tsing, A. L. (2012). On nonscalability: The living world is not amenable to precision-nested scales. *Common Knowledge*, 18(3): 505–524.

Van Baar, H. (2017). Evictability and the biopolitical bordering of Europe. *Antipode*, 49(1): 212–230.

Van der Ploeg, I. (1999). The illegal body: EURODAC and the politics of biometric identification. *Ethics and Information Technology*, 1(4): 295–302.

Vaughan-Williams, N. (2015). *Europe's Border Crisis: Biopolitical Security and Beyond.* Oxford: Oxford University Press.

Walters, W. (2006). Border/control. *European Journal of Social Theory, 9*(2): 187–203.

Walters, W. (2015). Migration, vehicles, and politics: Three theses on viapolitics. *European Journal of Social Theory, 18*(4): 469–488.

Walters, W. (2016). Microphysics of power redux. In P. Bonditti, D. Bigo & F. Gros (eds) *Foucault and the Modern International.* New York: Palgrave Macmillan, 57–75.

Walters, W. & Luthi, B. (2016). The politics of cramped space: Dilemmas of action, containment and mobility. *International Journal of Politics, Culture & Society, 29*(4): 359–366.

Weheliye, A. G. (2014). *Habeas Viscus: Racializing Assemblages, Biopolitics, and Black Feminist Theories of the Human.* Durham, NC: Duke University Press.

Whyte, Z. (2011). Enter the myopticon: Uncertain surveillance in the Danish asylum system. *Anthropology Today, 27*(3): 18–21.

Xiang, B. & Lindquist, J. (2014). Migration infrastructure. *International Migration Review, 48*: 122–148.

Zetter, R. (2007). More labels, fewer refugees: Remaking the refugee label in an era of globalization. *Journal of Refugee Studies, 20*(2): 172–192.

Index

alliances, 110, 138–142
   transversal, 24, 116, 135, 138, 141, 146, 147, 156–58
agency, 12, 46, 47, 131, 132, 147, 136–138, 144–146, 151
Aradau, C., 8, 25, 48, 61, 157, 160
archive, 73, 74, 77, 79, 131, 135, 149, 150, 158
asylum
   claim, 28, 36, 53, 58, 59, 68, 87, 88, 93, 122
   regime, 14, 39, 58–59, 64, 89, 91, 93, 131
autonomy, 64, 65, 88–92, 94, 128

Balibar, E., 4, 5, 70, 140, 146, 160
biometrics, 13, 28, 46, 51, 69, 73–76, 78–83, 133
biopolitics, 1, 4, 10, 11, 39, 48, 103–106, 117, 151
border
   controls, 12, 9, 36, 38, 43, 55, 83, 119, 131, 132, 148
   regime, 10, 50, 54, 61, 106, 132, 134, 136, 152
Butler, J., 20, 23, 52, 137, 139–42, 161

Calais, 1, 15, 16, 19, 47, 109, 115–19, 152, 157
camp, 26, 27, 34, 35, 119, 121, 122, 124, 134
chokepoints, 13, 81, 87
circulation, 10, 13, 74–76, 78–81, 87, 91, 97–99, 103, 104, 127, 128
citizen, 5, 7, 9, 12, 44, 47, 87, 88, 90, 116, 126, 132, 135, 136, 138, 142, 145–47, 155
collective subjects, 3–6, 15–20, 23, 24, 37, 38, 105–112, 131, 138, 139, 142, 143, 152, 156, 157
critique, 21, 92, 93, 132, 153–56

data
   circulation, 81, 87, 96–99
   extraction, 1, 4, 14, 30, 31, 51, 67, 74–78, 82–85, 87, 89

database, 28, 30, 63, 65, 74–82, 86, 96, 97
De Genova, N., 2, 4, 10, 19, 29, 32, 46, 132, 163
Deleuze, G., 6, 26, 76, 157, 163
disobediences, 14, 131, 133, 134, 144, 146, 148, 149, 151, 155, 158
dispersal, 9, 102, 108–118, 122–129
Dublin Regulation, 14, 58, 59, 77, 81, 107, 108, 118, 120, 133–35

EURODAC, 28, 41 n7, 62, 63, 73, 74, 80, 81, 121
eviction, 118, 124, 126, 129, 150

Fassin, D., 4, 134, 164
freedom, 24, 89–92, 127, 129, 133–135, 137
Fanon, Frantz, 7, 49, 50, 67, 70, 161
flow, 18, 19, 32, 33, 38, 76, 77
Foucault, M., 3, 5, 10, 18–22, 26, 27, 31, 44, 45, 51, 70, 91, 103–106, 133, 150, 164
frictions, 13, 61, 65, 81, 114
Frontex, 27, 28, 30, 32, 63, 69, 77, 80, 81, 121

genealogy, 1, 9, 14, 21, 23, 24, 78, 102, 106, 109–112, 115, 131, 157
governmentality, 4, 9, 10, 30–32, 46–48, 51, 69, 75, 89–94, 103–106, 127–29

Hacking, I., 31, 83, 84, 165
Honig, B., 1, 134, 166
hotspot, 53, 54, 62–63, 80–82, 94, 119, 121–23, 133, 134
humanitarianism, 3, 14, 38, 66, 88, 90, 91–93, 101, 117, 118, 120, 122
   refugee, 54, 83, 91–93
   financial, 85, 87
Huysmans, J., 25, 102, 107, 157, 166

individualism, 45, 131, 138, 144
infrastructures, 63, 87, 93, 120, 128, 147
invisibility, 35, 95–97, 110, 125, 135, 145, 146, 149, 156
Isin, E., 2, 143, 144, 166

Lampedusa, 28, 61–62, 121, 134, 149
Lesvos, 54, 61, 63, 81, 94, 156
Linebaugh, P., 20, 24, 142 148, 167

Mahmood, S., 12, 137, 138, 167
McNevin, A., 133, 143, 168
Mediterranean, 8, 27, 37, 39, 79, 95–97, 154–56
memory, 14, 131, 135, 146–150, 158
Mezzadra, S. 3, 4, 7, 10, 16, 17, 85, 133, 153, 168
mob, 6, 9, 13, 16, 20–25, 40, 108, 111, 157
movement, 1, 2, 9, 12, 13, 19, 22, 32–35, 60–64, 77, 78, 102–107, 113, 117, 120–23, 132, 134, 139, 145–51, 158
multiplicity, 5, 6, 16–20, 26–37, 40, 54, 65, 84, 87, 88, 95, 135, 141, 145, 151, 157

Negri, T., 139, 141, 142, 165

objectivation, 3, 4, 44, 51, 52, 69, 70, 75–77, 84, 85, 87, 99, 153

political technology, 50, 61, 67, 102, 106, 107, 110, 116, 129
Puar, J., 12, 48

Rediker, M. 23, 24, 142, 167, 169
refuge, 1, 2, 36, 103, 150
resistances, 10, 22, 44, 75, 81, 86, 94, 120, 133, 156

Schengen, 37, 57, 119, 133, 150
security, 3, 5, 8, 10, 31, 48, 79, 83, 89, 91, 93 103–105, 123

singularities, 3, 5, 18, 20, 30, 31, 44–46, 55, 67, 71, 74, 98, 153
solidarity, 116, 120, 131, 134–136, 141, 147–49, 154, 156
Stoler, A. L., 71, 135, 170
struggle, 6, 7, 12, 13, 19, 23, 35, 36, 41 n2, 47, 62, 92–94, 133–36, 140–43, 145–50, 155
subjectivation, 2–4, 6, 8, 17, 44, 46–48, 51, 70, 78, 79, 126, 152, 153
subjectivity, 3,5, 8, 44–46, 55, 74, 76, 78, 127, 132, 136–38, 146, 152

technologies, 9, 79, 83, 85, 86, 91, 93, 95, 98, 99, 102, 108, 127
  biometric, 76, 78
  digital, 14, 74, 75, 83, 87, 92, 93, 98, 99
  political, 4, 9–11, 14, 16, 46, 47, 51, 54, 67, 89, 109, 152, 153
temporality, 4, 18, 36, 54, 63, 64, 68, 79, 88, 103, 114, 144, 145, 148, 154

value, 76, 83, 88, 89, 93
Ventimiglia, 1, 15, 16, 19, 31, 55, 81, 119–23, 134, 136, 145, 156, 157
violence, 3, 11, 12, 28, 45, 48, 53–55, 85, 118, 153–56
visibility, 4, 32, 33, 52, 55, 57, 59, 75, 95–99, 109, 14, 125, 140, 144–47
vulnerability, 38, 47, 52–55, 82, 90, 137

Walters, W., 32, 37, 60, 67, 95, 117, 133, 148, 171